Firm Foundations of Growth

Scan to see all titles in the series.

East Asia and Pacific Development Studies

Firm Foundations of Growth

Productivity and Technology in East Asia and Pacific

Francesca de Nicola
Aaditya Mattoo
Jonathan Timmis

WORLD BANK GROUP

ISBN (paper): 978-1-4648-2200-1
ISBN (electronic): 978-1-4648-2221-6
DOI: 10.1596/978-1-4648-2200-1

Cover image: © Mit Jai Inn, "Untitled," 2025, oil on canvas, 120 × 120 cm. Image courtesy of Gallery
VER in Bangkok, Thailand. Used with permission. Further permission required for reuse.

About the artist: Mit Jai Inn (b. 1960) is a pioneering figure in Thai contemporary art. He has exhibited
widely across Asia, Australia, and Europe. His work challenges media boundaries by merging painting and
sculpture while exploring themes of transformation, space, and materiality.

Cover design: Guillaume Musel, Pi COMM, France / Bill Pragluski, Critical Stages, LLC

Library of Congress Control Number: 2025935439

EAST ASIA AND PACIFIC DEVELOPMENT STUDIES

The EAST ASIA AND PACIFIC DEVELOPMENT STUDIES explore economic issues in one of the most vibrant regions at a time of rapid technological change. Topics range from improving productivity and jobs to advancing services reform, and from enhancing education and health care to facilitating the green transition. Each volume blends analysis, examples, and policy lessons of interest to scholars, policy makers, and practitioners.

TITLES IN THE SERIES

Firm Foundations of Growth: Productivity and Technology in East Asia and Pacific (2025)

Future Jobs: Robots, Artificial Intelligence, and Digital Platforms in East Asia and Pacific (2025)

Green Technologies: Decarbonizing Development in East Asia and Pacific (2025)

Services Unbound: Digital Technologies and Policy Reform in East Asia and Pacific (2024)

Fixing the Foundation: Teachers and Basic Education in East Asia and Pacific (2023) (World Bank East Asia and Pacific Regional Report)

All books in this series are available for free in the World Bank's Open Knowledge Repository at https://hdl.handle.net/10986/42047.

Contents

Figures

Maps

Tables

Foreword

For decades, the East Asia and Pacific (EAP) region has been seen as a model of economic development. Rapid growth has raised wages and lifted millions out of poverty. However, three-quarters of this growth in the 21st century has been driven by significant investments in physical capital, such as buildings, machines, and equipment, and less than one-fifth by increases in productivity.

In a series of new books, the EAP region of the World Bank is examining how technological advances are impacting services, productivity, jobs, and the transition to low-carbon economies. This book focuses on firms as the foundations of productivity growth and creators of better jobs. Through a firm-level lens, it explores the constraints and policies needed to boost firm productivity.

The book finds that EAP's slow productivity growth is largely explained by the slowing productivity growth within established firms, especially those most productive—"the national frontier." On average, 10 percent of the most-productive firms accounted for 50 percent of aggregate productivity growth. However, the productivity of national frontier firms is falling further behind the most-productive firms globally in the digital sectors that are at the forefront of innovation. For example, in the digital manufacturing sectors, between 2005 and 2015, the productivity of the global frontier increased by 76 percent, whereas national frontier firms in Indonesia, Malaysia, the Philippines, and Viet Nam increased their productivity by only 34 percent on average. The weak performance of the national frontier matters because these firms account for a large share of output and jobs and are instrumental to the diffusion of new technologies to other firms.

The fact that frontier firm productivity growth has slowed during a period of rapid global technological change raises a puzzle. Firms in EAP have benefited enormously from earlier waves of technological progress. For example, advances in communication technologies allowed the proliferation of global value chains that spurred the East Asian manufacturing-led growth miracle. However, the technologies of today differ from those of yesterday. The best firms globally have shifted their business models, from investing in tangible capital, like factories or machines, toward investing in intangibles, like data or business processes. In advanced economies, investment in data increased from 0.5 to 0.7 percent of GDP between 2011 and 2018; however, data investment has stagnated at around 0.1 percent in EAP. An era of rapid technological change offers huge opportunities but also raises the risk of being left behind.

This book argues that policy needs to give frontier firms both the incentives and capabilities to innovate. Firm-level analysis reveals that impediments to competition in goods and services are inhibiting innovation incentives, especially for frontier firms. For example, services reforms in Viet Nam are associated with a more than 5 percent increase in the productivity of frontier firms in these same services sectors as well as of downstream manufacturing firms. The adoption of sophisticated technologies and productivity growth requires high-quality management skills and modern digital infrastructure. However, even basic skills are rare, with less than a quarter of workers in Cambodia, Mongolia, the Philippines, Thailand, and Viet Nam able to use the "copy and paste" function in a document.

Synchronizing reforms will help reap the synergies among enhanced human capital, infrastructure, and competition. For example, both openness to foreign competition and access to fiber broadband in the Philippines individually increased firm adoption of data analytics, but their combined impact is more than double.

As readers navigate this book, they will find new firm-level evidence on the factors behind the productivity slowdown and the policies that can reinvigorate productivity growth. It is my hope that this book will spur new dialogue among policy makers, researchers, and firms on how to realize the promise of technology to revamp the productive potential of the EAP region.

Manuela V. Ferro
Vice President, East Asia and Pacific
The World Bank

Acknowledgments

This book is a product of the Office of the Chief Economist, East Asia and Pacific Region (EAPCE) of the World Bank. It is a revised and expanded version of the special focus on "Firm Foundations of Growth," originally featured in the World Bank's "East Asia and Pacific Economic Update" (April 2024).

We are grateful for valuable contributions from Kiatipong Ariyapruchya, Arlan Brucal, Xavier Cirera, Tim DeStefano, Daisuke Fukuzawa, Duong Trung Le, Mariem Malouche, and Antonio Soares Martins Neto. Nesma Ali, Yiyi Bai, Parth Chawla, Charmaine Crisostomo, Benedict Evangelista, Serene Ho, Hieu Nguyen, Tsolmon Otgon, and Trang Thanh Tran provided excellent support on data used in the analysis. Elwyn Davies, Leonardo Iacovone, and Siddharth Sharma kindly provided comments and shared statistics on firm-level data from countries outside the EAP region.

Manuela V. Ferro provided valuable guidance and helpful comments. We are grateful for stimulating discussions and comments from Omar Arias, Dandan Chen, Andrea Coppola, Tatiana Didier, Ndiame Diop, Sebastian Eckardt, Kim Edwards, Benedictus Eijbergen, Yasser El-Gammal, Julia Fraser, Alvaro Gonzalez, Faya Hayati, Alexander Kremer, Lars Moller, Lalita Moorty, Rinku Murgai, Zafer Mustafaoglu, Cecile Niang, Marcin Piatkowski, Habib Rab, Alberto Rodriguez, Ralf Van Doorn, Gonzalo Varela, Anna Wellenstein, and Fabrizio Zarcone, as well as from members of the World Bank's East Asia and Pacific Management Team. We are grateful to Richard Kneller (Nottingham University) for serving as external reviewer.

We thank Maria Laura Gonzalez Canosa for leading the communications strategy, as well as Narya Ou and Cecile Wodon for their administrative support. Mary Anderson copy edited the manuscript, and Ann O'Malley proofread the book. Christina Ann Davis was the production editor. Cindy A. Fisher and Patricia Katayama provided advice and guidance on the publication process. Geetanjali S. Chopra, Ngan Hong Nguyen, Yi Gu, and other members of the External Communications and Relations team helped with dissemination.

The cover features "Untitled" (2025) by Mit Jai Inn, an oil on canvas, 120 × 120 cm artwork created by the artist for this publication. We are grateful to Mit Jai Inn for creating this piece and granting permission for its use on the cover and to Natthanat Taweepanyawong from Gallery VER in Bangkok, Thailand, for providing the high-quality image and supporting this collaboration. We would also like to thank Kanitha Kongrukgreatiyos from the External Communications and Relations team for facilitating the introduction to the gallery.

This book features spotlights on specific country experiences, each titled "Out of the Box." For contributions to these sections, we would like to thank Perry Ferrer, Preethi Nair, and Babu Padmanabhan for their insightful discussions and for agreeing to be featured in the book.

About the Authors

Francesca de Nicola is a senior economist in the Economic and Market Research Unit of the International Finance Corporation. Her current research focuses on productivity, innovation, and the green transition. She started her career at the International Food Policy Research Institute. She has published in journals such as the *Journal of Development Economics, Quantitative Economics,* and *Energy Economics.* She holds a PhD in economics from Johns Hopkins University and a master's degree in economics from Bocconi University.

Aaditya Mattoo is chief economist of the East Asia and Pacific Region of the World Bank. He specializes in development, trade, and international cooperation and provides policy advice to governments. Previously, he was the research manager, Trade and International Integration, at the World Bank. Before he joined the World Bank, he was an economic counselor at the World Trade Organization and taught economics at the University of Sussex and Churchill College, Cambridge University. He has published in academic and other journals, and his work has been cited in *The Economist, Financial Times, The New York Times,* and *Time Magazine.* He holds a PhD in economics from the University of Cambridge and an MPhil in economics from the University of Oxford.

Jonathan Timmis is a senior economist in the Office of the Chief Economist, East Asia and Pacific Region of the World Bank, where he researches the areas of digitalization and technological change, productivity, and globalization. Before joining the World Bank, he worked for the International Finance Corporation and the Organisation for Economic Co-operation and Development's Productivity and Business Dynamics Division; he was also an Overseas Development Institute Fellow in Rwanda. He has published in academic journals such as the *Review of Economics and Statistics, Journal of Economic Geography,* and *Journal of Development Economics,* and his work has been cited by *The Economist* and the *Harvard Business Review.* He holds a PhD and a master's degree in economics from the University of Nottingham.

Overview

The productivity puzzle

In the East Asia and Pacific (EAP) region, total factor productivity growth has slowed over the past two decades (refer to figure O.1).[1] Why this slowdown has come at a time of rapid technological progress is a puzzle. This book examines the issue through novel firm-level analysis, identifying the factors behind the slowdown and what policies would reignite productivity—a vital driver of economic growth.

Productivity growth is driven more by increases *within* firms than by reallocation *between* firms. Aggregate productivity growth is a dynamic process involving three factors: productivity growth within existing firms, the reallocation of market share to more-productive firms, and firm entry and exit. Correctly diagnosing the sources of the productivity slowdown matters for prescribing the right policies. For example, the limited role of reallocation and entry could reflect barriers to competition. In EAP countries on average, around three-quarters of aggregate productivity is due to productivity improvements within existing firms (refer to figure O.2).

> **Aggregate productivity growth has slowed in developing East Asia.**

FIGURE O.1   TFP growth trends in EAP and other selected countries, 1995–2022

Annual percentage change

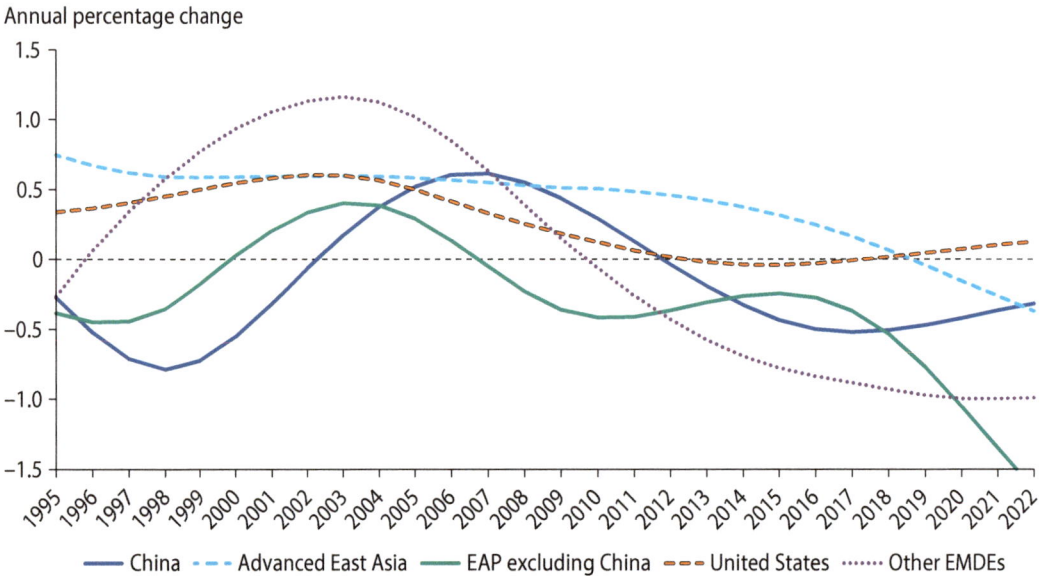

Source: Original figure for this publication using data from the Conference Board's Total Economy Database.
Note: The figure reflects trends in total factor productivity growth after applying a Hodrick-Prescott filter to remove short-term fluctuations. The negative growth for recent periods is not always robust to different choices of filters and trimming of time periods; however, the productivity slowdown is a general finding. "Advanced" refers to high-income countries, according to World Bank income classifications. EAP = East Asia and Pacific; EMDEs = emerging markets and developing economies, as defined by the International Monetary Fund (IMF 2019); TFP = total factor productivity.

Firm entry and exit or reallocation are important during periods of reform. For example, around the time of China's World Trade Organization (WTO) accession in 2001, almost half of its aggregate growth was due to new firms entering the market. The relative importance of productivity growth within firms has also been observed in countries such as India, the United States, and countries in Eastern Europe and Latin America.

> **Productivity growth in EAP has been driven primarily by increases in productivity within firms rather than reallocation between firms.**

FIGURE O.2   Decomposition of aggregate productivity growth in selected EAP countries

Percentage share

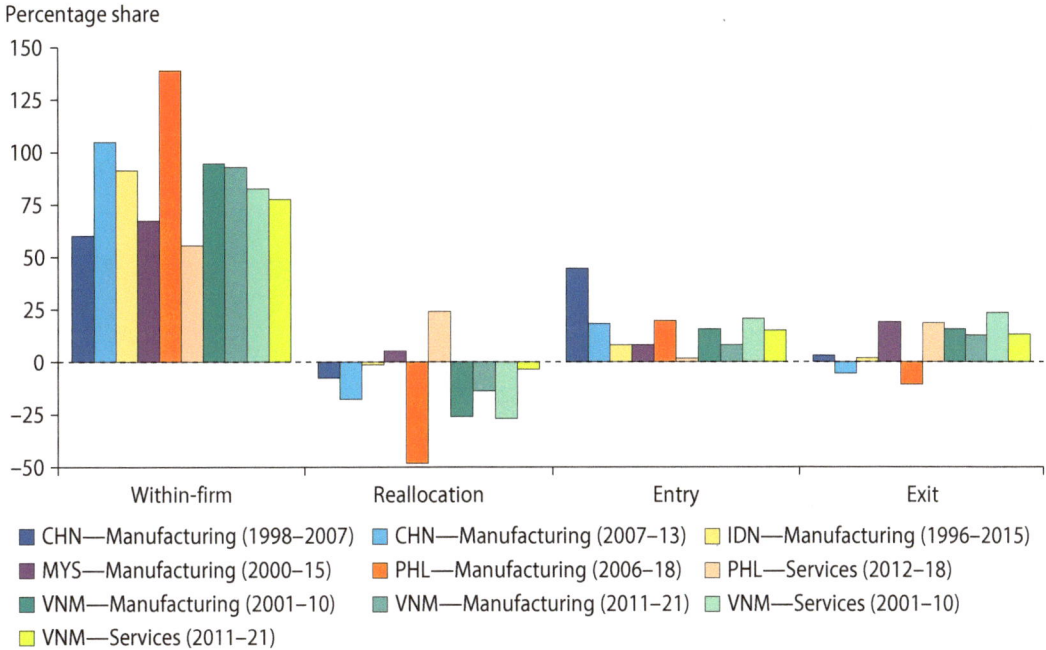

Legend:
- ■ CHN—Manufacturing (1998–2007)   ■ CHN—Manufacturing (2007–13)   □ IDN—Manufacturing (1996–2015)
- ■ MYS—Manufacturing (2000–15)   ■ PHL—Manufacturing (2006–18)   ■ PHL—Services (2012–18)
- ■ VNM—Manufacturing (2001–10)   ■ VNM—Manufacturing (2011–21)   ■ VNM—Services (2001–10)
- □ VNM—Services (2011–21)

Sources: Original figure for this publication using the specified statistical office microdata for Indonesia (IDN), Malaysia (MYS), the Philippines (PHL), and Viet Nam (VNM); Brandt et al. (2020) for China (CHN).
Note: Decompositions are calculated at the two-digit level and aggregated using value-added weights based on Foster, Haltiwanger, and Krizan (2001) decomposition. The figure reflects the average of 5 or 6 yearly productivity changes, over the periods shown in the legend (5 or 6 years depending upon country data availability). "Entry" reflects only entry of young firms; older firms entering in the microdata due to sampling changes have been excluded.

Productivity growth has been slower within the more-productive firms than the less-productive firms. Figure O.3 shows changes in the productivity distribution for each EAP country as repeated cross-sections to allow for changes in the composition of firms over time through entry and exit. The productivity of the most-productive firms within a sector (national frontier) in China, Indonesia, Malaysia, the Philippines, and Viet Nam has increased by less than the productivity of the rest of the firms in each respective country. These findings hold in both manufacturing and services. The relative stagnation of the most-productive firms is also observed in developing countries beyond EAP, although to a lesser extent.[2] These findings may suggest catch-up by the relatively backward firms, which is in itself desirable, but the slow growth of the frontier firms raises concerns, as discussed later.

In the EAP region, the productivity growth of frontier manufacturing and services firms has been slower than that of other firms.

FIGURE O.3   Productivity growth along the firm productivity distribution, EAP countries

a. Manufacturing firms, 1998–2019   **b. Services firms, 2010–19**

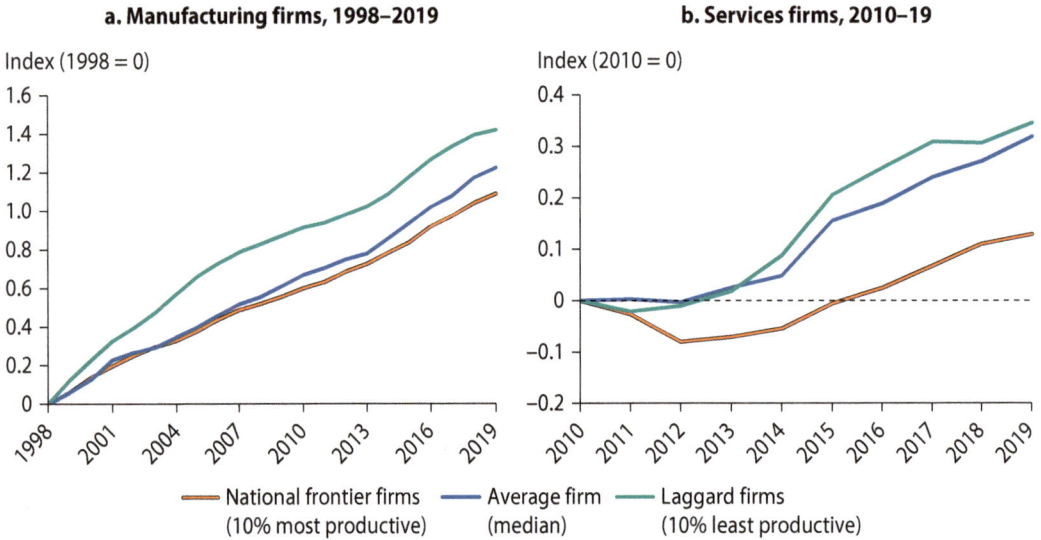

—— National frontier firms (10% most productive)   —— Average firm (median)   —— Laggard firms (10% least productive)

Source: Original figure for this publication using statistical office microdata for manufacturing firms in China, Indonesia, Malaysia, the Philippines, and Viet Nam and for services firms in the Philippines and Viet Nam.
Note: The figure reflects cross-sectional percentiles of the firm productivity distribution within countries, by two-digit industry, over time. "National frontier firms" refer to the 90th percentile of the firm productivity distribution and "laggard firms" to the 10th percentile. Annual changes reflect an unweighted average across countries and two-digit industries with available data.

The performance of frontier firms in global context

In the digital-intensive sectors—at the forefront of global innovation—the most-productive EAP firms ("the national frontier") are falling further behind the world's most-productive firms ("the global frontier"). Despite the global productivity slowdown, the global frontier has continued its rapid productivity growth, especially in digital-intensive sectors like electronics, pharmaceuticals, research and development, and information technology services.

These global trends contrast with the EAP national frontier. For example, in digital manufacturing sectors, the productivity of the global frontier increased by 76 percent between 2005 and 2015, whereas the national frontier firms in Indonesia, Malaysia, the Philippines, and Viet Nam increased their productivity by only 34 percent on average (refer to figure O.4). For less-digital-intensive sectors, the gap between the national and global frontier is less stark.

> The national frontier in EAP countries is falling behind the global frontier, especially in digital sectors.

FIGURE O.4   **Productivity gaps between the global frontier and national frontier in EAP countries, by digital sector intensity, 2003–19**

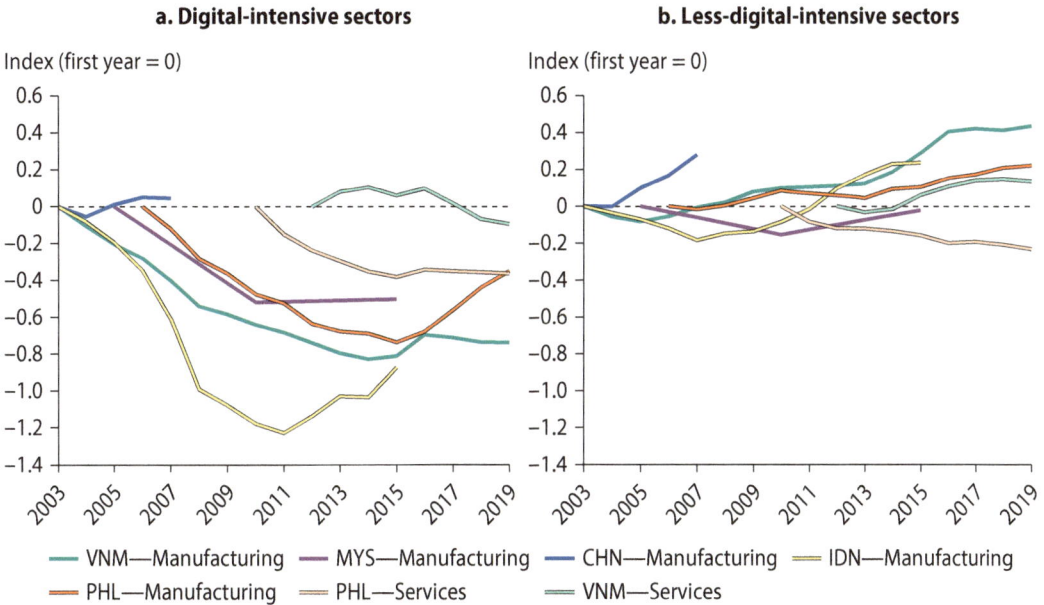

a. Digital-intensive sectors

b. Less-digital-intensive sectors

Index (first year = 0)

Legend:
- VNM—Manufacturing
- MYS—Manufacturing
- CHN—Manufacturing
- IDN—Manufacturing
- PHL—Manufacturing
- PHL—Services
- VNM—Services

Source: Original figure for this publication based on calculations using statistical office microdata (national frontier) and Criscuolo 2023 (global frontier).

Note: "National frontier" refers to the 90th percentile of the firm productivity distribution for each country and industry and "global frontier" to the 95th percentile of the firm productivity distribution across high-income economies within an industry (refer to box 3.1). The distance between the national and global frontier productivity is normalized to 0 in the first year, such that negative numbers reflect the national frontier falling further behind the global frontier relative to the first year, and positive numbers reflect the national frontier catching up with or exceeding the global frontier. Sector "digital intensity" is defined according to Eurostat's Digital Intensity Index, which classifies high-technology manufacturing and high-knowledge-intensive services as "digital-intensive sectors" (refer to box 3.2) and other manufacturing and services sectors as "less-digital-intensive sectors." CHN = China; IDN = Indonesia; MYS = Malaysia; PHL = Philippines; VNM = Viet Nam.

In this regard, the gap between EAP's and the world's most technologically sophisticated firms has widened, much more so than the gap between other EAP firms and their global counterparts (refer to figure O.5). Whereas firms in advanced economies are rapidly investing in data-driven business models—with investment increasing from 0.5 percent to 0.7 percent of gross domestic product between 2011 and 2018—investment in data has stagnated at around at 0.1 percent in the EAP region (refer to figure 3.12 in chapter 3).[3] The relative lack of sophistication of national technological leaders is also observed in low- and middle-income countries beyond the EAP region, although to a somewhat lesser degree.

> Gaps in technology use between developing East Asia and advanced countries are wider for more-sophisticated firms.

FIGURE 0.5   **Technology gap between firms in developing and advanced EAP countries**

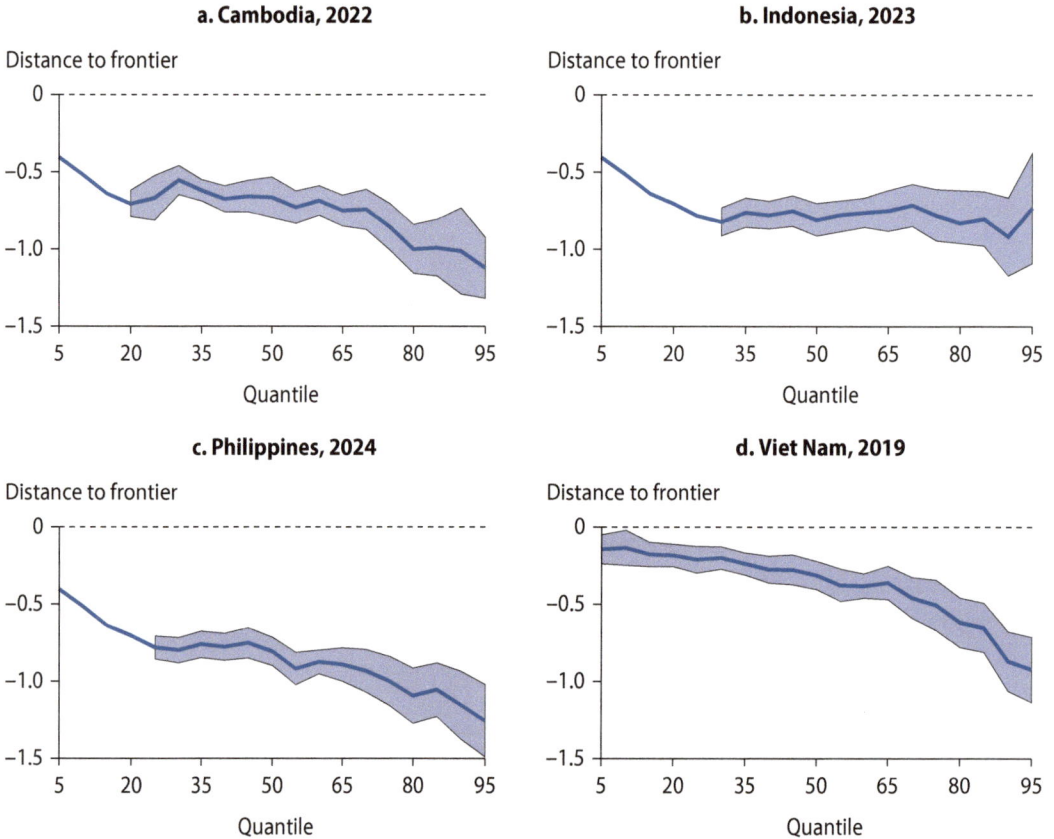

a. Cambodia, 2022

Distance to frontier

Quantile

b. Indonesia, 2023

Distance to frontier

Quantile

c. Philippines, 2024

Distance to frontier

Quantile

d. Viet Nam, 2019

Distance to frontier

Quantile

Source: Original figure for this publication using World Bank Firm-level Adoption of Technology (FAT) survey data from Cirera et al. (forthcoming).

Note: The figure reflects the sophistication of the most-common general business function technology (intensive margin) for both manufacturing and services sectors. The distributions of firms in Cambodia, Indonesia, and Viet Nam are shown in a percentile-to-percentile comparison with the distribution of firms in the most-advanced country (Republic of Korea) in the FAT data. For example, "distance to frontier" at the 95th percentile compares the top 5 percent most-sophisticated firms in each country with the top 5 percent in Korea. More negative numbers indicate larger technology gaps with Korean firms. Shaded areas represent the 95 percent confidence interval.

About one-third of the national frontier firms in the EAP region are the subsidiaries of multinationals, and even their performance falls below the global frontier. These subsidiaries tend to use more-advanced technologies than other national frontier firms but less-advanced technologies than the firms at the global frontier. There are at least two reasons for the relative backwardness. First, multinational enterprises (MNEs) that invest in developing countries are often not the most-sophisticated global firms—reducing the scope for spillovers of technology or productivity (refer to figure O.6). The parent MNEs of affiliates in emerging economies tend to have nearly 11 percent lower labor productivity and are 14 percent less likely to use artificial intelligence (AI).[4] Second, technology diffusion within MNEs is often incomplete. For example, although cloud computing has been widely adopted, about half of MNE subsidiaries have not adopted AI even when the headquarters did so (refer to figure O.7). One reason is that the multinational affiliates in developing countries may lack the capabilities to adopt the advanced technologies or business practices of their parent firms, as discussed later.

> **Affiliates in emerging economies tend to be part of less-productive and less technologically advanced multinationals.**

FIGURE O.6 Technology and labor productivity gaps between MNE affiliates in advanced and emerging economies, 2022

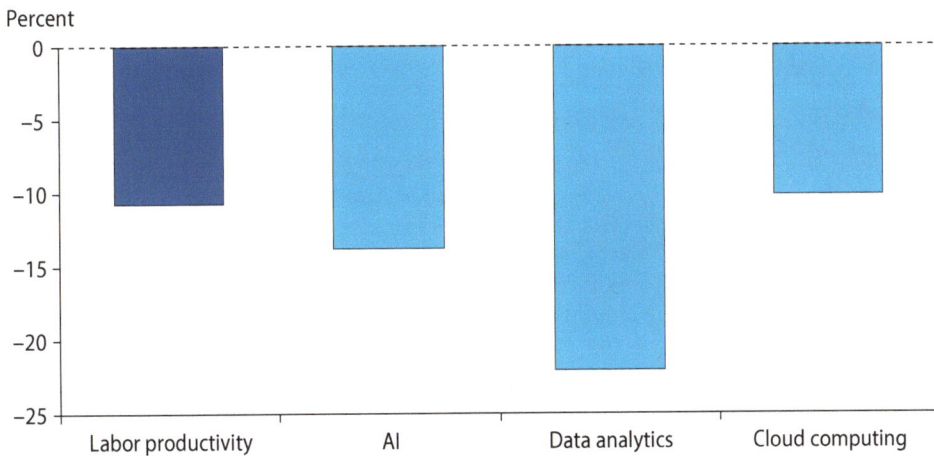

Source: Original figure for this publication using Spiceworks Computer Intelligence Technology Database data.
Note: The figure reflects 2022 data for 22 high-income economies and 7 emerging economies ("emerging" is according to IMF [2019] classifications). Regressions control for the country of origin of the parent MNE and reflect foreign affiliates of MNEs (that is, affiliates in countries other than the parent firm's). "Labor productivity" reflects multinational group revenue (in US dollars) per worker in 2020. "AI" use reflects machine learning. "Data analytics" reflects the use of enterprise resource planning software. "Cloud computing" reflects using Infrastructure as a Service (for example, servers, storage, networking, and virtualization). AI = artificial intelligence; MNE = multinational enterprise.

> **AI diffuses only partially within multinationals.**

FIGURE O.7   **Share of MNE subsidiaries using AI or cloud computing, by usage level, 2022**

a. AI

Share of subsidiaries within
an MNE using AI (%)

b. Cloud computing

Share of subsidiaries within an
MNE using cloud computing (%)

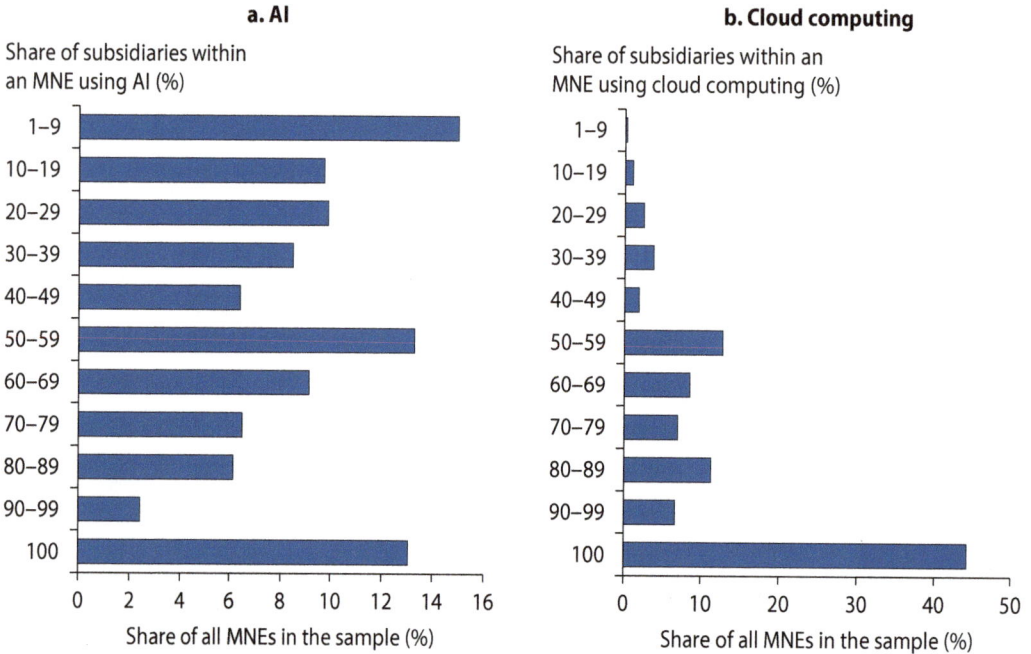

Source: Original figure for this publication using Spiceworks Computer Intelligence Technology Database data.
Note: The figure reflects 2022 data for 22 high-income economies and 7 emerging economies ("emerging" is according to IMF [2019] classifications). The figure also reflects MNEs with at least 1 subsidiary using "AI" or cloud computing (that is, excluding 0 percent share of subsidiaries). For example (panel a), in about 15 percent of the MNEs, only 1–9 percent of the subsidiaries use AI. Panel a reflects 4,229 MNEs, and panel b, 27,204 MNEs. Use of AI reflects machine learning. "Cloud computing" reflects using Infrastructure as a Service (for example, servers, storage, networking, and virtualization). AI = artificial intelligence; MNE = multinational enterprise.

The importance of national frontier firms

The poor performance of the frontier firms matters because they account for a large share of output and jobs, pay higher wages, and facilitate the diffusion of better technologies to other domestic firms. The national frontier firms shape aggregate productivity because of their relative size. They account for more than one-third of employment and more than one-half of value-added market share in the EAP region (refer to figure O.8). These frontier firms also pay triple the wages of the least-productive 10 percent of firms. In addition, the sluggishness of the national frontier firms raises concerns about the future growth of all firms. Because new knowledge and technologies typically arrive first at the frontier and then spill over to the rest of the firms, revitalizing the national frontier firms matters for the future growth of all firms. At a time of digital transitions, this is likely of heightened importance.

National frontier firms matter because of their size.

FIGURE O.8   **Share of sector value added and employment of EAP firms, by productivity decile**

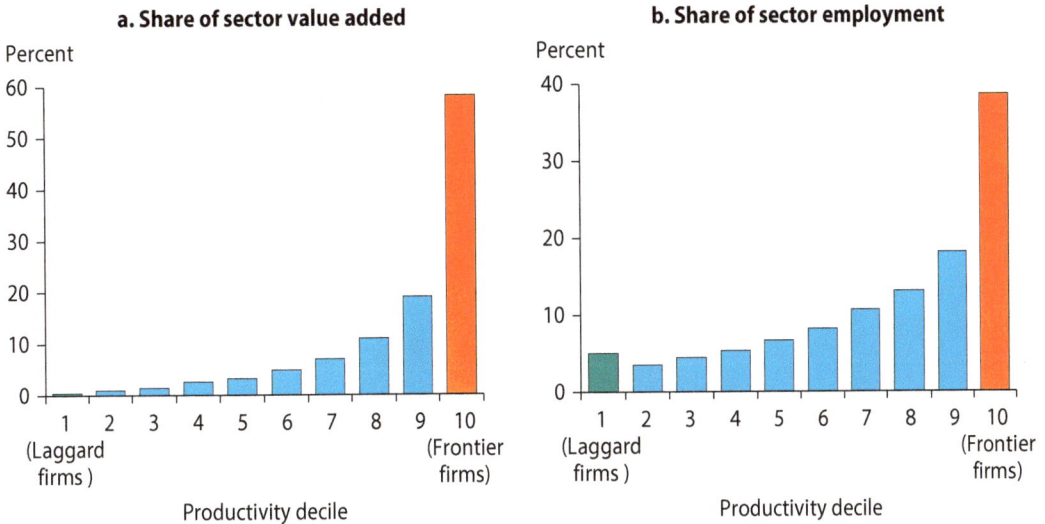

a. Share of sector value added

b. Share of sector employment

Source: Original figure for this publication based on calculations using statistical office microdata for China, Indonesia, Malaysia, the Philippines, and Viet Nam, as detailed in chapter 1, box 1.1.
Note: The share in two-digit industry employment or value added of the laggard and frontier firms (the bottom and top 10 percent by total factor productivity, respectively) are calculated within each country and industry and year. Unweighted average shown for all country industries. Data are from 1998–2007 for China, 1996–2015 for Indonesia, 2000–15 for Malaysia, 2006–18 for the Philippines, and 2001–21 for Viet Nam.

Why are the leaders not leading?

The EAP region's relative inertia may be because frontier firms lack adequate incentives (such as the spur of international competition) and the relevant capabilities (such as access to high-quality skills and infrastructure). EAP frontier firms are more likely than less-productive firms to identify as key constraints barriers to trade, paucity of skills, and weakness in the transport and telecommunications infrastructure (refer to figure O.9).

More-productive firms report trade regulations, poor workforce skills, and weak transport or telecommunications infrastructure as important constraints to business operations.

FIGURE O.9   Severity of constraints to manufacturing business operations in developing EAP countries, by labor productivity quartile (versus bottom quartile)

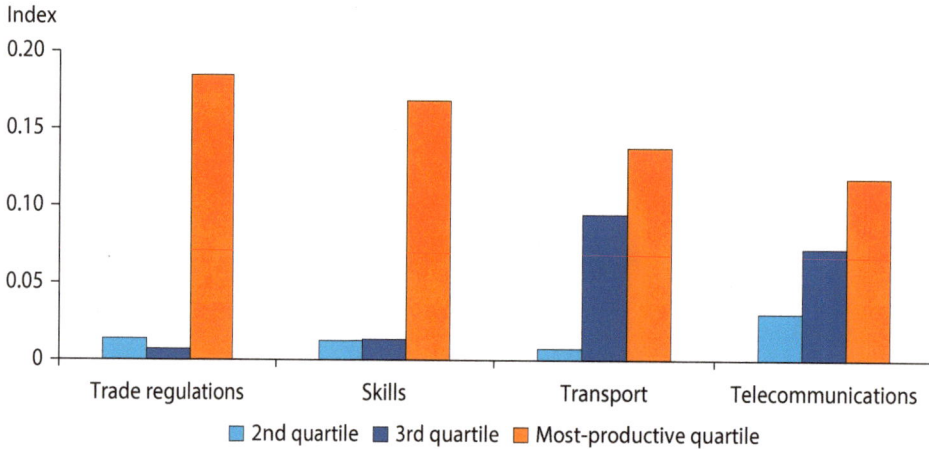

Source: Original figure for this publication based on calculations using World Bank Enterprise Surveys.
Note: The figure reflects data for 11 developing East Asia and Pacific countries from Enterprise Surveys between 2009 and 2023. Labor productivity quartiles of manufacturing firms are calculated within each country and year (applying sampling weights). Scores reflect the severity of constraint reported by firms (on a 0–4 scale) within each quartile, relative to the bottom quartile (least-productive firms). The figure presents the results of firm-level regressions of reported constraints on labor productivity quartiles, controlling for firm size and country and year fixed effects.

Firms require the right incentives

Impediments to competition are inhibiting the incentive to innovate, especially among the frontier firms, and preventing the reallocation of resources toward more-productive firms. Less exposure to competition—from openness to trade and investment, for instance—reduces the incentives for frontier firms to innovate to stay ahead of their competitors (Aghion, Antonin, and Bunel 2021; Aghion et al. 2009). In contrast, laggard firms grow in less-competitive sectors because it is easier for them to catch up with other firms.

Frontier firms in EAP that are more exposed to competition show faster productivity growth. Foreign-owned frontier firms showed 3.4 percent faster annual productivity growth than other frontier firms (refer to figure O.10, panel a), and their presence led to faster productivity growth than other frontier firms in the same sector (refer to figure O.10, panel b). In contrast, state-owned enterprises (SOEs) have 3.5 percent slower productivity growth, and their presence reduced the productivity growth of other frontier firms.

Higher SOE presence in EAP is associated with lower TFP growth of frontier firms, and higher foreign-firm presence is associated with higher TFP growth.

FIGURE O.10   Correlation between productivity growth of EAP frontier firms and the presence of state-owned or foreign-owned firms

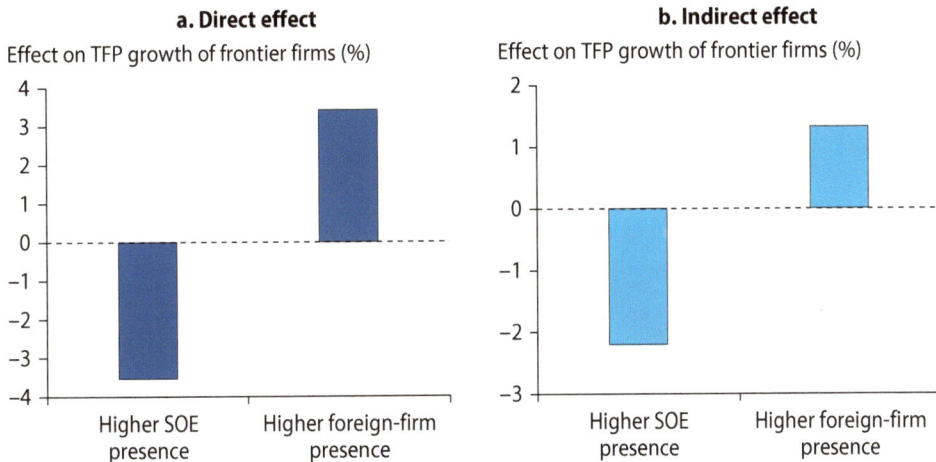

Source: Original figure for this publication using calculations based on statistical office microdata for China, Indonesia, the Philippines, and Viet Nam. Refer to box 1.1 for years of data.

Note: State ownership data are available only for China and Indonesia; foreign ownership data are available for all four countries. "Direct effect" of foreign ownership (panel a) reflects the difference in annual TFP growth between foreign-owned and domestic-owned frontier firms. "Frontier firms" are the most-productive 10 percent of firms within a country and industry. "Indirect effect" (panel b) represents the differential annual TFP growth for domestic-owned frontier firms in industries with 10 percent higher foreign ownership (measured as the share of industry sales due to foreign-owned firms). The direct and indirect effects of higher state ownership are defined similarly. The figure reflects an unweighted average across countries. All estimated effects are statistically significant at the 95 percent level. SOE = state-owned enterprise; TFP = total factor productivity.

Although manufacturing tariffs are relatively low in EAP countries, nontariff measures in manufacturing and restrictions on services trade limit competition. Services trade restrictions are higher in most EAP countries than in countries of a similar level of development (refer to figure O.11, panel b), and this is also true of nontariff measures in manufacturing (figure O.11, panel a). Furthermore, product market regulations in China and Indonesia are 50 percent more restrictive than in the United States (OECD 2023). Some EAP markets, for example in Viet Nam, are dominated by SOEs that can also influence competitive conditions. One symptom of weakening competition in EAP is the dramatic decline in the number of start-ups over the past two decades, especially in digital-intensive sectors, and the region is increasingly full of aging incumbents. For example, in Viet Nam's digital sectors, the share of young firms has declined from around half of industry employment in 2011 to less than a third in 2021 (refer to chapter 4, figure 4.4).

> Most EAP countries restrict goods and services trade more than other economies at comparable levels of development.

FIGURE O.11   Extent of nontariff barriers and services trade restrictions in EAP countries relative to developing countries elsewhere

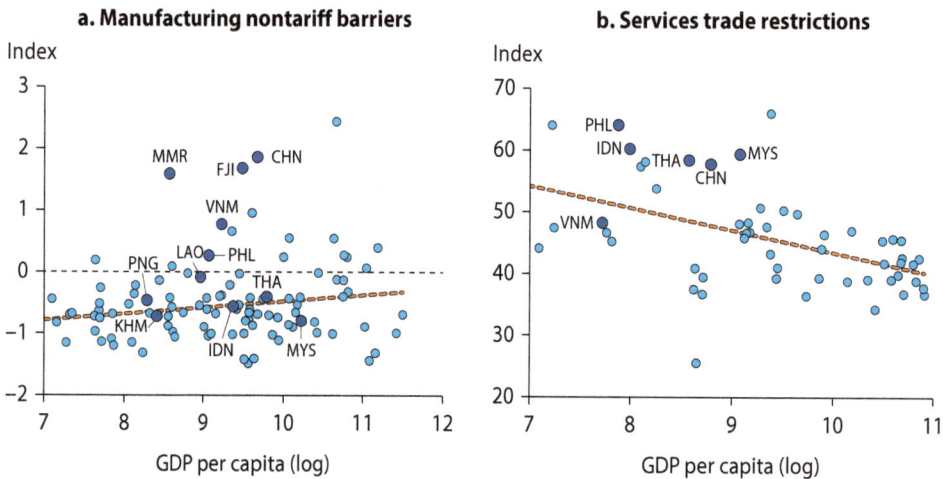

a. Manufacturing nontariff barriers

b. Services trade restrictions

Sources: Original figure for this publication based on calculations using UNCTAD TRAINS NTM data and CEPII BACI trade data (panel a); World Bank 2024 (panel b).

Note: The index in panel a is the average difference between the number of border NTMs applied by an economy in each product and the average number of measures applied to that product based on 2021 TRAINS NTM dataset. Averages are computed by weighing each product by its importance in world trade. Following Ederington and Ruta (2016), border NTMs cover all price and quantity control measures (for example, quotas, bans, prohibitions, nonautomatic licenses); preshipment inspections; and port of entry or direct consignment requirements; as well as other customs monitoring and surveillance requirements; customs inspection, processing, and servicing fees; additional taxes; and charges levied in connection to services provided by the government (for example, stamp tax and statistical tax). The index in panel b is the average Services Trade Restrictions Index (of the World Bank and World Trade Organization) per country in 2021 or last available year. BACI = Base pour l'Analyse du Commerce International; CEPII = Centre for Prospective Studies and International Information; CHN = China; FJI = Fiji; IDN = Indonesia; KHM = Cambodia; LAO = Lao PDR; MMR = Myanmar; MYS = Malaysia; NTMs = nontarrif measures; PHL = the Philippines; PNG = Papua New Guinea; THA = Thailand; TRAINS = Trade Analysis Information System; UNCTAD = United Nations Conference on Trade and Development; VNM = Viet Nam.

Firms require the right capabilities

The adoption of sophisticated technologies and productivity growth require a broad range of skills and high-quality digital infrastructure. In EAP, frontier firms with a higher share of educated workers showed faster productivity growth than other frontier firms (refer to chapter 5, figure 5.4). New technologies in Vietnamese manufacturing raised productivity but only among firms with sufficiently skilled workers (refer to chapter 4, figure 4.16). Access to fiber broadband in the Philippines is associated with the adoption of more-sophisticated technologies (such as data analytics) and higher firm productivity (refer to chapter 5, figure 5.6).

Access to modern data infrastructure and the necessary skills to use it are uneven in EAP. Whereas access to mobile broadband is widespread in EAP, high-speed fiber is unevenly available across and within countries (refer to map O.1). The region shows wide variations in the availability of data centers needed to store, share, and process data via the cloud. Data localization and variations in data privacy laws limit access to cross-border data and cloud computing. Furthermore, even basic digital skills are rare, with less than a quarter of workers in Cambodia, Mongolia, the Philippines, Thailand, and Viet Nam able to use the "copy and paste" function in a document (refer to chapter 4, figure 4.12).

Management skills also play a crucial role in leveraging new technologies. The average firms in both high-income and low- and middle-income EAP countries are, on average, less well managed than in the United States (refer to figure O.12). However, even the best-managed firms in low- and middle-income EAP countries are behind the best-managed firms in high-income EAP countries and far behind those in the United States.

High-speed broadband is unevenly available within and across EAP countries.

MAP O.1   Fixed broadband speeds in EAP countries, 2023

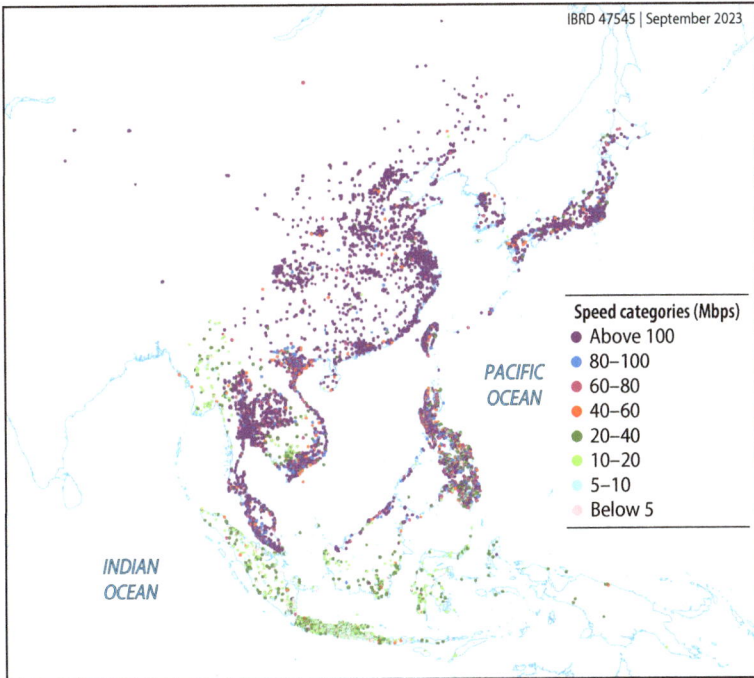

Source: IBRD 47545, December 2023, using Ookla fixed broadband speedtest data from 2023-Q2.
Note: Mbps = megabits per second.

> The best-managed firms in developing EAP countries have skills far below the best in high-income economies.

FIGURE O.12   Management skill gaps between EAP firms and US firms

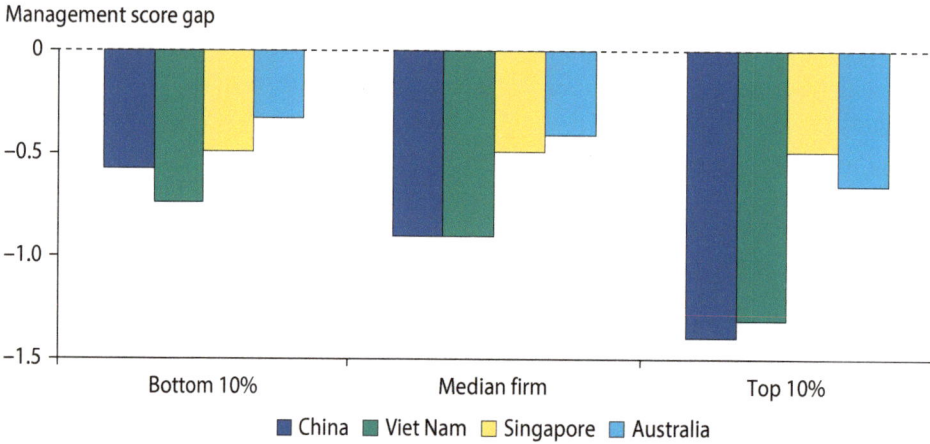

Management score gap

■ China ■ Viet Nam ■ Singapore ■ Australia

Source: Original figure for this publication based on the regression coefficients reported in Table 1 of Maloney and Sarris (2017).

Note: The figure reflects the gap in management scores between the best-managed firms (top 10 percent) in selected EAP countries and those in the United States. The bottom 10 percent and median are defined similarly.

How can policy boost technology adoption and productivity growth?

Policy reforms and support can help generate both the incentives to invest in technology to improve productivity and the capabilities to do so. Policies should focus first on doing no harm by eliminating impediments to entry and competition that inhibit the incentive to improve. Second, policies should seek to support the common good through horizontal policies to build human capital and infrastructure and create the capacity to improve. Third, in some cases, policy may seek to do specific good, such as through targeted industrial policies.

Reforms to spur competition

Eliminating impediments to entry and competition in goods and services markets can accelerate productivity growth. Tariff liberalization in Viet Nam around the time of its WTO accession (refer to figure O.13, panel a) raised the productivity of frontier and other firms, especially in downstream sectors that use these imported inputs (refer to figure O.13, panel b). While EAP goods markets are relatively open, liberalization of remaining tariffs and the relatively opaque nontariff measures could increase exposure to competition at home and equip firms to compete abroad. Elimination of restrictions on entry and operation in services, too, could have a pro-competitive impact (World Bank 2024). For example, services reforms in Viet Nam are associated both with more than 5 percent growth in the productivity of frontier firms in these same sectors and with more than 10 percent productivity growth in the frontier downstream manufacturing firms (refer to figure O.14).

Opening goods to competition can increase productivity in these manufacturing sectors as well as downstream sectors that use these inputs.

FIGURE O.13   Correlation between firm productivity and tariff reform in Viet Nam

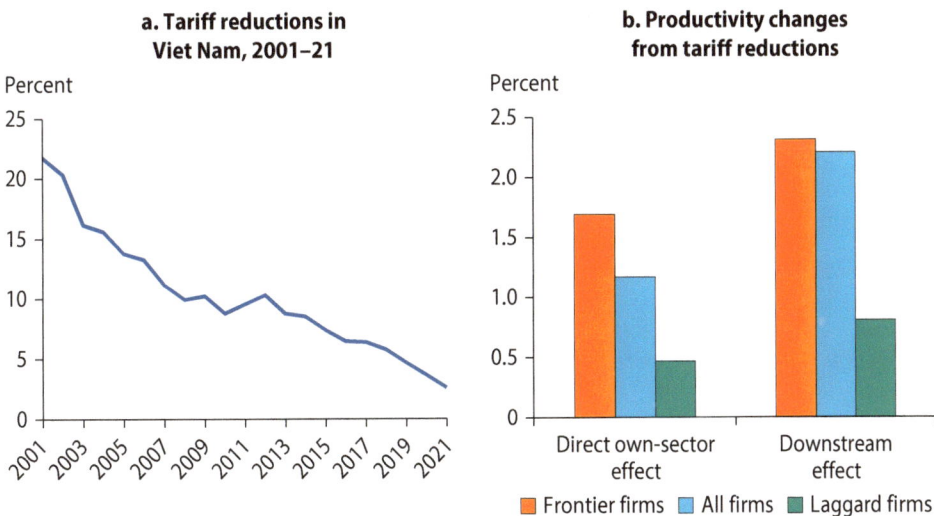

a. Tariff reductions in Viet Nam, 2001–21

b. Productivity changes from tariff reductions

Frontier firms   All firms   Laggard firms

Sources: Original figure for this publication using calculations based on enterprise surveys for manufacturing firms, General Statistics Office of Viet Nam; tariff data from McCaig, Pavcnik, and Wong (2023).
Note: "Frontier firms" are defined as the top 10 percent in TFP within an industry and "laggard firms" as the bottom 10 percent. Coefficients reflect the estimated increase in productivity for a 1 standard deviation decrease in tariffs. The coefficients on laggard firms are not statistically different from 0, all other coefficients are statistically significant at the 99 percent level. Panel a shows the effectively applied tariff rates over time; unweighted average by two-digit industry. Panel b presents the within-firm changes in TFP as a result of output tariff changes (labeled "direct own-sector effect") or input tariff changes (labeled "downstream effect"). The input tariffs have been calculated using the tariffs for each two-digit manufacturing sector, weighted by the corresponding share of inputs purchased from these sectors. The inputs are taken from the 2002 input-output tables for Viet Nam from the 2023 Organisation for Economic Co-operation and Development Inter-Country Input-Output tables. TFP = total factor productivity.

> Opening services to competition in Viet Nam increased productivity in these services sectors as well as in downstream manufacturing sectors that use services inputs.

FIGURE O.14   **Correlation between firm productivity and services reform in Viet Nam**

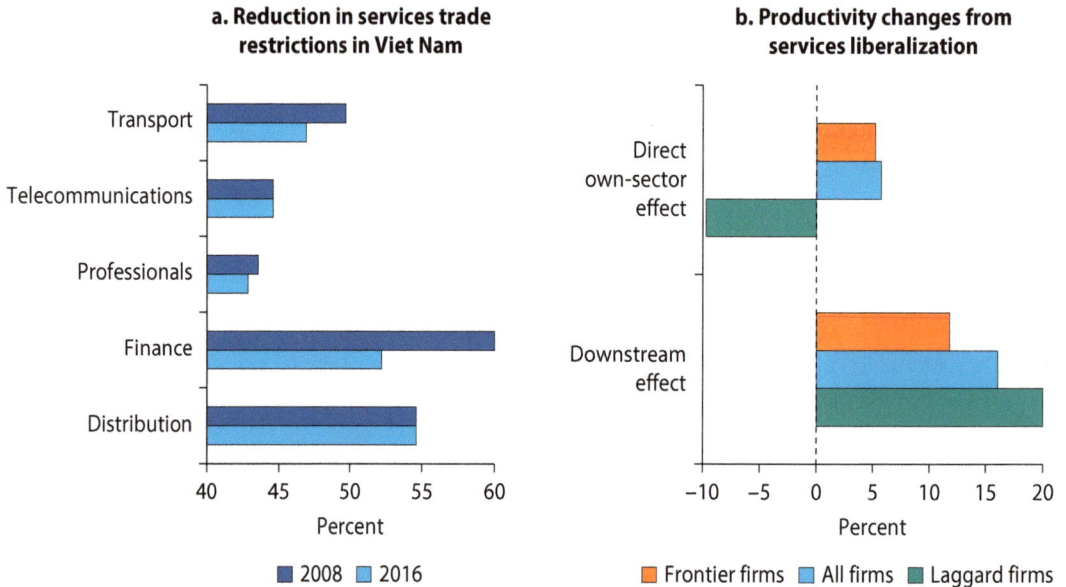

a. Reduction in services trade restrictions in Viet Nam

b. Productivity changes from services liberalization

Legend: ■ 2008 ■ 2016   ■ Frontier firms ■ All firms ■ Laggard firms

Source: Original figure for this publication based on estimations using data from 2008 and 2016 enterprise surveys, General Statistics Office of Viet Nam.

Note: The figure presents within-firms estimates of changes in total factor productivity between 2008 and 2016 and changes in the STRI of the World Bank and World Trade Organization. Coefficients reflect the estimated increase in productivity for a 1 standard deviation decrease in STRI. All coefficients are statistically significant at the 95 percent level. "Frontier firms" are defined as the top 10 percent most-productive firms within an industry, and "laggard firms" are the bottom 10 percent. The main explanatory variable is the change in STRI values in the trade, transport, finance, professionals, and telecommunications sectors between 2016 and 2008 in the "direct own-sector effect," and the change in the "downstream" STRI for manufacturing sectors in "downstream effect." The downstream STRI is a sector-specific measure for each two-digit manufacturing sector, calculated by the average STRI of the 5 services sectors, weighted by the corresponding purchasing value from each manufacturing sector. The regression sample in "direct own-sector effect" consists of all enterprises operating in the trade, transport, finance, professionals, and telecommunications sectors, and all manufacturing enterprises in "downstream effect," in 2008 and 2016. STRI = Services Trade Restrictions Index.

Reforms to enhance human capital

Improving human capital is imperative and has at least three dimensions. First is fixing the foundation of basic skills on which more-advanced skills can be built (World Bank 2023). Investing in teacher training is estimated to produce benefits in terms of discounted lifetime earnings that are 10 times larger than the costs.

Second is equipping workers with the skills that complement new technologies as well as the ability to innovate. Technology also tends to displace workers who cannot take advantage of the technology in their jobs. Investments in tertiary education, therefore, need to emphasize the development of workers' advanced cognitive, technical, and socioemotional skills.

Third is enhancing the abilities of managers. Differences in management quality are an important contributor to productivity differences across countries, and recent research suggests that management quality can be improved. For example, firms provided with management consulting in Colombia improved their management practices and increased employment (Iacovone, Maloney, and McKenzie 2022). Both intensive 1:1 consulting and cheaper consulting in small groups of firms led to improvements in management practices of a similar magnitude (8–10 percentage points) and in firm sales, profits, and labor productivity.

Infrastructure and the synergies between reforms

Synchronizing reforms can help exploit the synergies between enhanced human capital, infrastructure, and competition. Both openness to foreign competition and access to fiber broadband for firms in the Philippines increased technology adoption, but their combined impact was more than double (refer to figure O.15). Widening access to higher education in China led to increases in technology adoption and productivity, and these gains were especially large for foreign-owned firms (Che and Zhang 2018). Trade liberalization in Indonesia led to productivity-enhancing increases in foreign direct investment, and these gains were especially large for firms with more-skilled workforces (Blalock and Gertler 2009).

In some cases, policy may seek to do specific good through targeted industrial policies, which have been deployed both globally and in the EAP region. Such policies make economic sense when, for example, there are learning spillovers or coordination failures. The Republic of Korea offers an example of successful implementation of industrial policy: Temporary subsidies had a large and significant effect on firm sales as much as 30 years after subsidies ended (Choi and Levchenko, 2021; Lane 2024). However, industrial policy interventions may misfire, and extensive investments may yield limited results at best. China's investments in the shipbuilding industry echo patterns observed in other countries: Entry subsidies were wasteful (attracting small and inefficient firms), and production subsidies yielded negative net returns (Barwick, Kalouptsidi, and Zahur 2024). Historically, industrial policy is more likely to succeed when interventions are transparent, credibly tied to performance, and protected from political influence—and do not limit openness to domestic, and ideally international, competition.

> Firm productivity and data analytics use are strongly associated with having both access to fiber broadband and foreign ownership.

FIGURE O.15   Comparisons of productivity and investments in data and software in relation to foreign ownership or fiber broadband capability in the Philippines, 2013–21

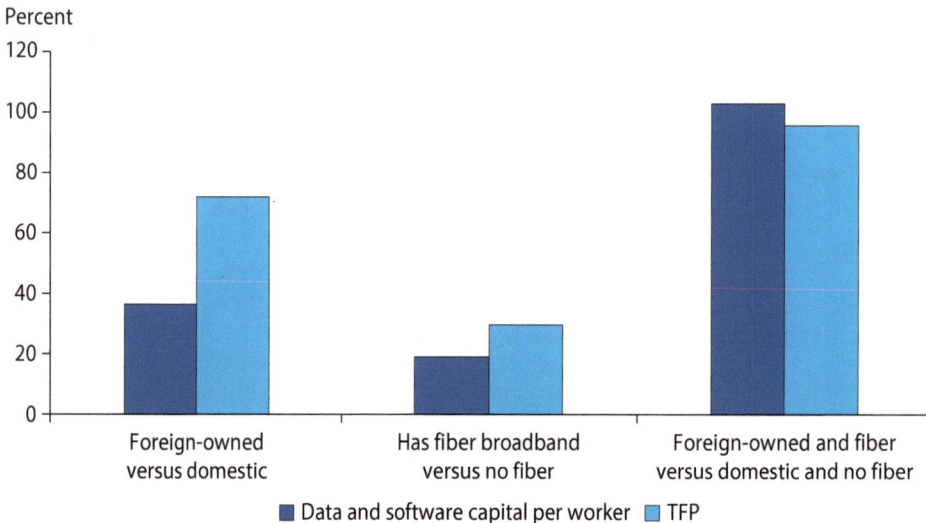

Source: Original figure for this report based on calculations using the Annual Survey of Philippine Business and Industry and Census of Philippine Business and Industry databases of the Philippines Statistical Authority.
Note: The figure shows the percentage increase in firm TFP or in data and software capital per worker associated with foreign-owned firms compared with domestically owned firms, firms with fiber broadband compared with those without fiber, and foreign-owned firms with fiber broadband compared with domestic-owned firms without fiber. Regressions control for two-digit industry and year fixed effects. TFP = total factor productivity.

Notes

1. Throughout the book, "productivity" refers to total factor productivity: the residual measure of improvements in technology and organization that cannot be explained by changes in capital or labor inputs. Where the book considers labor productivity, it is referred to as such. "Labor productivity" is defined as value added per worker.
2. "Developing" economies are low- and middle-income economies according to World Bank income classifications.
3. "Advanced" economies are high-income economies according to World Bank income classifications.
4. "Emerging" economies are defined according to International Monetary Fund classifications (IMF 2019).

References

Aghion, P., C. Antonin, and S. Bunel. 2021. *The Power of Creative Destruction: Economic Upheaval and the Wealth of Nations*. Cambridge, MA: Harvard University Press.

Aghion, P., R. Blundell, R. Griffith, P. Howitt, and S. Prantl. 2009. "The Effects of Entry on Incumbent Innovation and Productivity. *Review of Economics and Statistics* 91 (1): 20–32.

Barwick, P. J., M. Kalouptsidi, and N. B. Zahur. 2024. "Industrial Policy: Lessons from Shipbuilding." *Journal of Economic Perspectives* 38 (4): 55–80.

Blalock, G., and P. J. Gertler. 2009. "How Firm Capabilities Affect Who Benefits from Foreign Technology." *Journal of Development Economics* 90 (2): 192–99.

Brandt, L., J. Litwack, E. Mileva, L. Wang, Y. Zhang, and L. Zhao. 2020. "China's Productivity Slowdown and Future Growth Potential." Policy Research Working Paper 9298, World Bank, Washington, DC.

Che, Y., and L. Zhang. 2018. "Human Capital, Technology Adoption and Firm Performance: Impacts of China's Higher Education Expansion in the Late 1990s." *The Economic Journal* 128 (614): 2282–320.

Choi, J., and A. A. Levchenko, 2021. "The Long-Term Effects of Industrial Policy," NBER Working Papers 29263. National Bureau of Economic Research, Cambridge, MA.

Cirera, X., D. Comin, and M. Cruz. 2022. *Bridging the Technological Divide: Technology Adoption by Firms in Developing Countries*. Washington, DC: World Bank.

Cirera, X., D. Comin, M. Cruz, K. M. Lee, and A. Soares Martins Neto. Forthcoming. "Distance and Convergence to the Technology Frontier." Research Paper, World Bank, Washington, DC.

Criscuolo, C. 2023. "Productivity Growth and Structural Change in the Era of Global Shocks." PowerPoint, KDI–Brookings Joint Seminar: Productivity in a Time of Change, April 11. https://www.brookings.edu/wp-content/uploads/2023/04/2.1-KDI-Brookings-Jointt -Seminar-revised-ppt_Chiara-Criscuolo.pdf.

Ederington, J., and M. Ruta. 2016. "Non-Tariff Measures and the World Trading System." Policy Research Working Paper Series 7661, World Bank, Washington, DC.

Iacovone, L., W. Maloney, and D. McKenzie. 2022. "Improving Management with Individual and Group-Based Consulting: Results from a Randomized Experiment in Colombia." *Review of Economic Studies* 89 (1): 346–71.

IMF (International Monetary Fund). 2019. *World Economic Outlook 2019: Global Manufacturing Downturn, Rising Trade Barriers*. Washington, DC: IMF.

Lane, N. 2024. "Manufacturing Revolutions: Industrial Policy and Industrialization in South Korea." Working Paper No. 11388, CESifo, Munich.

Maloney, W. F., and M. Sarrias. 2017. "Convergence to the Managerial Frontier." *Journal of Economic Behavior and Organization* 134: 284306.

McCaig, B., N. Pavcnik, and W. F. Wong. 2023. "Foreign and Domestic Firms: Long Run Employment Effects of Export Opportunities." Working Paper No. 10168, CESifo, Munich.

OECD (Organisation for Economic Co-operation and Development). 2023. 2023 Product Market Regulation Indicators. Database, OECD, Paris. https://www.oecd.org/en/topics/sub-issues/product-market-regulation.html.

World Bank. 2023. *The Business of the State*. Washington, DC: World Bank.

World Bank. 2024. *World Development Report 2024: The Middle-Income Trap*. Washington, DC: World Bank.

Abbreviations

AI	artificial intelligence
ASEAN	Association of Southeast Asian Nations
BACI	Base pour l'Analyse du Commerce International
CEPII	Centre for Prospective Studies and International Information
CiTB	Computer Intelligence Technology Database
DII	Digital Intensity Index
EAP	East Asia and Pacific
EMDEs	emerging markets and developing economies
ERP	enterprise resource planning
EU	European Union
FAT	World Bank Firm-level Adoption of Technology
FDI	foreign direct investment
GDP	gross domestic product
HHI	Herfindahl-Hirschman Index
HICs	high-income countries
IMF	International Monetary Fund
IT	information technology
MICs	middle-income countries
MNEs	multinational enterprises
NTMs	nontariff measures
OECD	Organisation for Economic Co-operation and Development
p.p.	percentage points

PIM   perpetual inventory method
PPP   purchasing power parity
SOEs   state-owned enterprises
STRI   Services Trade Restrictions Index
TFP   total factor productivity
TRAINS   Trade Analysis Information System
UNCTAD   United Nations Conference on Trade and Development
US   United States
WTO   World Trade Organization

The Productivity Puzzle | 1

Key messages

- Productivity is the key driver of labor income in the long run.
- Income growth in the East Asia and Pacific (EAP) region over the past two decades has been driven by capital accumulation rather than productivity growth, despite the rapid emergence of new technologies.
- The region's limited increases in aggregate productivity have come predominantly from improvements within existing firms rather than from firm entry or from scaling-up by productive firms.

The importance of productivity

The EAP region benefited from rapid growth during the 2000s—raising wages and lifting millions out of poverty. However, the sustainability of growth depends upon its source. Although the region's growth in per capita income has surpassed that of most other emerging-market and developing economies in the past two decades,[1] growth was driven primarily by investing in capital rather than by total factor productivity (TFP) growth (refer to figure 1.1). Understanding the sources of declining productivity growth in EAP economies would help governments to design policies that support long-term growth.

Growth in labor productivity can arise from these channels:

- Greater capital or capital deepening;
- Human capital improvements through education and skill-enhancement;
- Higher TFP—that is, the part of production attributable to innovation because it cannot be explained by increases in quantities of labor or physical and human capital.

Developing countries can experience catch-up growth by investing more in physical capital (such as buildings, machines, and equipment) as well as human capital (through more and better education and training). But capital investment ultimately exhibits decreasing returns, although their onset is probably much further away in the case of human capital. In the long run, total factor productivity—the efficiency with which inputs are transformed into outputs—is the key driver of growth.[2]

Empirical evidence suggests that EAP's regional labor productivity growth has been driven predominantly by capital accumulation rather than TFP growth. As discussed in this chapter, capital deepening explains three-fourths of the labor productivity growth in 2002–19, both in China and in other EAP countries (refer to figure 1.1). In contrast, TFP improvements contributed to less than one-fifth of labor productivity growth. The large contribution of capital deepening and relatively small contribution of TFP is a long-standing feature of EAP growth, as reflected in earlier evidence using

Regional labor productivity growth has been driven by capital accumulation rather than TFP growth.

FIGURE 1.1   **Decomposition of labor productivity, by country and income group**

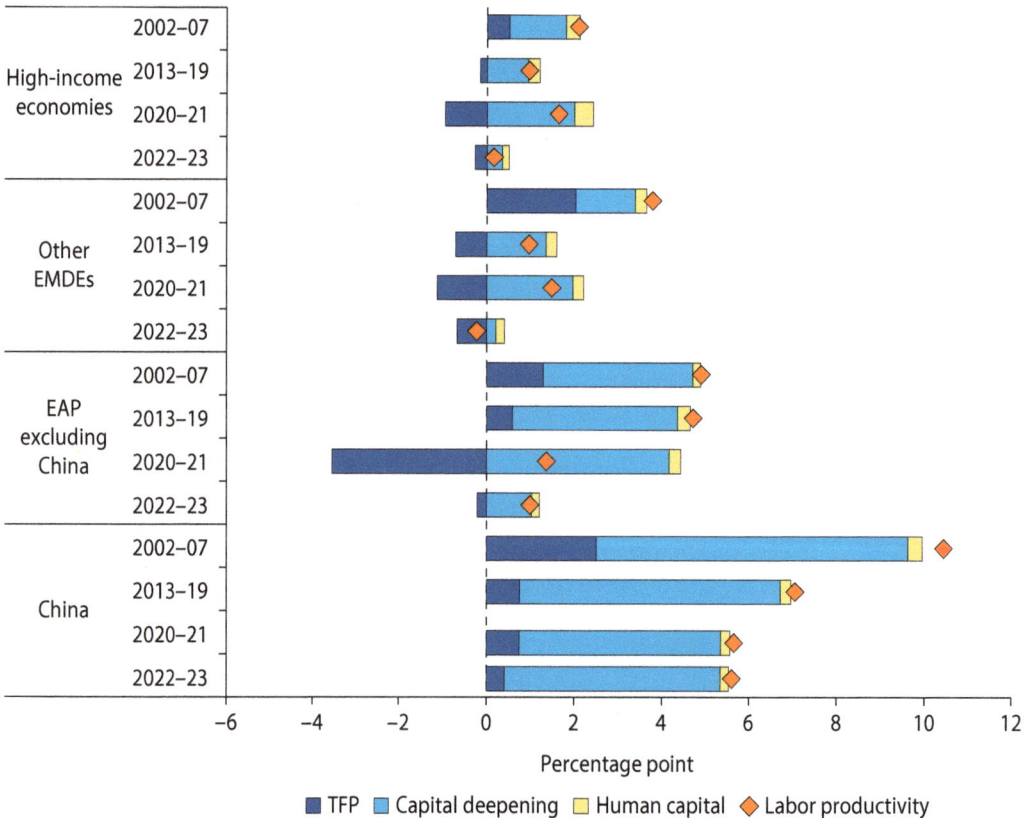

Source: Original figure for this publication compiled from datasets of the Conference Board's Total Economy Database.

Note: The figure shows unweighted medians. (EAP excluding China reflects 7 countries). EMDEs = emerging markets and developing economies, as defined by the International Monetary Fund (IMF 2019). TFP = total factor productivity.

data from the 1960s to the 1980s (Young 1994). The contribution of human capital accumulation to labor productivity growth has also been relatively low, although measuring human capital can be challenging.[3] Catalyzing productivity must be a policy priority—future living standards depend on it.

This chapter examines the challenge of productivity growth through novel firm-level analysis, the factors behind its slowdown, and the policies that could reignite TFP growth.

Sources of the productivity slowdown

Economies in EAP have experienced a productivity slowdown since the 2008–09 Global Financial Crisis, like most of the rest of the world. Although productivity growth has slowed globally, the slowdown has been more acute in developing East Asia and has occurred even in previously rapidly growing economies such as China (refer to figure 1.2). In fact, productivity growth has been slower in developing East Asia than in the region's advanced economies and the United States, suggesting that convergence with high-income country levels has slowed as well. Furthermore, the slowdown in TFP has led to a deceleration in labor productivity and wage growth, offsetting the impact of capital deepening. But what explains the productivity slowdown? And what can be done to revive productivity growth?

> **Aggregate productivity growth has slowed in developing East Asia.**

FIGURE 1.2   TFP growth trends in EAP and other selected countries, 1995–2022

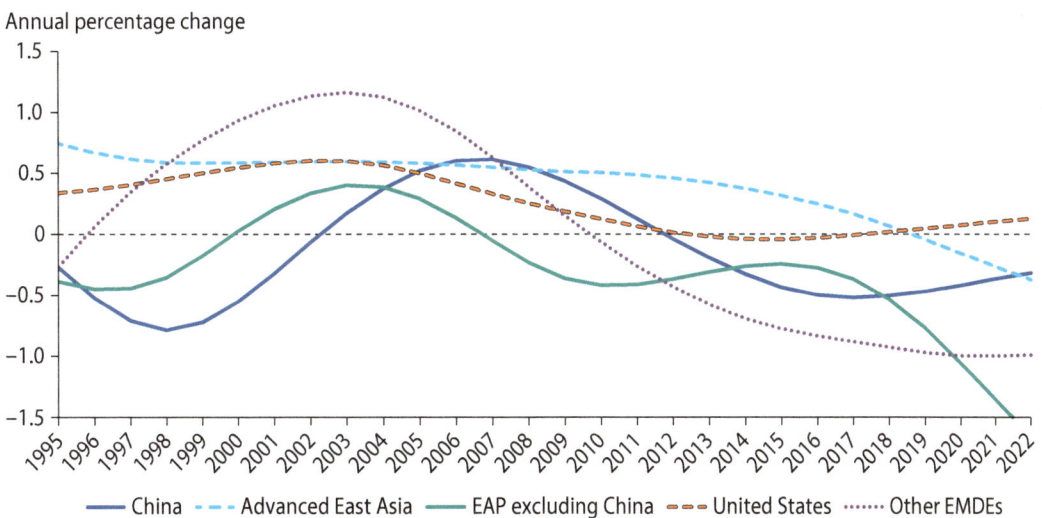

Source: Original figure for this publication compiled from datasets of the Conference Board's Total Economy Database.
Note: The figure reflects the trend in TFP growth after applying a Hodrick-Prescott filter to remove short-term fluctuations. The negative growth for recent periods is not always robust to different choices of filters and trimming of time periods; however, the productivity slowdown is a general finding. "Advanced" refers to high-income countries, according to World Bank income classifications. EMDEs = emerging markets and developing economies, as defined by the International Monetary Fund (IMF 2019). TFP = total factor productivity.

Aggregate productivity growth is a dynamic process involving productivity growth within firms, the reallocation of activity to more-productive firms, and entry and exit (refer to figure 1.3). Aggregate productivity, measured as TFP, is the sum of each underlying firm's TFP weighted by the firm's size (value added).[4] Aggregate productivity increases if existing firms become more productive (the "within-firm" component of figure 1.3)—for instance, by using new technologies or improving management practices. Aggregate productivity also increases if more-productive firms scale up or if less-productive firms shrink, reflecting the reallocation of value-added market share toward the more-productive firms (the "reallocation" component).[5] The dynamic process of entry and exit can also raise productivity through the entry of more-productive firms and the exit of less-productive ones (the "entry" and "exit" components). We aggregate these components using sector value-added weights to take account of changes in the structure of the economy.[6] We first decompose aggregate productivity growth into these components. We then take a closer look at the within-firm component, contrasting the growth of frontier and laggard firms.[7]

Correctly diagnosing the sources of the productivity slowdown matters for prescribing the right policies. For example, when productivity-enhancing exit is not happening, reforms aimed at facilitating firms' exit can boost productivity. Li and Ponticelli (2022) provide evidence that expediting insolvency resolution in China shifted employment away from sectors dominated by zombie firms, spurred new business entry, and improved capital productivity. Diagnosing the causes of the slowdown requires reliable firm-level data, which is unevenly available in the region (refer to box 1.1).

FIGURE 1.3   Sources of aggregate productivity growth

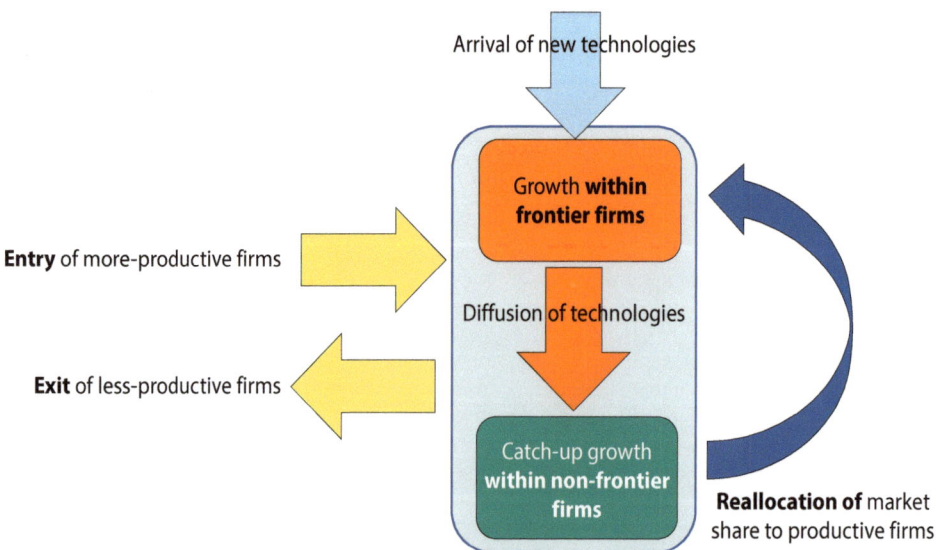

Source: Original figure for this publication.
Note: "Frontier firms" refer to the most-productive firms within a country and industry, defined as the 90th percentile of the firm productivity distribution.

Box 1.1 Availability of microdata in the East Asia and Pacific region

This book calculates and presents harmonized statistics using comprehensive firm-level data from statistical offices in the region, applying the same methods and data-cleaning steps across all the datasets. The statistical offices' microdata used in this report are representative but with some caveats: First, several countries have minimum firm-size thresholds. Second, because the data reflect the formal sector, they do not always capture the bottom of the firm distribution. In the productivity analysis, we focus on firms with at least 20 employees to enable comparability. The methods applied in this report may differ from those applied by statistical offices, so we may not be able to replicate aggregate trends, but the trends in this report are comparable across countries.

Although the East Asia and Pacific (EAP) region collects rich microdata, the availability of these data varies across countries. The usefulness of microdata is magnified when the data can be linked—whether to follow the same firms across time or to link to other firm data (such as linking firm productivity, technology surveys, or trade data). The Philippines Statistics Authority restricts availability to in-person access for approved research projects but is transparent in the process—the surveys, sampling strategy, and data dictionaries are available online—and allows linking of all its firm-level datasets.

For most other countries, data availability and access procedures may be less transparent, and matching different data can be impossible (often because control of different datasets rests with different ministries). These difficulties limit the potential for research. For instance, we have access to only cross-section data for Mongolia and Thailand, which prevents their inclusion in productivity decompositions. For Malaysia, we have information only for the manufacturing sector and could not obtain firm surveys on technology use. Accordingly, the latter parts of this book that examine mechanisms are biased toward the Philippines.

The sets of microdata used in this report, and the years of data, are as follows:

- *China:* National Bureau of Statistics "Above-Scale" Industrial Firms (manufacturing, 1998–2013)
- *Indonesia:* Statistik Industri (manufacturing, 1996–2015)
- *Malaysia:* Economic Census (manufacturing, 2000, 2005, 2010, 2015)

(continued)

Box 1.1   Availability of microdata in the EAP region *(Continued)*

- *Mongolia:* Cross-section Establishment Census (manufacturing and services, 2011, 2016, 2021)
- *The Philippines:* Annual Survey of Philippine Business and Industry and Census of Philippine Business and Industry (manufacturing, 2006–21; services, 2010–21)
- *Thailand:* Cross-section Business and Industry Census (manufacturing, 2012, 2017, 2022; services, 2012, 2022)
- *Viet Nam:* General Statistics Office Enterprise Survey (manufacturing and services, 2001–21).

The following data appear to exist but have not been accessible for inclusion in this volume:

- *Cambodia:* Economic Census (2011, 2022)
- *Lao People's Democratic Republic:* Economic Census (2006, 2013, 2020)
- *Malaysia:* Economic Census (services, 2000–15, 2020); Annual Economic Surveys (2000–22); Surveys on Usage of ICT and E-commerce by Establishment (biannually since 2015)
- *Thailand:* Panel data, Business and Industry Census (2022); Establishment Survey on the Use of ICT (2012, 2017, 2021)
- *Timor-Leste:* Business Activity Survey (2010–22).

Decomposition of productivity growth

In many EAP economies, productivity growth is mostly due to improvements in productivity within existing firms. For EAP countries on average, around three-quarters of aggregate productivity is due to within-firm growth, and for every country it reflects at least 50 percent of the aggregate (refer to figure 1.4).[8] Using labor productivity or alternative productivity decomposition methods as robustness checks, the analysis similarly finds that the within-firm component explains most aggregate productivity growth (refer to figure 1.5 and appendix figure A.1). The challenges of measuring capital are explained in appendix box A.2.

Productivity growth in EAP has been driven primarily by increases in productivity within firms.

FIGURE 1.4   Decomposition of aggregate productivity growth, selected EAP countries

Percentage share

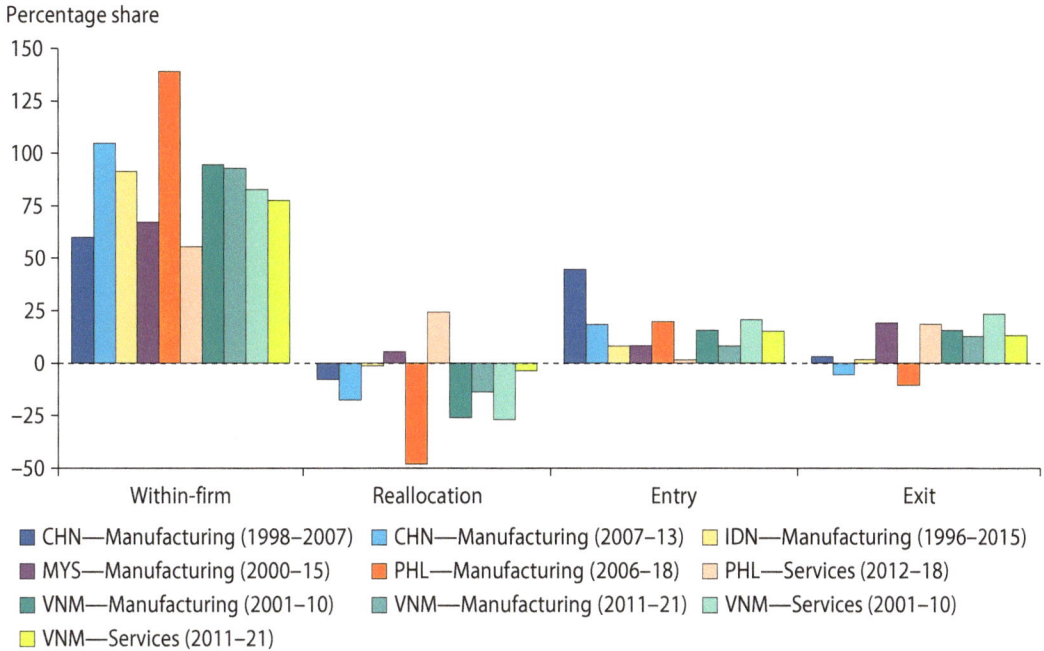

Sources: Original figure for this publication using the specified statistical office microdata for Indonesia (IDN), Malaysia (MYS), the Philippines (PHL), and Viet Nam (VNM); Brandt et al. (2020) for China (CHN).
Note: Decompositions are calculated at the two-digit level and aggregated using value-added weights based on Foster, Haltiwanger, and Krizan (2001) decomposition. The figure reflects the average of 5 or 6 yearly productivity changes, over the periods shown in the legend (5 or 6 years depending upon country data availability). "Entry" reflects only entry of young firms; older firms entering in the microdata due to sampling changes have been excluded.

The portion attributable to firm exit and reallocation is small (refer to box 1.2). This may suggest that resources are trapped in less-productive firms that should shrink or exit, which would enable more-productive firms to scale up and increase their market share. In fact, after China's World Trade Organization accession in 2001, almost half of the country's aggregate productivity growth came from new firms entering the market although within-firm growth still accounted for the bulk of growth. (Reallocation within existing and exiting firms contributed negligibly.)[9] Other studies suggest that alleviating firms' misallocation of capital and labor resources or production inputs across firms (and sectors) can potentially yield significant productivity gains—as high as 80 percent in Indonesia and around 20 percent in Malaysia (de Nicola, Loayza, and Nguyen 2024).

> Labor productivity growth in EAP has also been driven primarily by increases in labor productivity within firms.

FIGURE 1.5   Decomposition of labor productivity growth, selected EAP countries

Percentage share

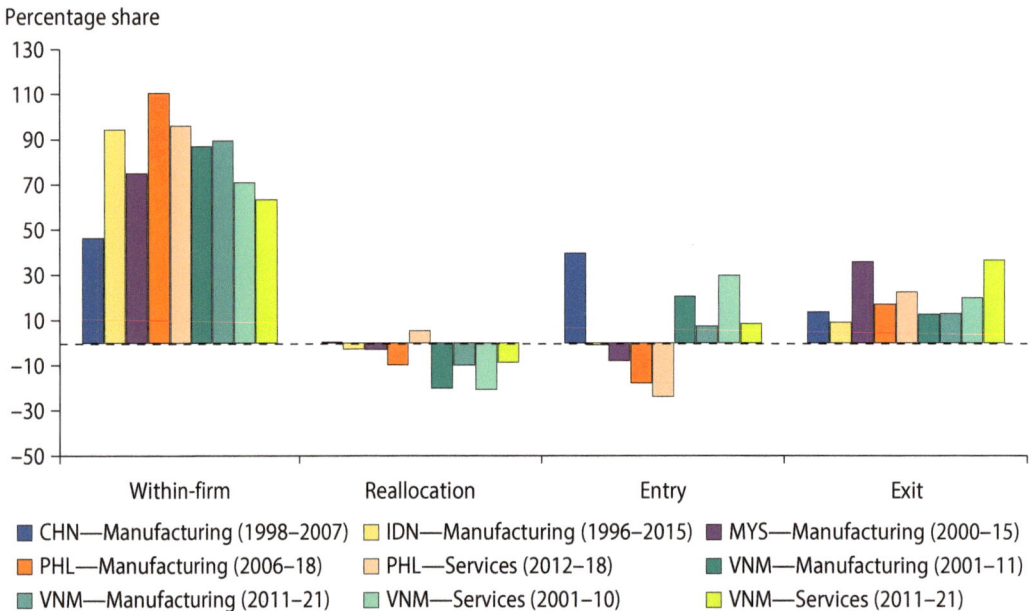

- CHN—Manufacturing (1998–2007)
- IDN—Manufacturing (1996–2015)
- MYS—Manufacturing (2000–15)
- PHL—Manufacturing (2006–18)
- PHL—Services (2012–18)
- VNM—Manufacturing (2001–11)
- VNM—Manufacturing (2011–21)
- VNM—Services (2001–10)
- VNM—Services (2011–21)

Source: Original figure for this publication using the specified statistical office microdata for China (CHN), Indonesia (IDN), Malaysia (MYS), the Philippines (PHL), and Viet Nam (VNM).
Note: "Labor productivity" is defined as real value-added per worker. Decompositions are calculated at the two-digit level and aggregated using value-added weights based on Foster, Haltiwanger, and Krizan (2001) decomposition. The figure reflects the average of 5 or 6 yearly productivity changes over the periods mentioned in the legend (5 or 6 years depending upon country data availability). Entry reflects only entry of young firms; older firms entering in the microdata due to sampling changes have been excluded.

Box 1.2   The reallocation puzzle

Productivity growth can be decomposed into four components: within-firm reallocation, between-firm reallocation, entry, and exit. Conventional wisdom suggests that moving resources from less-productive to more-productive firms should drive substantial productivity gains. Yet our empirical evidence indicates that reallocation between firms has a limited role in most countries. How can we interpret this?

More-productive firms are larger than less-productive firms in all EAP countries for which we have data (refer to figure B1.2.1). Before considering reallocation, that is changes in value added, it is helpful to first consider value-added levels. In other words, are more-productive firms larger in terms of their levels of value added? We find that

(continued)

Box 1.2   The reallocation puzzle *(Continued)*

a firm's value added is strongly related to its productivity. EAP firms that are twice as productive are on average 130 percent larger in terms of value added than other firms within the same industry and country. For all EAP countries for which we have data, we find firms that are twice as productive are, on average, at least twice as large.[a]

> **Firms that are twice as productive are more than twice as large in terms of value added in EAP.**

FIGURE B1.2.1   Relationship between firm value added and productivity in EAP countries

Value added (log. demeaned)

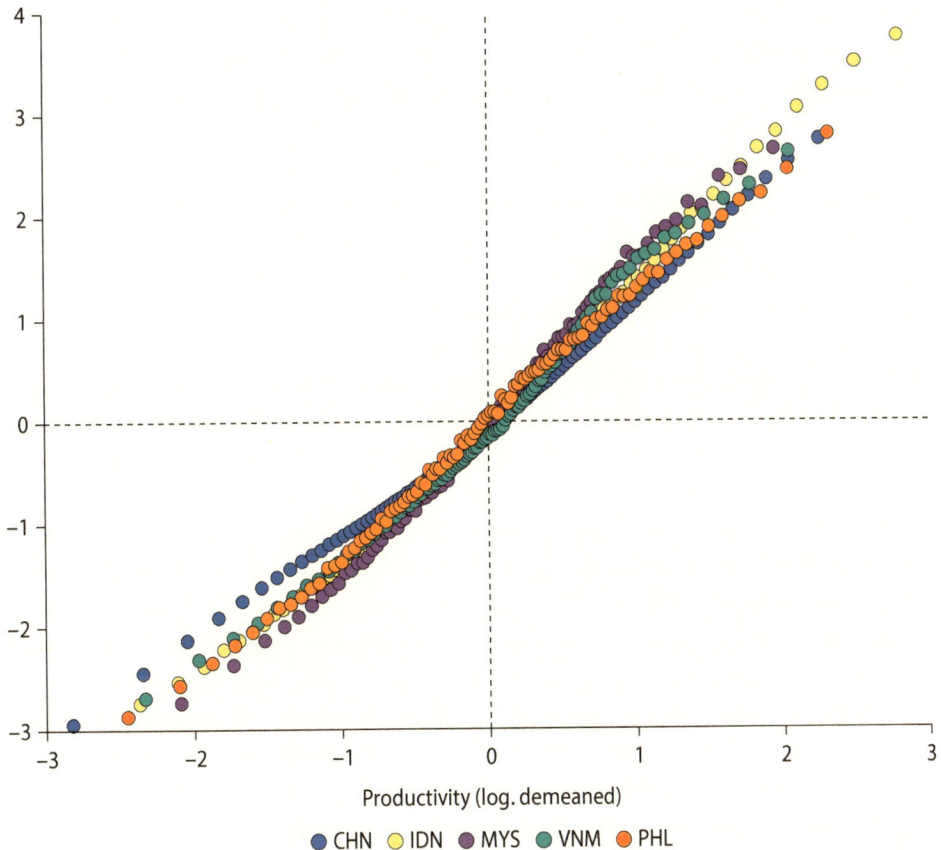

Productivity (log. demeaned)

● CHN   ○ IDN   ● MYS   ● VNM   ● PHL

Source: Original figure for this publication using statistical office microdata for China (CHN), Indonesia (IDN), Malaysia (MYS), the Philippines (PHL), and Viet Nam (VNM). Refer to box 1.1 for years of data.
Note: The figure shows the cross-section relationship between firm value added and firm productivity, comparing firms within the same country and industry. Firm value added and firm productivity are demeaned, subtracting the average value added or productivity of firms in that two-digit industry and country. For readability, firm productivity has been grouped into 100 categories and the average firm value added reported for that category.

(continued)

Box 1.2 The reallocation puzzle *(Continued)*

Productivity growth in most regions has been driven primarily by increases in productivity within firms, possibly because policy restrictions inhibit reallocation between firms. Using microdata for other countries in other regions reveals that most of the productivity gains are due to within-firm changes (refer to figure B1.2.2). This finding holds for Bulgaria, Colombia, Croatia, India, Romania, Serbia, and the United States, mirroring findings for EAP countries (refer to figure 1.4).

Studies in other regions using labor productivity rather than total factor productivity often arrive at similar conclusions. Using manufacturing firm data for Brazil, Bazzi, Muendler, and Rickey (2014) find that the within-firm component explains most of the growth in labor productivity between 1987 and 2009. Similarly, the within-firm

> Productivity growth in other regions has also been driven primarily by increases in productivity within firms.

FIGURE B1.2.2 **Decomposition of productivity growth outside the EAP region**

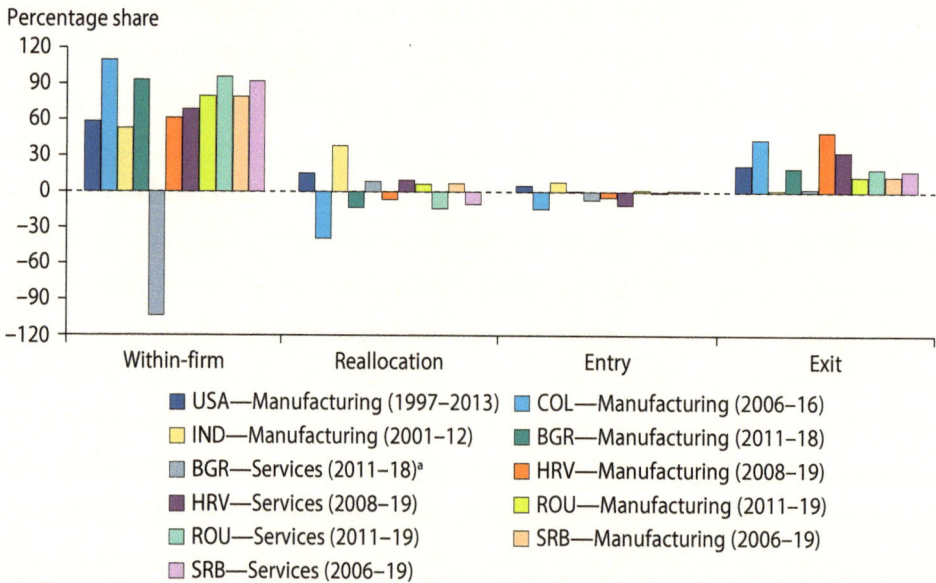

Percentage share

Legend:
- ■ USA—Manufacturing (1997–2013)
- ■ COL—Manufacturing (2006–16)
- □ IND—Manufacturing (2001–12)
- ■ BGR—Manufacturing (2011–18)
- ■ BGR—Services (2011–18)[a]
- ■ HRV—Manufacturing (2008–19)
- ■ HRV—Services (2008–19)
- ■ ROU—Manufacturing (2011–19)
- ■ ROU—Services (2011–19)
- ■ SRB—Manufacturing (2006–19)
- ■ SRB—Services (2006–19)

Sources: Calculations using statistical office microdata, with grateful acknowledgment of other World Bank teams; Pancost and Yeh (2022) for US data.

Note: "Productivity" is TFP. Decompositions are calculated at the two-digit level and aggregated using value-added weights based on Foster, Haltiwanger, and Krizan (2001) decomposition. The figure reflects the average of 5 yearly productivity changes, over the periods shown in the legend. "Entry" reflects only entry of young firms; older firms included in the microdata due to sampling changes have been excluded. BGR = Bulgaria; COL = Colombia; IND = India; HRV = Croatia; ROU = Romania; SRB = Serbia; USA = United States; TFP = total factor productivity.

a. Unlike other countries in the figure, Bulgaria's aggregate services TFP change is negative.

(continued)

Box 1.2 **The reallocation puzzle** *(Continued)*

component dominates the other components (entry, exit, or reallocation) of labor productivity growth for the manufacturing sectors in Chile, Colombia, Mexico, and Peru between 1995 and 2012 (Brown et al. 2018).

That reallocation becomes an important driver of productivity growth after reforms are implemented in developing economies (as discussed later) suggests that the persistence of input and product market restrictions could frustrate the movement of factors between firms.

Reallocation between firms is most pronounced during periods of transition following reforms. This relationship is evident in the experience of Colombia and several Eastern European countries (Bartelsman, Haltiwanger, and Scarpetta 2004; Eslava et al. 2004). For example, in Colombia from 1993 to 2012, a period of substantial structural reforms, about half of productivity growth was via entry and exit (Cusolito and Maloney 2018).

Reform periods also spur productivity improvements within firms. During the liberalization in Eastern Europe, around half of the aggregate productivity gains came from within-firm improvements (Bartelsman, Haltiwanger, and Scarpetta 2004). And in the case of reforms in India in the 1990s, most productivity growth occurred within plants (Bollard, Klenow, and Sharma 2013; Harrison, Martin, and Nataraj 2013; Sivadasan 2009). Once the transition is complete, one would expect further productivity gains to come mostly from improvements within firms instead of further reallocation between firms.

In less-distorted economies such as the United States, most product innovation is within firms. Innovation is one of the main drivers of productivity growth, and incumbent firms are largely driving innovation in high-income economies. Garcia-Macia, Hsieh, and Klenow (2019) infer the sources of innovation from employment dynamics of US firms and argue that incumbent firms drive around 80 percent of total product innovation. In contrast, only 20 percent of innovation is from new entrants—emphasizing that most productivity growth arises not from dramatic shifts in the market landscape but from continuous improvement and refinement by established firms. Their findings are consistent with Argente, Lee, and Moreira (2024), who find that adding and dropping products during the Great Recession was mostly within incumbents and was associated with improved-quality products, larger productivity gains, and faster growth.

Competition's disciplining effect may also contribute to within-firm increases in productivity. The latest empirical evidence challenges the view that entrants drive

(continued)

Box 1.2   The reallocation puzzle *(Continued)*

growth and incumbents are inert. As argued by Aghion and Howitt (1992) and more recently highlighted in *World Development Report 2024: The Middle-Income Trap* (World Bank 2024), entrants do create value themselves, but they also force incumbents to adapt or exit. In fact, competition threats per se induce incumbents to improve products and production processes, promoting productivity growth. Also, incumbents may be better equipped to make improvements because they can bring scale and invest in upgraded products, management practices, and technologies for new markets. Scale allows incumbents to become more efficient and specialize in multiple product lines (Akcigit and Kerr 2018). For example, as Backus (2020) finds, an increase in competition in the ready-mix concrete industry caused productivity upgrades among incumbent firms through greater specialization and managerial inputs.

Note that the effect of competition can be heterogeneous across incumbent firms. Firms that are close to the technology frontier innovate to stay ahead of their competitors, whereas laggard firms are discouraged and innovate less (Aghion, Antonin, and Bunel 2021; Aghion et al. 2005, 2009). Later chapters return to this point.

Measurement challenges can obscure the role of reallocation. Although the aforementioned factors may dwarf the extent to which reallocation between firms contributes to productivity growth in EAP, measurement challenges may also be a reason. Kehrig and Vincent (2019) highlight the challenges in measuring reallocation effects over longer periods. Aggregate data often fail to separate the productivity gains due to sectoral shifts from within-sector dynamics driven by entry, competition, and innovation. Much of what appears to be limited sectoral reallocation may instead reflect mismeasured within-sector dynamics.

a. The correlation between firm value added and firm productivity within a country and two-digit industry is 1.14 for China, 1.30 for Indonesia, 1.47 for Malaysia, 1.27 for Philippines manufacturing, 1.09 for Philippines services, 1.41 for Viet Nam manufacturing, and 1.17 for Viet Nam services.

Because most productivity growth was due to within-firm growth, the slowdown in aggregate productivity is also likely due to a slowdown in within-firm growth. Indeed, research on manufacturing firms in Thailand finds that the bulk of the fall in manufacturing productivity between 2006 and 2011 was due to declining productivity within firms, with reallocation and entry or exit contributing negligibly (Paweenawat, Chucherd, and Amarase 2017; World Bank 2020).

The role of new technologies

Why the productivity slowdown has come at a time of rapid technological progress is puzzling. Many new technologies such as automation, broadband internet, and e-commerce are diffusing rapidly (refer to figure 1.6). These technologies tend to arrive first at the frontier, potentially increasing productivity within frontier firms and spurring reallocation through increases in their scale. Adoption of new technologies does matter for productivity, with evidence from the Philippines showing this is particularly the case for services sector firms (refer to figure 1.7). In the use of data analytics, for instance, productivity increases are three times higher in services than in manufacturing.

Chapter 2 explores how technology adoption and productivity improvements are intertwined—shedding further light on the puzzling conjunction of rapid technological progress and the productivity slowdown.

New technologies have diffused rapidly in the EAP region.

FIGURE 1.6   Diffusion of robots and broadband in EAP countries

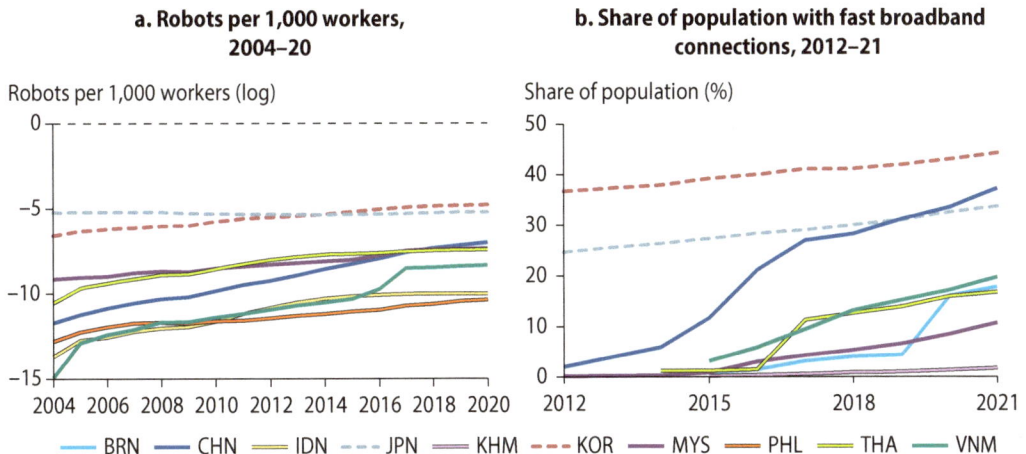

a. Robots per 1,000 workers, 2004–20

b. Share of population with fast broadband connections, 2012–21

Sources: Original figure for this publication based on calculations using International Federation of Robotics and World Development Indicators data (panel a); calculations using International Telecommunication Union data (panel b).
Note: "Fast broadband" is defined as connections of >10 megabits per second (Mbps). BRN = Brunei; CHN = China; IDN = Indonesia; JPN = Japan; KHM = Cambodia; KOR = Korea, Rep.; MYS = Malaysia; PHL = the Philippines; THA = Thailand; VNM = Viet Nam.

New technologies matter for within-firm productivity growth in the Philippines.

FIGURE 1.7   **Within-firm changes in TFP from increases in IT capital or in data and software capital per worker, by industry type, the Philippines, 2010–21**

Change in TFP (%)

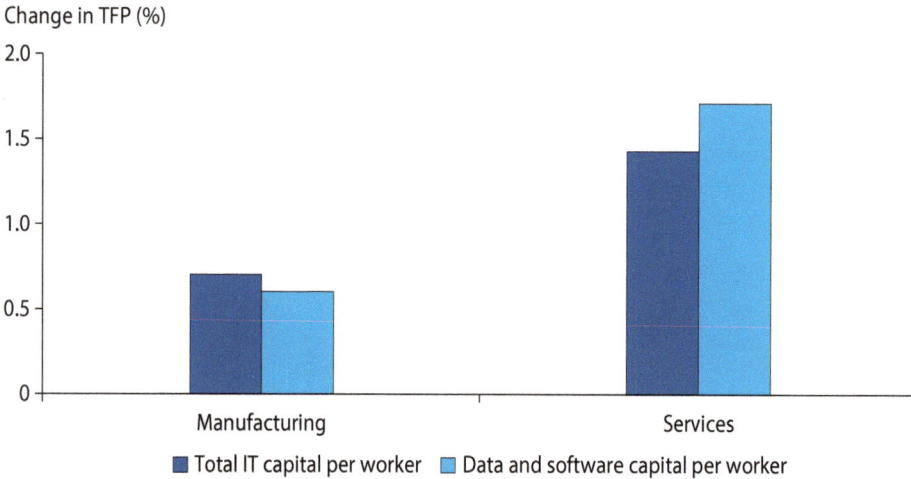

Source: Original figure for this publication using the Annual Survey of Philippine Business and Industry and the Census of Philippine Business and Industry microdata from the Philippine Statistics Authority.
Note: The figure measures a 1 standard deviation increase in information technology capital or data and software capital per worker. Within-firm estimates from regressions controlling for firm and year fixed effects. IT = information technology; TFP = total factor productivity.

Notes

1. "Developing" economies refer to low- and middle-income economies, and "advanced" to high-income economies, by World Bank income classifications. "Emerging" economies are defined according to International Monetary Fund classifications (IMF 2019).
2. "Productivity" and "aggregate productivity" refer to total factor productivity unless "labor productivity" is specified.
3. For example, recent work suggests that the contribution of human capital accumulation to labor productivity growth in developing economies may be underestimated because existing growth-accounting decompositions do not properly account for learning outcomes (Angrist et al. 2021). For a further discussion, refer to appendix box A.1.
4. Specifically, we compute these decompositions within each two-digit industry, using firm TFP and firm size (value added). We aggregate two-digit industries using industry value-added shares in the economy. The use of value-added weights to aggregate firm TFP follows convention in the literature (for example, Melitz and Polanec 2015; Olley and Pakes 1996).

5. Note that there may be interdependence between these sources of aggregate growth. For instance, greater scope for reallocation through flexible product and factor markets can incentivize firms to make sunk investments, which can raise both within-firm productivity and the scale of productive firms. Furthermore, the threat of competition from firm entry can incentivize within-firm innovations to stay ahead of the competition. Subsequent chapters return to these points.

6. This chapter does not explicitly isolate the role of changes in these sectoral weights for the decompositions (that is, structural change); instead, it focuses on firm-level changes within sectors. However, these structural changes can be important after periods of reform, especially the move from agriculture toward the higher-productivity manufacturing or services sectors (McMillan, Rodrik, and Sepúlveda 2016). We exclude agriculture from our analysis owing to limited data availability across EAP countries.

7. "Frontier" and "laggard" firms are defined as those with the highest (90th percentile) and lowest (10th percentile) productivity levels, respectively, which the next chapter discusses further.

8. Within-firm growth has the dominant role despite examination of changes over five-year periods or more—which, by construction, will give a larger weight to entry and exit than annual changes—because entrants will encompass any firm up to five years old.

9. Note that we have decomposed the entry component into entry of new young firms and entry into the sample of older firms (the latter likely reflecting sampling changes), and figure 1.4 reflects only the former. Including the latter for China would increase the contribution of entrants to around 60 percent and reduce the contribution within firms to about 40 percent.

References

Aghion, P., C. Antonin, and S. Bunel. 2021. *The Power of Creative Destruction: Economic Upheaval and the Wealth of Nations*. Cambridge, MA: Harvard University Press.

Aghion, P., N. Bloom, R. Blundell, R. Griffith, and P. Howitt. 2005. "Competition and Innovation: An Inverted-U Relationship." *Quarterly Journal of Economics* 120 (2): 701–28.

Aghion, P., R. Blundell, R. Griffith, P. Howitt, and S. Prantl. 2009. "The Effects of Entry on Incumbent Innovation and Productivity." *Review of Economics and Statistics* 91 (1): 20–32.

Aghion, P., and P. Howitt. 1992. "A Model of Growth Through Creative Destruction." *Econometrica* 60 (2): 323–51.

Akcigit, U., and W. R. Kerr. 2018. "Growth Through Heterogeneous Innovations." *Journal of Political Economy* 126 (4): 1374–443.

Angrist, N., S. Djankov, P. K. Goldberg, and H.A. Patrinos. 2021. "Measuring Human Capital Using Global Learning Data. *Nature* 592: 403–8.

Argente, D., M. Lee, and S. Moreira. 2024. "The Life Cycle of Products: Evidence and Implications." *Journal of Political Economy* 132 (2): 337–90.

Backus, M. 2020. "Why Is Productivity Correlated with Competition?" *Econometrica* 88 (6): 2415–44.

Bartelsman, E., J. Haltiwanger, and S. Scarpetta. 2004. "Microeconomic Evidence of Creative Destruction in Industrial and Developing Countries." Policy Research Working Paper 3464, World Bank, Washington, DC.

Bazzi, S., M-A. Muendler, and L. Rickey. 2014. "Sources of Labor Productivity Changes in Brazil." Unpublished working paper.

Bollard, A., P. Klenow, and G. Sharma. 2013. "India's Mysterious Manufacturing Miracle." *Review of Economic Dynamics* 16 (1): 59–85.

Brandt, L., J. Litwack, E. Mileva, L. Wang, Y. Zhang, and L. Zhao. 2020. "China's Productivity Slowdown and Future Growth Potential." Policy Research Working Paper 9298, World Bank, Washington, DC.

Brown, J. D., G. A. Crespi, L. Iacovone, and L. Marcolin. 2018. "Decomposing Firm-level Productivity Growth and Assessing Its Determinants: Evidence from the Americas." *Journal of Technology Transfer* 43: 1571–606.

Cusolito, A. P., and W. F. Maloney. 2018. *Productivity Revisited: Shifting Paradigms in Analysis and Policy*. Washington, DC: World Bank.

de Nicola, F., N. Loayza, and H. Nguyen. 2024. "Productivity Loss and Misallocation of Resources in Southeast Asia." *Journal of the Asia Pacific Economy* 29 (4): 2152–69.

Eslava, M., J. Haltiwanger, A. Kugler, and M. Kugler. 2004. "The Effects of Structural Reforms on Productivity and Profitability Enhancing Reallocation: Evidence from Colombia." *Journal of Development Economics* 75 (2): 333–71.

Foster, L., J. C. Haltiwanger, and C. J. Krizan. 2001. "Aggregate Productivity Growth: Lessons from Microeconomic Evidence." In *New Developments in Productivity Analysis*, edited by C. R. Hulten, E. R. Dean, and M. J. Harper. Chicago: University of Chicago Press.

Garcia-Macia, D., C-T. Hsieh, and P. J. Klenow. 2019. "How Destructive Is Innovation?" *Econometrica* 87 (5): 1507–41.

Harrison, A., L. A. Martin, and S. Nataraj. 2013. "Learning Versus Stealing: How Important Are Market-Share Reallocations to India's Productivity Growth?" *The World Bank Economic Review* 27 (2): 202–28.

IMF (International Monetary Fund). 2019. *World Economic Outlook 2019: Global Manufacturing Downturn, Rising Trade Barriers*. Washington, DC: IMF.

Kehrig, M., and N. Vincent. 2019. "Good Dispersion, Bad Dispersion," Report No. w25923. National Bureau of Economic Research, Cambridge, MA.

Li, B., and J. Ponticelli. 2022. "Going Bankrupt in China." *Review of Finance* 26 (3): 449–86.

McMillan, M., D. Rodrik, and C. Sepúlveda, eds. 2016. *Structural Change, Fundamentals, and Growth: A Framework and Case Studies*. Washington, DC: International Food Policy Research Institute.

Melitz, M. J., and S. Polanec. 2015. "Dynamic Olley-Pakes Productivity Decomposition with Entry and Exit." *RAND Journal of Economics* 46 (2): 362–75.

Olley, G. S., and A. Pakes. 1996. "The Dynamics of Productivity in the Telecommunications Equipment Industry." *Econometrica* 64 (6): 1263–97.

Pancost, N. A., and C. Yeh. 2022. "Decomposing Aggregate Productivity." Working Paper CES-22-25, Center for Economic Studies, US Census Bureau, Washington, DC.

Paweenawat, A., T. Chucherd, and N. Amarase. 2017. "Uncovering Productivity Puzzles in Thailand: Lessons from Microdata." PIER Discussion Paper 73, Puey Ungphakorn Institute for Economic Research, Bangkok.

Sivadasan, J. 2009. "Barriers to Competition and Productivity: Evidence from India." *BE Journal of Economic Analysis and Policy* 9 (1): 1–66.

World Bank. 2020. "Thailand Manufacturing Firm Productivity Report." World Bank, Washington, DC.

World Bank. 2024. *World Development Report 2024: The Middle-Income Trap.* Washington, DC: World Bank.

Young, A. 1994. "Lessons from the East Asian NICs: A Contrarian View." *European Economic Review* 38 (3–4): 964–73.

The Importance of National Frontier Firms

2

Key messages

- The performance of the most-productive national frontier firms shapes aggregate productivity because of their relative size.
- The frontier firms account for a large share of output and jobs, pay higher wages, and facilitate the diffusion of better technologies to other domestic firms.
- However, the market share of frontier firms is falling, implying that reallocation of value added is not leading to aggregate productivity gains in the East Asia and Pacific region.

Frontier firms drive aggregate productivity

National frontier firms account for the bulk of aggregate productivity growth in the East Asia and Pacific (EAP) region.[1] "Frontier firms" are the most-productive firms within a country and industry (refer to appendix box A.3). In EAP, the firms in the top 10 percent of productivity account for 50 percent of aggregate productivity growth within firms (refer to figure 2.1).[2] Similarly, frontier firms in the United Kingdom were responsible for 63 percent of the annual growth in UK labor productivity between 2011 and 2019 (Romei 2023). Therefore, to diagnose slowdown in aggregate productivity growth, one must examine the firms' performance at the frontier.

> **Frontier firms drive aggregate productivity.**

FIGURE 2.1   Contribution to aggregate within-firm productivity growth in EAP, by productivity decile

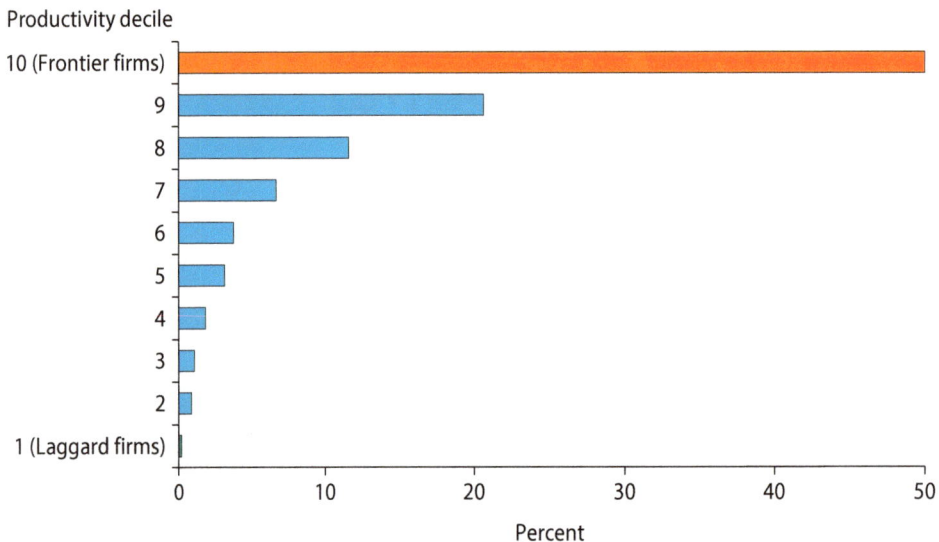

Productivity decile

Source: Original figure for this publication using calculations based on statistical office microdata for China, Indonesia, Malaysia, the Philippines, and Viet Nam.
Note: The contribution to within-firm productivity growth is decomposed into the contribution by firm productivity decile in the initial year of a 5- to 6-year change. The figure reflects the average of 5 or 6 yearly productivity changes, depending upon country data availability: 1998–2007 for China, 1996–2015 for Indonesia, 2000–15 for Malaysia, 2006–18 for the Philippines, and 2001–21 for Viet Nam. Decompositions are calculated at the two-digit level and aggregated using value-added weights based on Foster, Haltiwanger, and Krizan (2001) decomposition. The figure reflects the unweighted average of aggregate manufacturing and services across the 5 EAP countries in the sample.

Size matters: The large impact of frontier firms

The frontier firms shape aggregate productivity because of their relative size. They account for an outsize share of new job creation, investment, production, and exports. More-productive firms tend to be larger than less-productive firms in EAP, so the performance of frontier firms disproportionately matters for aggregate outcomes. The relationship between size and productivity is stronger in manufacturing than in services; consequently, the manufacturing frontier firms account for a larger share of aggregate growth than services frontier firms (56 percent and 30 percent, respectively).

Within each industry, the most-productive 10 percent of firms account for more than one-third of employment or new job creation in each of the EAP countries for which we have firm-level data (refer to figure 2.2, panel b). The frontier firms also disproportionately create high-quality jobs because they pay higher wages—on average, nearly 50 percent higher than at nonfrontier medium or large firms (refer to figure 2.4). Frontier firms also account for nearly 40 percent of capital investment, almost one-half of total exports, and more than half of industry value added (refer to figure 2.2, panel a).

> **Frontier firms drive aggregate productivity because of their size.**

FIGURE 2.2   Share of sector value added and employment of EAP firms, by productivity decile

a. Share of sector value added

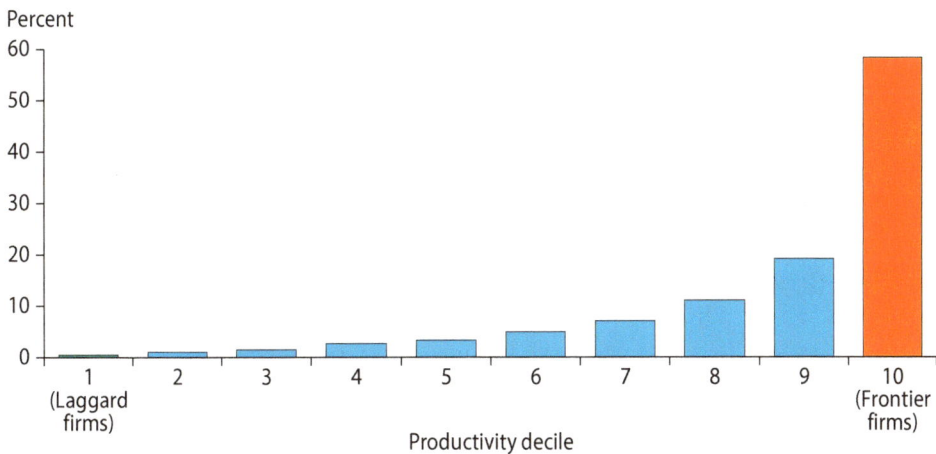

b. Share of sector employment

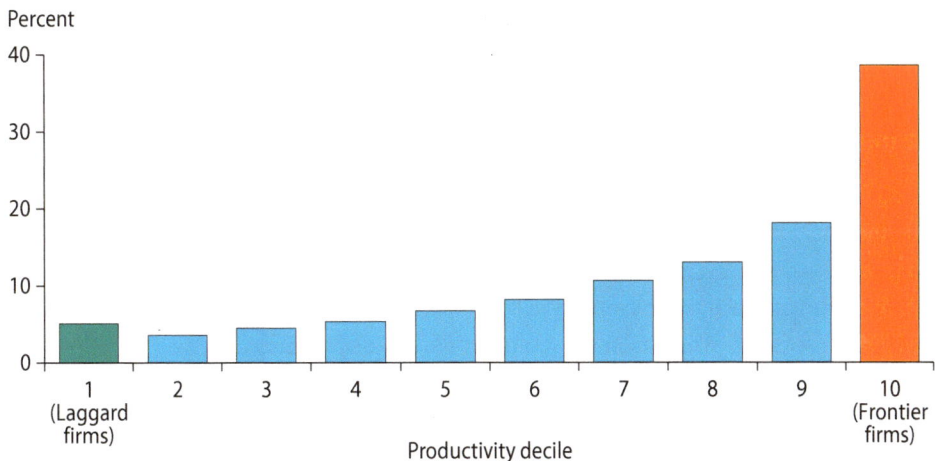

Source: Original figure for this publication using calculations based on statistical office microdata for China, Indonesia, Malaysia, the Philippines, and Viet Nam.

Note: The share in two-digit industry employment or value added of the laggard and frontier firms (the bottom and top 10 percent by total factor productivity, respectively) are calculated within each country and industry and year. Unweighted average shown for all country industries. Data are from 1998–2007 for China, 1996–2015 for Indonesia, 2000–15 for Malaysia, 2006–18 for the Philippines, and 2001–21 for Viet Nam.

From a static perspective, the concentration of more economic activity in productive firms is good news. However, reallocation and productivity growth more generally depend on productivity-enhancing dynamics, as the next section discusses.

Frontier firms also matter for aggregate productivity because of their dynamic role in technology diffusion. They are generally the first to adopt new technologies and business models. These technologies then tend to diffuse gradually through supply chains and customer networks while also spurring imitation among competitors (refer to box 2.1). Modern supply chains are often characterized by long-term relationships, which help incentivize suppliers to innovate and learn from their customers (refer to Out of the Box 1).

Box 2.1   Frontier firms and technology diffusion: Examples from Viet Nam

Halimex beer

Halimex, a Vietnamese state-run brewery, was established in 1966 but continued until the 2000s to produce most of its products by labor-intensive processes that were perceived as far below international standards. In 2003, Carlsberg (a Danish multinational) acquired a 25 percent stake and provided modern equipment and machinery to set up a new plant as well as the transfer of critical expertise in production and marketing. The technology level of the new plant was much higher than the technology used in the old breweries at that time. Halimex and its canned beer, Halida, quickly became a success. With the new know-how, technology, and experience acquired through Carlsberg's investment, Halimex established an offshoot brewery (Viet Ha), which adopted many of the technologies and practices from its parent company.

Honda motorcycles

Honda's 1996 entry into Viet Nam's motorcycle industry had a dramatic impact on both the industry itself and its network of suppliers. Honda built advanced factories featuring precision robots, computer-controlled machines, highly automated assembly lines, state-of-the-art paint shops, and quality-control workshops. The company combined sophisticated production technologies with skills training, not only in working with the machines but also in management and marketing. In addition, Honda developed a network of suppliers in Viet Nam that included other foreign-owned firms as well as domestic suppliers. Honda passed its quality standards down to suppliers along with technical support and management skills training—creating both the incentive and capacity for upgrading domestic supply chains.

Source: Original box for this publication with information from Estrin and Meyer 2004.

Out of the Box 1   How the EMS Group exemplifies long-term relationships and innovation

EMS Group is a leading electronics manufacturing firm and human resources service provider based in the Philippines. Established in 2004, the company now employs more than 16,000 people and supplies major multinational enterprises in the electronics, telecommunications, automotive, medical, and semiconductor industries. Its product offerings include the assembly of circuit boards and electronic products, as well as services related to product design, semiconductor testing, and human resources. This box summarizes an interview for this publication with the chairperson and CEO of EMS Group.

What is EMS's overall business strategy?

EMS's strategy is centered on innovation and long-term customer relationships. The company recognizes that technology evolves rapidly, and therefore, EMS must innovate constantly to keep pace with its customers' needs and to stay competitive. The pace of innovation appears to be accelerating: when the firm was founded, it operated on a 5-year plan but now focuses 1–2 years ahead.

EMS places great emphasis on fostering long-term relationships, having supplied many of its customers for more than a decade. Such relationships are common in supply chains for complex and highly customized products (such as electronics or automobiles) because it is often impossible to write a perfect contract for supplying such complex inputs. In such cases, firms rely partly on trust, and the future value of the long-term relationship incentivizes suppliers to make sunk investments in innovation today (Macchiavello 2022).

How does EMS learn from its customers?

In a rapidly changing technology sector, anticipating the demands of customers is a constant challenge, and EMS follows a two-pronged approach to do so. At the executive level, EMS engages in frequent discussions with high-level management of its customers to understand industry trends and their strategic priorities. At the operational level, account managers maintain daily interactions with customers, providing detailed real-time insights into production challenges, market trends, or research and development. EMS combines the bottom-up and top-down information to predict shifts in its customers' demands such as for emerging products and technologies.

(continued)

Out of the Box 1   How the EMS Group exemplifies long-term relationships and innovation *(Continued)*

What are the biggest challenges EMS faces?

EMS is wedded to its customers because it produces highly customized products via long-term relationships. If demand falls from a particular customer, EMS is exposed because it is not easy to sell this product elsewhere. And because its customers are abroad, geopolitical risks and international trade uncertainty have a direct impact on its operations. For instance, trade policies affecting EMS's Chinese customers have led to sudden changes in demand for its products.

Another major challenge is the limited domestic supply chains in the Philippines. The Philippines has free trade agreements with various nations, which makes the country an attractive platform to export to the region. However, some manufacturing inputs are difficult to source locally, so making certain products can be challenging.

How does EMS address these challenges?

To mitigate the risks of relying on a limited number of product lines, EMS has diversified its production portfolio. It is not as easy to expand the number of customers for its existing product range because customer relationships are long-term ones and products are specific to each customer. Instead, the company has expanded into production of new products that require skill sets and methods similar to those it already uses. This approach allows EMS to remain resilient when demand shifts in its traditional markets.

EMS has also extended beyond traditional manufacturing to offer human resources services, deploying skilled employees to clients abroad. Some EMS clients, especially in advanced East Asian countries, face labor shortages due to an aging population. Sending employees abroad strengthens client relationships while providing career opportunities for Filipino workers. EMS has offered these services for a variety of skilled positions, including accounting and software development. To prevent operational disruptions due to labor mobility, EMS has implemented structured training programs and uses the opportunity to move abroad as an incentive to help motivate its workers. When employees transition abroad, the company ensures that replacements are trained well in advance, allowing operations to continue smoothly.

Source: Box original for this publication based on an interview with EMS.

Highest productivity but falling market share

Reallocation of value added is not leading to aggregate productivity gains in EAP because the market share of frontier firms is falling. Reallocation depends on more-productive firms scaling up their value-added market share and on the least-productive firms shrinking or exiting. However, EAP firms are not exhibiting these dynamics. As noted in chapter 1, reallocation has contributed negligibly to aggregate productivity. Here, we identify the frontier as the main cause.

Firms of medium productivity are increasing their value-added market share somewhat more than those of lower productivity. However, the problem is at the tails of the distribution. The market share of laggard firms is rising by at least as much as those of medium productivity, and crucially the most-productive firms' share is declining (refer to figure 2.3).

Reallocation of value added is not increasing productivity because frontier firms are losing market share.

FIGURE 2.3   Growth of value-added market share, by productivity decile

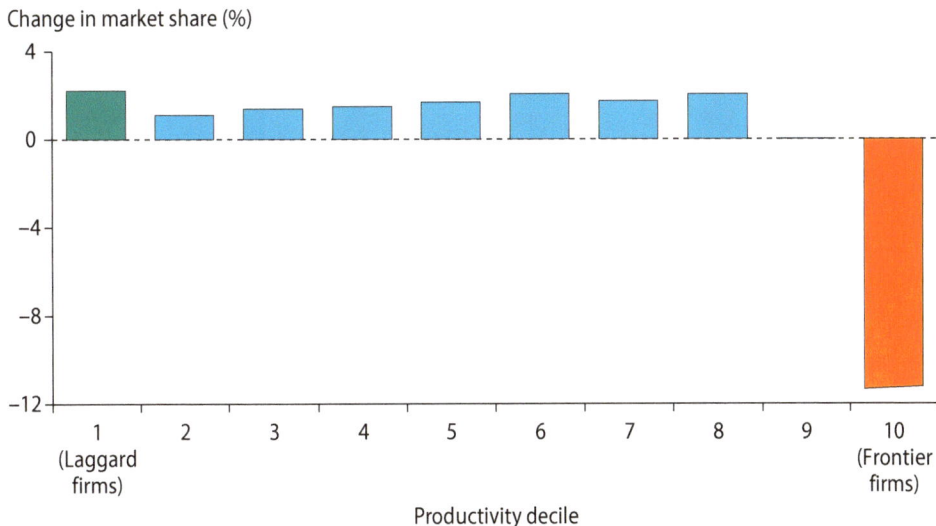

Change in market share (%)

Source: Original figure for this publication using calculations based on statistical office microdata for China, Indonesia, Malaysia, the Philippines, and Viet Nam.

Note: The figure reflects the average of 5 yearly changes in the share of industry value added among different productivity groups of firms in the initial year of a 5- to 6-year change (6 yearly changes in the Philippines). The figure reflects an unweighted average of country industries during these time periods: 1998–2007 for China, 1996–2015 for Indonesia, 2000–15 for Malaysia, 2006–18 for the Philippines, and 2001–21 for Viet Nam. Because the data reflect changes in market share, the changes in the figure sum to 0 by construction. The growth of value-added market share of the 9th productivity decile is close to 0.

Higher wages but slow employment growth

Jobs are important as the key source of labor income, and labor income increases when more people have higher-wage jobs. In EAP, the more-productive firms pay higher wages and employ more workers. Also, frontier firms (each industry's most-productive 10 percent) pay workers more than four times what they earn at laggard firms (the least-productive 10 percent) (refer to figure 2.4). In services firms in emerging economies elsewhere, the frontier-firm wage premium is of a similar magnitude, from about 1.9 times to more than 4.3 times higher (Nayyar, Hallward-Driemeier, and Davies 2021).

In the EAP region, when the productivity of a given firm increases, about a quarter of this improvement is shared with workers through higher wages. Frontier firms also employ about six times as many workers as laggard firms, and more-productive firms generally tend to be bigger employers (as shown earlier in figure 2.2, panel b).[3] So again from a static perspective, the concentration of jobs in more-productive firms is good news for worker incomes.

Frontier firms pay the highest wages.

FIGURE 2.4   **Average wages across EAP firms, by productivity level**

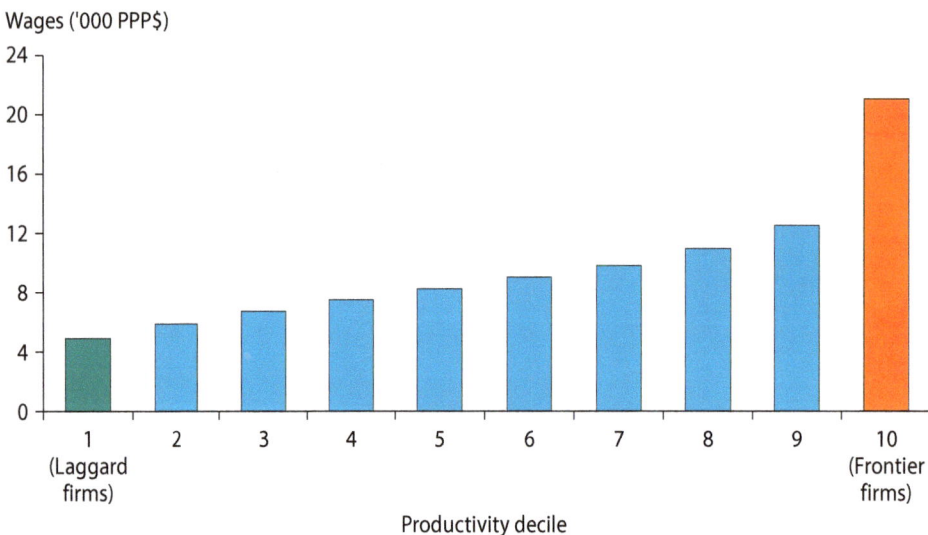

Wages ('000 PPP$)

Source: Original figure for this publication using calculations based on statistical office microdata for China, Indonesia, Malaysia, the Philippines, and Viet Nam.
Note: The figure reflects the average wages per worker, in constant purchasing power parity 2005 US dollars, for firms within different quantiles of total factor productivity within a given country, two-digit industry, and year. The figure depicts an unweighted average of country industries. Data are from 1998–2007 for China, 1996–2015 for Indonesia, 2000–15 for Malaysia, 2006–18 for the Philippines, and 2001–21 for Viet Nam. All data are for manufacturing firms except for the Philippines and Viet Nam, whose data encompass both manufacturing and services firms.

But are jobs being reallocated toward more-productive firms and away from less-productive firms in the region? Reallocation of jobs to more-productive firms is difficult to measure because of data limitations, but evidence suggests it is low in EAP. Accurately measuring reallocation requires data for the full firm distribution, which is typically not available in EAP countries (apart from the Philippines and Viet Nam in certain years). Based on the methodology proposed by Decker et al. (2020), however, it is possible to measure reallocation by assessing whether more-productive firms increase employment.

The good news is that less-productive firms within an industry do reduce employment and the more-productive firms employ more workers (refer to figure 2.5). The relationship appears to strengthen toward the extremes of the productivity distribution—the laggard and frontier firms. But the responsiveness of employment flows to productivity appears to be low relative to benchmarks in more-flexible labor markets, such as the United States, and it is not increasing over time (refer to figure 2.6). This finding suggests that the most-productive EAP firms struggle to scale up employment compared with more-frictionless benchmarks.

> **Jobs are reallocating away from laggard firms and toward the frontier.**

FIGURE 2.5   Average one-year employment growth in EAP firms, by productivity decile

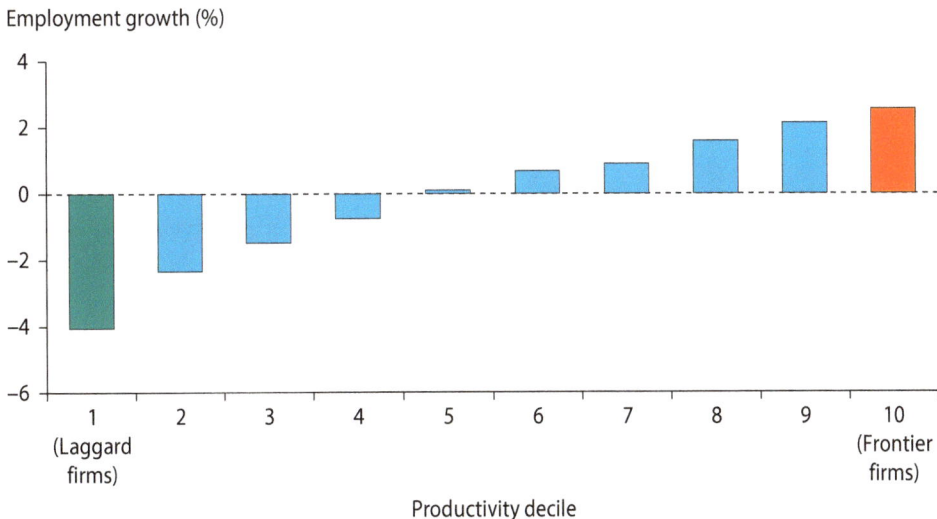

Source: Original figure for this publication using calculations based on statistical office microdata for China, Indonesia, Malaysia, the Philippines, and Viet Nam.
Note: The figure reflects the average 1-year employment growth for firms within different productivity deciles within a given country, two-digit industry, and year. The figure depicts an unweighted average of country industries. Data are from 1998–2007 for China, 1996–2015 for Indonesia, 2000–15 for Malaysia, 2006–18 for the Philippines, and 2001–21 for Viet Nam.

> Reallocation of employment toward more-productive firms is low in EAP relative to the United States.

FIGURE 2.6   Responsiveness of employment to TFP growth in EAP countries and the United States

Employment growth responsiveness to TFP (p.p.)

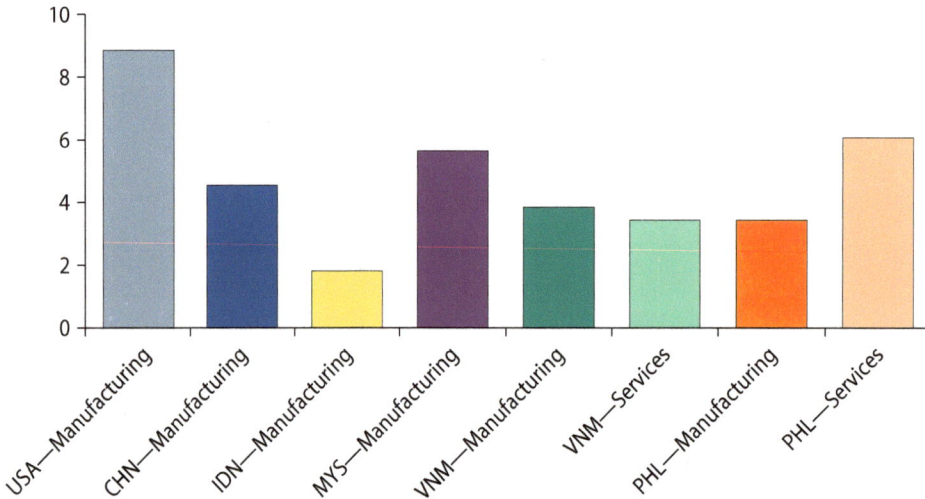

Sources: Original figure for this publication using calculations based on statistical office microdata for China, Indonesia, Malaysia, the Philippines, and Viet Nam; Decker et al. (2020) for US responsiveness. Refer to box 1.1 for years of data.
Note: The figure shows the p.p. increase in 1-year employment growth correlated with a 1 standard deviation higher (1-year lagged) TFP for manufacturing firms. Reflects 2013 or last available year of data (if earlier). CHN = China; IDN = Indonesia; MYS = Malaysia; PHL = the Philippines; p.p. = percentage point; TFP = total factor productivity; US = United States; VNM = Viet Nam.

The combination of slower value-added growth and faster employment growth implies that the frontier's labor productivity is stagnating. Chapter 3 returns to the frontier's aggregate productivity growth.

Notes

1. "Productivity" and "aggregate productivity" refer to total factor productivity, the residual measure of improvements in technology and organization that cannot be explained by changes in capital or labor inputs. "Labor productivity" is referred to as such, and "aggregate labor productivity" is defined as the amount of output per unit of labor input in a given economy.
2. Recall that the vast majority of aggregate productivity growth is driven within firms (refer to chapter 1).
3. Furthermore, calculations for this publication find that a doubling in productivity within a firm leads it to hire about 5 percent more workers, on average.

References

Decker, R. A., J. Haltiwanger, R. S. Jarmin, and J. Miranda. 2020. "Changing Business Dynamism and Productivity: Shocks Versus Responsiveness." *American Economic Review* 110 (12): 3952–90.

Estrin, S., and K. E. Meyer, eds. 2004. *Investment Strategies in Emerging Markets: New Horizons in International Business.* Cheltenham, UK: Edward Elgar Publishing.

Foster, L., J. C. Haltiwanger, and C. J. Krizan. 2001. "Aggregate Productivity Growth: Lessons from Microeconomic Evidence." In *New Developments in Productivity Analysis*, edited by C. R. Hulten, E. R. Dean, and M. J. Harper, 303–72. Chicago: University of Chicago Press.

Macchiavello, R. 2022. "Relational Contracts and Development." *Annual Review of Economics* 14 (1): 337–62.

Nayyar, G., M. Hallward-Driemeier, and E. Davies. 2021. *At Your Service? The Promise of Services-Led Development.* Washington, DC: World Bank.

Romei, V. 2023. "UK Productivity Growth Driven by Minority of High-Performing Companies." *Financial Times*, December 11.

The Performance of Frontier Firms in Global Context   3

Key messages

- Productivity growth has been slower within more-productive firms than less-productive firms in the East Asia and Pacific (EAP) region. This catch-up by the relatively backward firms is in itself desirable.
- However, the most-productive EAP firms (the "national frontier") are falling further behind the world's most-productive firms (the "global frontier") in the digital-intensive sectors at the forefront of global innovation. The best firms globally are rapidly adopting technologies related to data, but these technologies are diffusing more slowly among the leaders in EAP.
- The gap between the most technologically sophisticated firms in EAP and those globally has widened—and much more than the gap between other EAP national firms and their global counterparts.

Rapid productivity growth of global frontier firms

The slowdown in productivity growth has been global. But in advanced economies, laggards are struggling while frontier firms are leading and growing strong. This chapter takes a closer look at the within-firm component of productivity growth, presenting new evidence on the growth of frontier and laggard firms in East Asia and Pacific (EAP) and other regions.[1]

Across the world, the lag between when a technology was invented in one country and when it arrived in other countries had been declining until 2000. Historical data on technology use indicated that at least some firms in all countries had been enjoying faster access to new technologies (Cirera et al. 2021). Until 2000, new technologies were also being adopted earlier by EAP frontier firms (that is, a country's most-productive firms, as box 3.1 discusses), but they

---

Box 3.1   Who are the frontier firms?

The world's most-productive firms come from a range of Organisation for Economic Co-operation and Development (OECD) countries. The OECD defines these "frontier firms" as the most-productive 5 percent of firms in each industry globally (Andrews, Criscuolo, and Gal 2016; Criscuolo 2023). According to Orbis data for OECD economies, for example, Finland and the Republic of Korea have firms at the global frontier in most information and communication technology sectors, and Italy is well represented at the global frontier in the textiles industry (Andrews, Criscuolo, and Gal 2016).

Eleven OECD countries have at least one global frontier firm in three-quarters or more of the two-digit industries, but richer countries tend to have more global frontier firms. Global frontier firms are larger and more capital-intensive, have lower labor shares (wages as a share of value added), are more likely to be foreign owned, and are more likely to patent their products than other medium or large firms in advanced economies (Andrews, Criscuolo, and Gal 2016).

In East Asia and Pacific (EAP) countries, national frontier firms are smaller than their global counterparts. The national frontier in developing EAP, defined as the most-productive 10 percent of firms in each industry and country, also have distinct characteristics compared with the rest of the firms in their economies. Using microdata described in chapter 1, box 1.1, reveals that the national frontier firms are larger, more capital-intensive, and more information technology-capital-intensive; have higher data capital per worker and lower labor shares; are more likely to be foreign owned; and are more likely to export. However, even at the national frontier in manufacturing sectors, fewer than one-third of firms are foreign owned and about one-half the firms do not export. Furthermore, the national frontier firm in EAP is many orders smaller than the global frontier firms—approximately 10 times smaller in terms of sales (Andrews, Criscuolo, and Gal 2016).

were diffusing more slowly to other firms than in earlier decades. Furthermore, adoption lags among frontier firms in developing East Asia had been converging with Organisation for Economic Co-operation and Development country levels.

The pattern of frontier firms rapidly adopting technologies continues in advanced economies today.[2] Since the 2000s, although productivity growth has stagnated for most firms in advanced economies, the most-productive firms (constituting the global frontier) have continued to experience rapid productivity growth (refer to figure 3.1, panel a). The productivity divergence between firms has been attributed to frontier firms' investments in large fixed-cost technologies (such as data technologies) and management skills (Autor et al. 2020; Corrado et al. 2021) (refer to figure 3.2). In fact, the growth of the global frontier is particularly rapid in digital-intensive sectors (refer to figure 3.1, panel b). (For the classification of digital intensity, refer to box 3.2.) This rapid growth is potentially amplified by globalization, which allows more-productive firms to benefit from larger economies of scale (Andrews, Criscuolo, and Gal 2016).

> **In advanced economies, frontier firms have faster productivity growth than other firms, especially in digital sectors.**

FIGURE 3.1 **TFP growth of firms in advanced economies, by frontier status and sector, 2003–19**

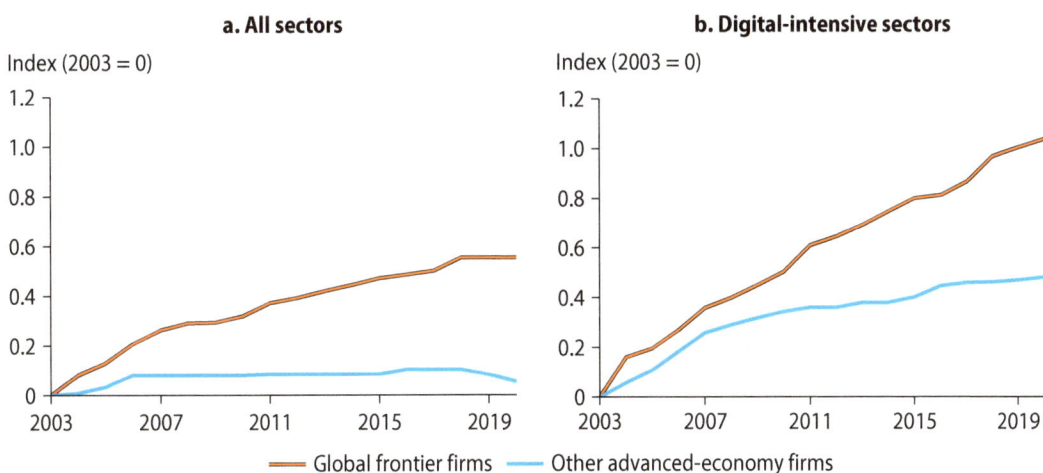

a. All sectors

b. Digital-intensive sectors

Legend: Global frontier firms — Other advanced-economy firms

Source: Original figure for this publication using data from Criscuolo (2023).
Note: Based on Orbis data for 24 Organisation for Economic Co-operation and Development economies. "Global frontier firms" reflect the top 5 percent globally most-productive firms within each two-digit manufacturing and services sector; "other advanced-economy firms" reflect the remainder. Unweighted average of industries. Sector digital intensity is defined according to a Eurostat index (refer to box 3.2). TFP = total factor productivity.

> In advanced economies, fixed costs of frontier firms have been increasing, in part because of investments in data technologies.

FIGURE 3.2 Fixed-cost and data investment increases among frontier firms in advanced economies

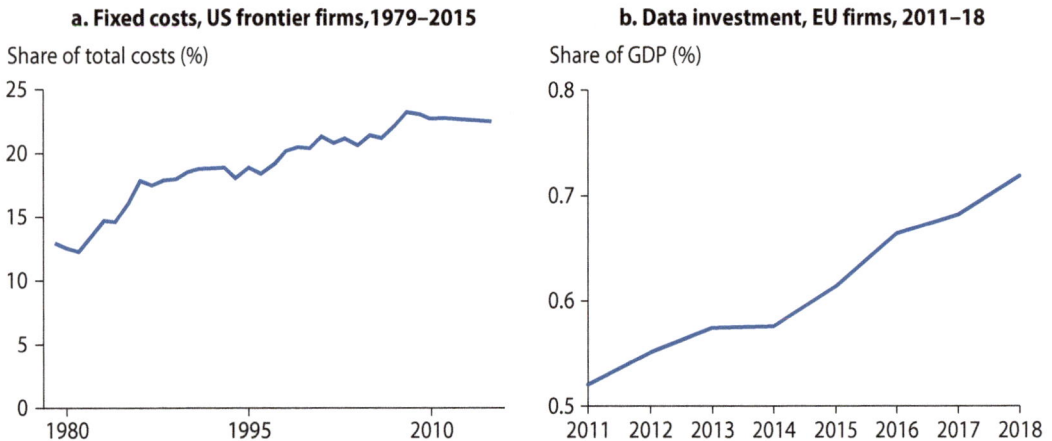

a. Fixed costs, US frontier firms, 1979–2015

b. Data investment, EU firms, 2011–18

Sources: De Ridder 2024 © *American Economic Review*, reproduced with permission (panel a); data investment data from Goodridge, Haskel, and Edquist (2022); and original figure for this publication using investment data from World Bank World Development Indicators (panel b).

Note: Panel a reflects firms listed on stock markets in the United States. Panel b reflects the aggregate sum of investment divided by the aggregate GDP in 16 EU economies. The authors are not aware of measures of fixed costs for EU firms. Without comparable estimates of data investment using Labor Force Surveys for the US, we focus on the EU as a benchmark. EU = European Union; US = United States.

The pattern of the global frontier productivity pulling away from the rest is not what standard economics theories would predict, given that laggard firms have a wider set of new technologies to adopt and greater scope for catch-up (Bartelsman, Haskel, and Martin 2008). Crucially, however, only laggard firms with sufficient absorptive capacity can take advantage of these opportunities (Griffith, Redding, and Van Reenen 2004). Frontier technologies today require experience and access in using data and the skills to leverage data in sophisticated business models—capabilities that nonfrontier firms cannot easily obtain.

The rise of data technologies has contributed to the rising scale of business in advanced economies (Bajgar et al. 2023; Bajgar, Criscuolo, and Timmis 2025; Crouzet and Eberley 2019). A key difference between intangibles (such as data technologies or management skills) and tangible assets is that intangibles involve high fixed costs and low marginal costs (Haskel and Westlake 2018). Such economies of scale are conducive to an enhanced scale of production. Although the resulting dominance of a few firms raises concerns about increasing industrial concentration, it also leads to employment of workers and capital in larger, more productive firms. This productive reallocation now accounts for around half of the aggregate productivity growth in Europe (Bighelli et al. 2023).[3]

Box 3.2   Classifying digital-intensive sectors

We classify digital-intensive sectors according to Eurostat's Digital Intensity Index (DII), which classifies manufacturing sectors into "high technology," "medium-high technology," "medium-low technology," and "low technology" groups, and classifies services into "knowledge-intensive services" and "less-knowledge-intensive services." This chapter refers to "digital-intensive" sectors, which correspond to the DII's "high-technology manufacturing" and "knowledge-intensive services." These sectors include pharmaceuticals manufacturing, computer and electronics manufacturing, publishing and broadcasting, telecommunications, computer programming, information technology (IT) services, and scientific research and development (respectively, divisions 21, 26, 59–63, and 72 of ISIC rev.4).

Measuring digital intensity is not straightforward and can depend upon whether one measures digital skills, use of digital capital such as IT or robots, or use of digital services such as cloud computing. However, we find similar results using the Organisation for Economic Co-operation and Development classification of Calvino et al. (2018), which reflects a composite of these different digital measures.

These Eurostat sector measures are based on European economies, which we take as a relatively undistorted benchmark. The sector ranking also appears to be a meaningful predictor of digital intensity of sectors in developing East Asia and Pacific countries. For the Philippines, where detailed sectoral data on technology use is available, we find that the two-digit industries with a higher number of computers per worker (a common proxy of aggregate IT capital) also tend to have a relatively high technological intensity ranking according to Eurostat's DII (with a correlation of 0.6 between a sector's computers per worker and the DII in both manufacturing and services).

Lagging productivity growth of EAP frontier firms

Since the 2000s, the national frontier firms in EAP are no longer leading productivity growth and are falling behind the best firms globally. Figures 3.3 and 3.4 show changes in the productivity distribution for each EAP country as repeated cross-sections, to allow for changes in the composition of firms over time through entry and exit.[4] In contrast to what is occurring in advanced economies, the productivity of the most-productive firms (national frontier) in China, Indonesia, Malaysia, the Philippines, and Viet Nam has increased by *less* than the rest of the firms in each respective country.[5] There are some differences in the timing of the changes across countries (for example, being more salient in recent years in the Philippines and in the 2000s in Viet Nam).

These findings are true in both manufacturing and services (refer to figure 3.5). Similar results are also obtained using labor productivity (rather than total factor productivity), enabling us to include data for Mongolia and Thailand (refer to figure 3.6 and appendix figure B.2). The trends do not change if we include all firm sizes rather than just medium and large firms.[6]

In the EAP region, the productivity growth of frontier manufacturing and services firms has been slower than that of other firms.

FIGURE 3.3   **Productivity growth along the firm productivity distribution, EAP countries**

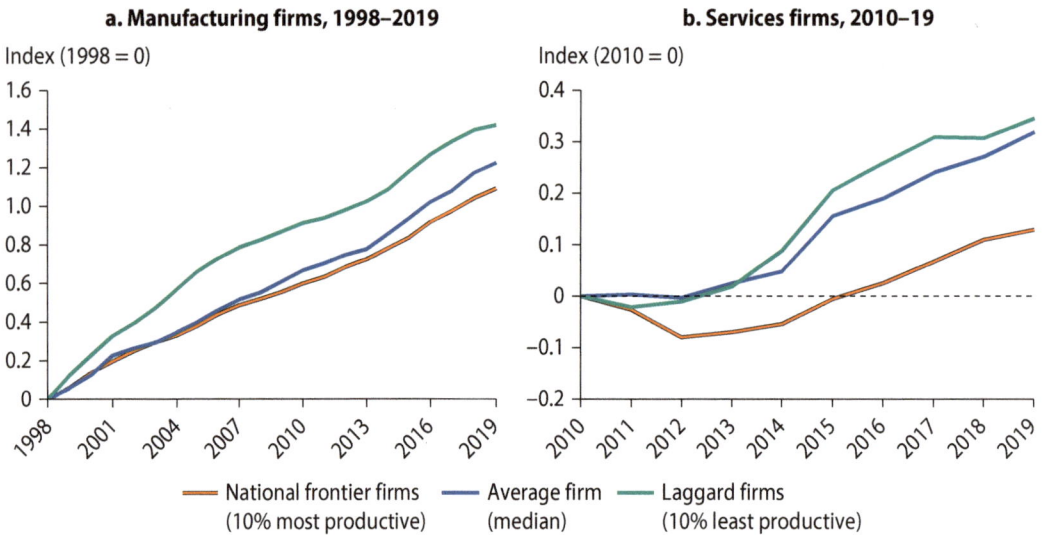

a. Manufacturing firms, 1998–2019

b. Services firms, 2010–19

— National frontier firms (10% most productive)   — Average firm (median)   — Laggard firms (10% least productive)

Source: Original figure for this publication using statistical office microdata for manufacturing firms in China, Indonesia, Malaysia, the Philippines, and Viet Nam and for services firms in the Philippines and Viet Nam.
Note: The figure reflects cross-sectional percentiles of the firm productivity distribution within countries, by two-digit industry, over time. "National frontier firms" refer to the 90th percentile of the firm productivity distribution and "laggard firms" to the 10th percentile. Annual changes reflect an unweighted average across countries and two-digit industries with available data.

The slower productivity growth of national frontier firms is true in every EAP country with available manufacturing data.

FIGURE 3.4   Manufacturing productivity growth along the firm distribution, by EAP country

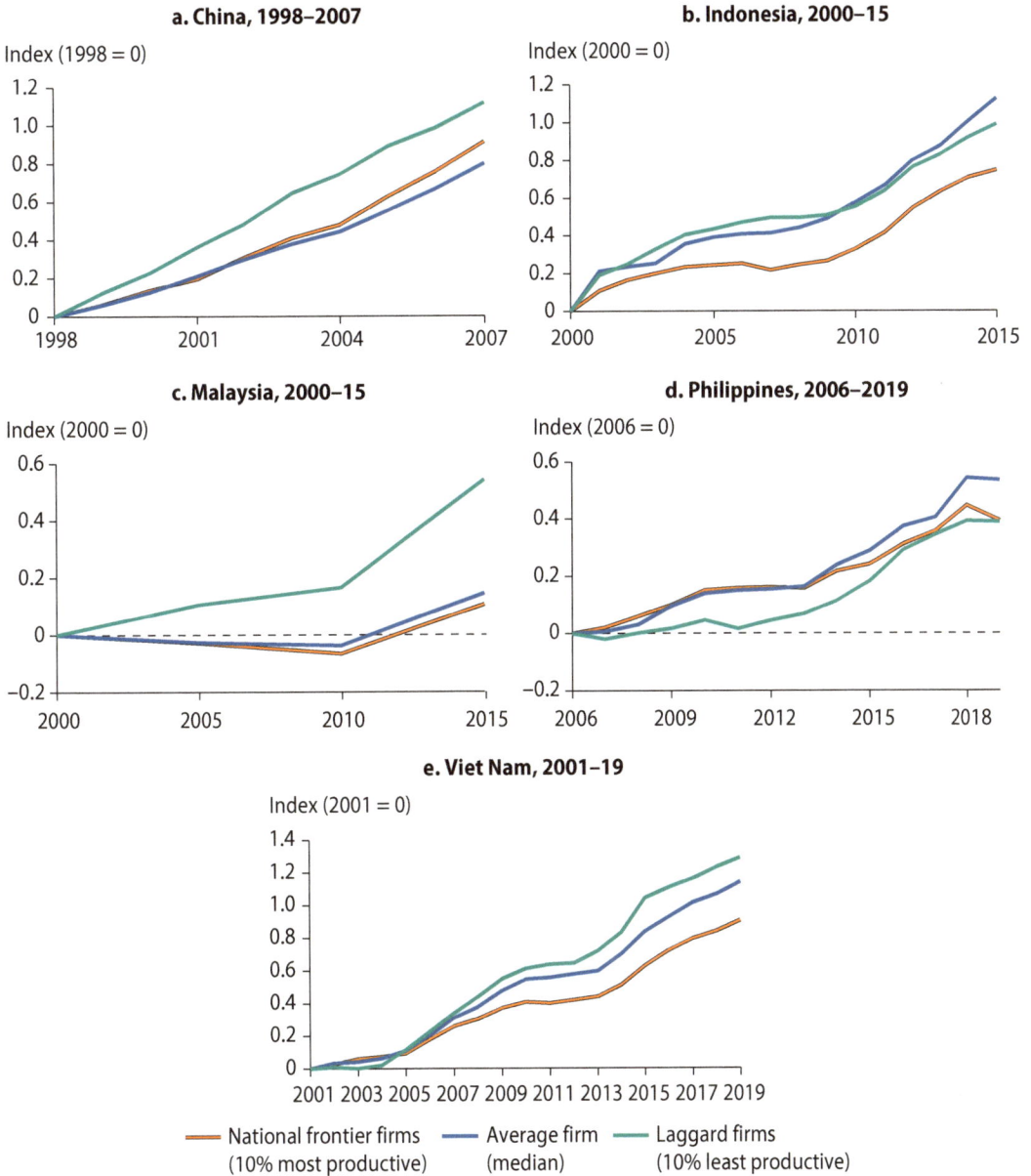

a. China, 1998–2007

Index (1998 = 0)

b. Indonesia, 2000–15

Index (2000 = 0)

c. Malaysia, 2000–15

Index (2000 = 0)

d. Philippines, 2006–2019

Index (2006 = 0)

e. Viet Nam, 2001–19

Index (2001 = 0)

National frontier firms (10% most productive)   Average firm (median)   Laggard firms (10% least productive)

Source: Original figure for this publication using statistical office microdata for manufacturing firms.
Note: Reflects cross-sectional percentiles of the manufacturing firm productivity distribution within countries, by two-digit industries, over time. "National frontier firms" refer to the 90th percentile of the firm productivity distribution and "laggard firms" to the 10th percentile. The figure reflects an unweighted average across two-digit industries.

> The slower productivity growth at the EAP national frontier is also true among services firms.

FIGURE 3.5   Services productivity growth along the firm distribution, by EAP country

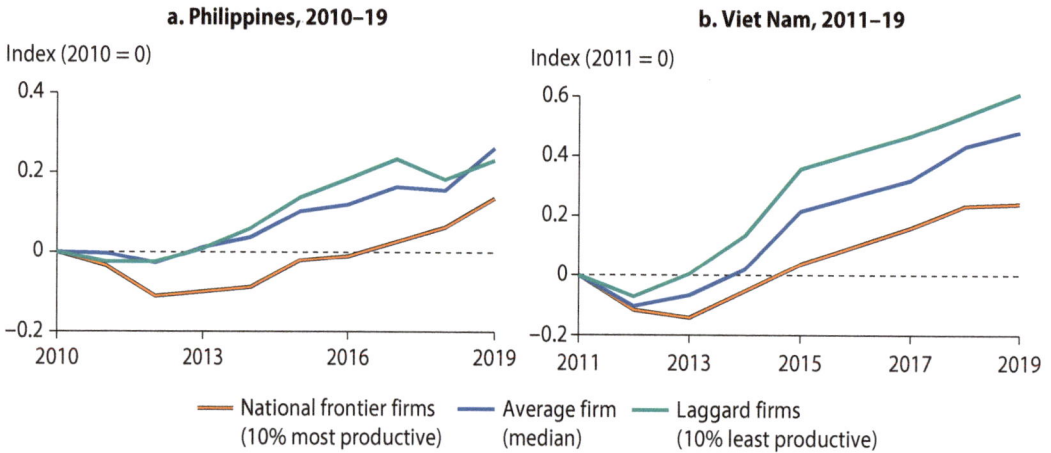

a. Philippines, 2010–19

b. Viet Nam, 2011–19

National frontier firms (10% most productive) — Average firm (median) — Laggard firms (10% least productive)

Source: Original figure for this publication using statistical office microdata for services firms.
Note: The figure reflects cross-sectional percentiles of the services firm productivity distribution within countries, by two-digit industries, over time. "National frontier firms" refer to the 90th percentile of the firm productivity distribution and "laggard firms" to the 10th percentile. Charts reflect an unweighted average across two-digit industries.

> The slower growth among EAP frontier firms also holds true for labor productivity.

FIGURE 3.6   EAP labor productivity growth along the firm distribution

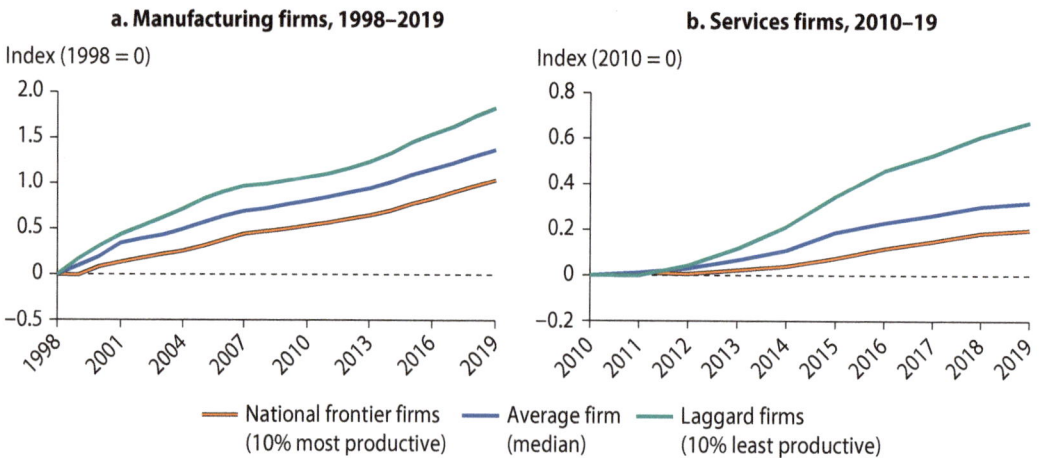

a. Manufacturing firms, 1998–2019

b. Services firms, 2010–19

National frontier firms (10% most productive) — Average firm (median) — Laggard firms (10% least productive)

Source: Original figure for this publication using statistical office microdata for manufacturing firms in China, Indonesia, Malaysia, Mongolia, the Philippines, Thailand, and Viet Nam (panel a), and for services firms in Mongolia, the Philippines, Thailand, and Viet Nam (panel b).
Note: The figure reflects cross-sectional percentiles of the firm labor productivity distribution within countries, by two-digit industry, over time. "Labor productivity" is defined as real value added per worker in 2005 PPP international dollars. "National frontier firms" refer to the 90th percentile of the firm labor productivity distribution and "laggard firms" to the 10th percentile. Annual changes reflect an unweighted average across countries and two-digit industries with available data. PPP = purchasing power parity.

In recent years, the productivity growth of the national frontier firms in EAP economies has been falling further behind the global frontier in digital-intensive sectors such as electronics (refer to figure 3.7, panel a)—the very same sectors in rich countries where the best firms are pulling away. For example, in digital-intensive manufacturing sectors between 2005 and 2015, the productivity of the global frontier increased by 76 percent, whereas the national frontier firms in Indonesia, Malaysia, the Philippines, and Viet Nam increased their productivity by only 31 percent on average. To maintain pace with the global frontier in digital sectors, the annual productivity growth of the national frontier would need to be more than 4 percent faster. For less-digital-intensive sectors, the gap between the national frontier firms and the global ones is less stark (refer to figure 3.7, panel b). Using more recent data on firms listed on stock markets, as a proxy for the frontier, suggests that the national frontier in EAP has continued to fall behind the global frontier since the COVID-19 pandemic (refer to box 3.3).

> **The national frontier in EAP countries is falling behind the global frontier, especially in digital-intensive sectors.**

FIGURE 3.7   **Productivity gaps between the global frontier and national frontier firms in EAP countries, by digital sector intensity, 2003–19**

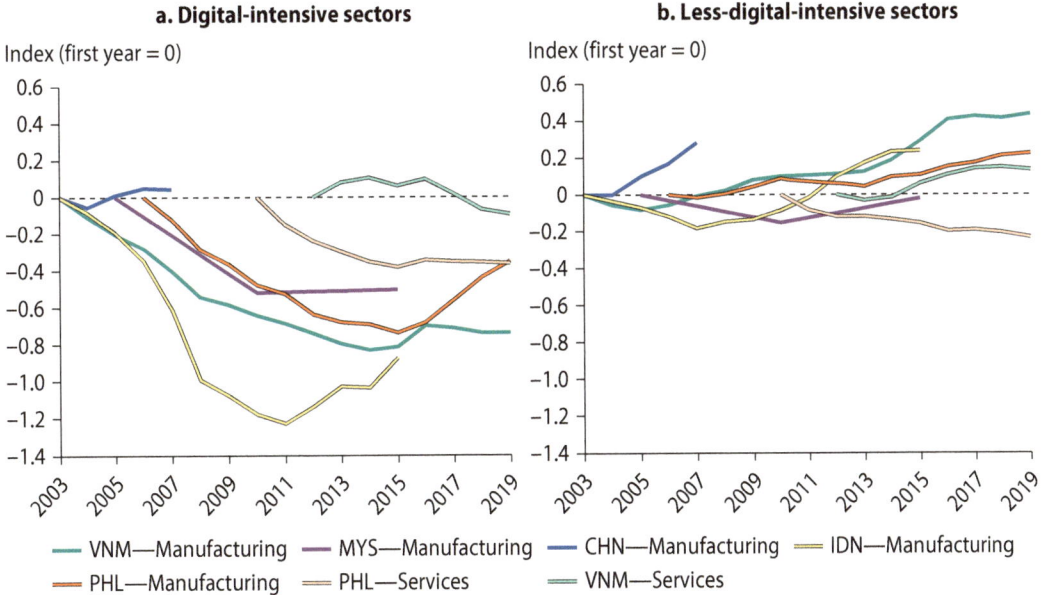

a. Digital-intensive sectors

b. Less-digital-intensive sectors

Legend:
- VNM—Manufacturing
- MYS—Manufacturing
- CHN—Manufacturing
- IDN—Manufacturing
- PHL—Manufacturing
- PHL—Services
- VNM—Services

Source: Original figure for this publication based on calculations using statistical office microdata (national frontier) and Criscuolo (2023) (global frontier).

Note: "National frontier" refers to the 90th percentile of the firm productivity distribution for each country and industry and "global frontier" to the 95th percentile of the firm productivity distribution across high-income economies within an industry (refer to box 3.1). The distance between the national and global frontier productivity is normalized to 0 in the first year, such that negative numbers reflect the national frontier falling further behind the global frontier relative to the first year, and positive numbers reflect the national frontier catching up with or exceeding the global frontier. Sector "digital intensity" is defined according to Eurostat's Digital Intensity Index, which classifies high-technology manufacturing and high-knowledge-intensive services as "digital-intensive sectors" (refer to box 3.2) and other manufacturing and services sectors as "less-digital-intensive sectors." CHN = China; IDN = Indonesia; MYS = Malaysia; PHL = Philippines; VNM = Viet Nam.

Box 3.3 Productivity of national frontier firms since the COVID-19 pandemic

The chapter has focused so far on time periods before the COVID-19 shock. In early 2020, almost overnight, the COVID-19 pandemic triggered increased dependence on digital technologies, which played a crucial role in helping firms weather the worst of the shock (Comin et al. 2022). As lockdowns spread and working-from-home rose, the pandemic incentivized many firms to adopt e-commerce to reach consumers online. Larger and more-productive firms were able to adopt new technologies to better manage supply chains or internal processes (World Bank 2022). Did this rapid wave of digital-technology adoption alter the productivity trend of frontier firms?

Answering this question would ideally use the representative statistical office microdata employed thus far in this report. Unfortunately, these data are hard to obtain and often available with significant time lags. Firms listed on stock markets are typically among an economy's most-productive firms, with their financial statements available until the previous year. We use listed firms as a proxy for the national frontier firms in the East Asia and Pacific (EAP) region and compare them with the benchmark of listed firms in the United States—our proxy for the global frontier here. Productivity is estimated using the same methods applied earlier (detailed in appendix A, box A.3); however, there may be some differences between the information reported to statistical offices and that reported in financial statements.

The productivity of listed firms in EAP has fallen further behind the listed firms in the United States, despite a temporary reversal in 2020. The productivity of listed firms in China, Indonesia, Malaysia, the Philippines, Thailand, and Viet Nam grew less quickly than listed firms in the United States over 2015–19 (refer to figure B3.3.1). After COVID-19 hit in 2020, the gap narrowed, but by 2021 the listed firms in most of the EAP countries (Thailand being the exception) continued to fall further behind the productivity of their US counterparts.

Firms in digital-intensive sectors fared relatively better when COVID-19 hit, but those in both digital-intensive and less-digital-intensive sectors fell further behind the United States after 2020 (refer to figure B3.3.2). Earlier, this chapter revealed that before COVID-19, EAP's national frontier was falling behind the global frontier in

(continued)

Box 3.3   Productivity of national frontier firms since the COVID-19 pandemic *(Continued)*

digital sectors. More-recent listed-firm data show that after COVID-19 hit, digital-intensive firms performed relatively better than those in the United States *during* 2020. However, from 2021 onward, both digital and nondigital sectors show a broadly similar trend of falling further behind the productivity of listed firms in the United States.

> The productivity gap between frontier firms in EAP and the United States has widened post–COVID-19.

FIGURE B3.3.1   Productivity gap between national EAP and US frontier firms, 2015–23

Index (2015 = 0)

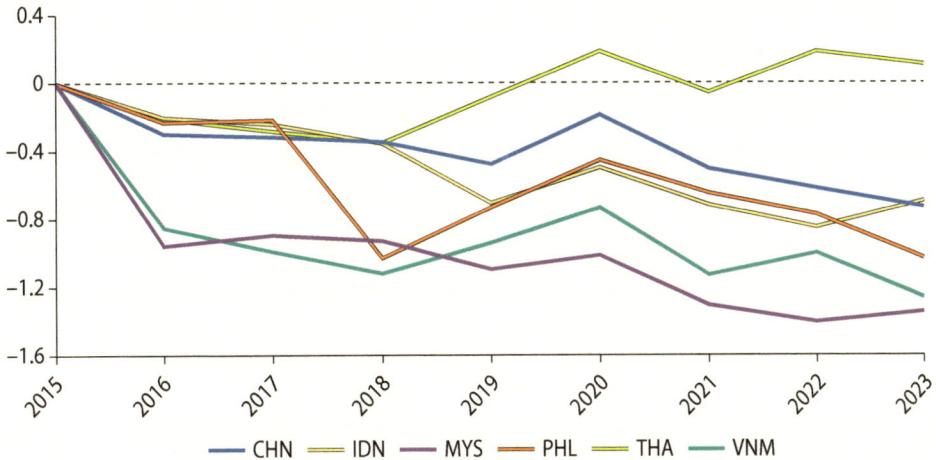

Source: Original figure for this publication using calculations based on Worldscope data for stock market-listed firms.
Note: "Productivity" is total factor productivity. The distance between national and global frontier productivity is normalized to 0 in 2015, such that negative numbers reflect the national frontier falling further behind the global frontier relative to 2015, and positive numbers reflect the national frontier catching up with or exceeding the global frontier. Reflects unweighted average for two-digit sectors across countries. CHN = China; IDN = Indonesia; MYS = Malaysia; PHL = the Philippines; THA = Thailand; VNM = Viet Nam.

(continued)

Box 3.3   Productivity of national frontier firms since the COVID-19 pandemic *(Continued)*

The productivity gap widened more for less-digital-intensive firms since the COVID-19 pandemic.

FIGURE B3.3.2   Productivity gap between EAP national and US frontier firms, by sector digital intensity, 2015–23

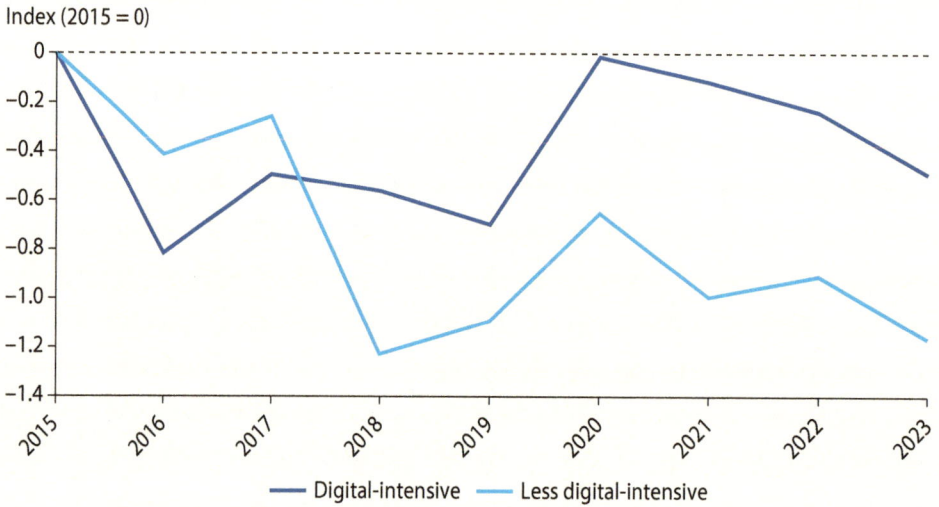

Source: Original figure for this publication using calculations based on Worldscope data for stock market-listed firms.
Note: "Productivity" is total factor productivity. The distance between national and global frontier productivity is normalized to 0 in 2015, such that negative numbers reflect the national frontier falling further behind the global frontier relative to 2015. The figure reflects unweighted average of two-digit sectors across China, Indonesia, Malaysia, the Philippines, Thailand, and Viet Nam. Sector "digital intensity" is defined according to Eurostat's Digital Intensity Index (refer to box 3.2).

The relative stagnation of the national frontier is also observed in developing countries beyond EAP, albeit to a lesser extent. Evidence on the trends in the national frontier (versus the global frontier) beyond EAP is limited. Evidence for Colombia and Mexico does not find any discernible change between the national and global frontiers in manufacturing between 2003 and 2011 (Araujo et al. 2016). Data for firms in Colombia; Europe (Bulgaria, Croatia, Romania, and Serbia); and India show that national frontier productivity has increased by less than the average firm and much less than laggards (refer to figure 3.8). Therefore, the pattern of the relative stagnation of the national frontier does not appear to be exclusive to the EAP region.

On the face of it, the convergence within national economies—as the average firm catches up with the national frontier—is good news. However, despite this catch-up, convergence gaps between the most- and least-productive firms remain large even in the final period for which we have data, the national frontier firms (the most-productive 10 percent) being on average around 10 times more productive than laggards in the same industry (the bottom 10 percent).

The sluggishness of the national frontier firms raises concerns about the future growth of *all* firms. Because new knowledge and technologies typically arrive first at the frontier and then spill over to the rest of the firms, revitalizing firms on the national frontier matters for the future growth of all firms. At a time of digital transitions, this is likely of heightened importance. The next section examines whether new technologies are diffusing to the frontier.

> **Productivity growth of frontier firms has also been relatively slow in other emerging economies.**

FIGURE 3.8   **Productivity growth along the firm distribution in selected non-EAP countries**

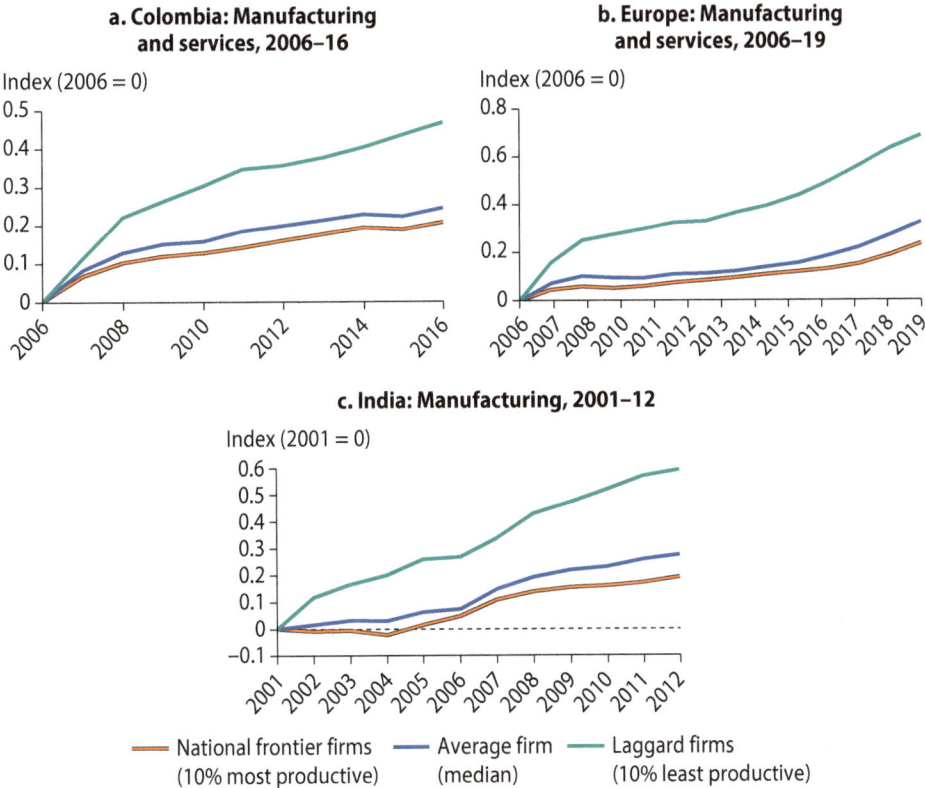

a. Colombia: Manufacturing and services, 2006–16

b. Europe: Manufacturing and services, 2006–19

c. India: Manufacturing, 2001–12

National frontier firms (10% most productive)   Average firm (median)   Laggard firms (10% least productive)

Source: Original figure for this publication using calculations based on statistical office microdata for manufacturing and services firms in Colombia, manufacturing and services firms in Europe (Bulgaria, Croatia, Romania, and Serbia), and manufacturing firms in India.

Note: The figure reflects cross-sectional percentiles of the firm productivity distribution within countries, by industry, over time. "National frontier firms" refer to the 90th percentile of the firm productivity distribution and "laggard firms" to the 10th percentile. Annual changes reflect an unweighted average across countries (for Europe) and two-digit industries with available data.

EAP frontier falling behind in advanced technology use

Whereas the average firm in EAP is somewhat behind the average firm in advanced economies, the region's most-sophisticated firms are far behind the most-sophisticated firms globally. Unsurprisingly, firms in developing East Asia are less sophisticated than those in the most-advanced country for which we have technology measures from the World Bank Firm-level Adoption of Technology (FAT) survey: the Republic of Korea. However, comparing the distribution of technology reveals that these technology gaps are wider in the more-sophisticated firms (refer to figure 3.9). The gap between the least-sophisticated firms in Cambodia, Indonesia, the Philippines, and Viet Nam and the least-sophisticated firm in Korea is relatively small (those with low quantile scores). But the gap widens as one compares the most-sophisticated firms in these countries—as indicated by the downward sloping line. In Cambodia, the Philippines, and Viet Nam, the gap with Korean firms is around twice as large for the most-sophisticated 5 percent of firms than for the bottom 5 percent, with a smaller difference for Indonesia.[7]

The national frontier's relative lack of sophistication is also observed beyond East Asia, although to a somewhat lesser degree. The large gaps in technology sophistication of the frontier are evident in Bangladesh, Georgia, and Ghana, although not in India (refer to figure 3.10). Advanced technologies are diffusing more slowly to the national leaders in the EAP region and some other developing countries than to the leaders in advanced countries.

For national leaders, there are substantial differences between having a technology and using it. The limited technology diffusion is particularly evident when measuring a firm's most commonly used technologies (as in figures 3.9 and 3.10). Firms use a bundle of technologies—for instance, combining written notes with electronic databases, or manual manufacturing tasks with automated machinery (Cirera et al. 2021). If one measures instead the most-advanced technology a firm *has* (whether it uses it frequently or not), the difference between national leaders in EAP and national leaders in advanced countries is much smaller. This suggests that the barriers for the most-sophisticated EAP firms are less about accessing advanced technologies and more about effective use. The challenge of embedding technologies within business processes is that it often requires substantial sunk investment in skills and organizational capital (Bloom, Sadun, and Van Reenen 2012; Brynjolfsson et al. 2008).

Gaps in technological use between developing East Asia and advanced countries are wider for more-sophisticated firms.

FIGURE 3.9   **Technology gap between firms in developing and advanced EAP countries, by sophistication level**

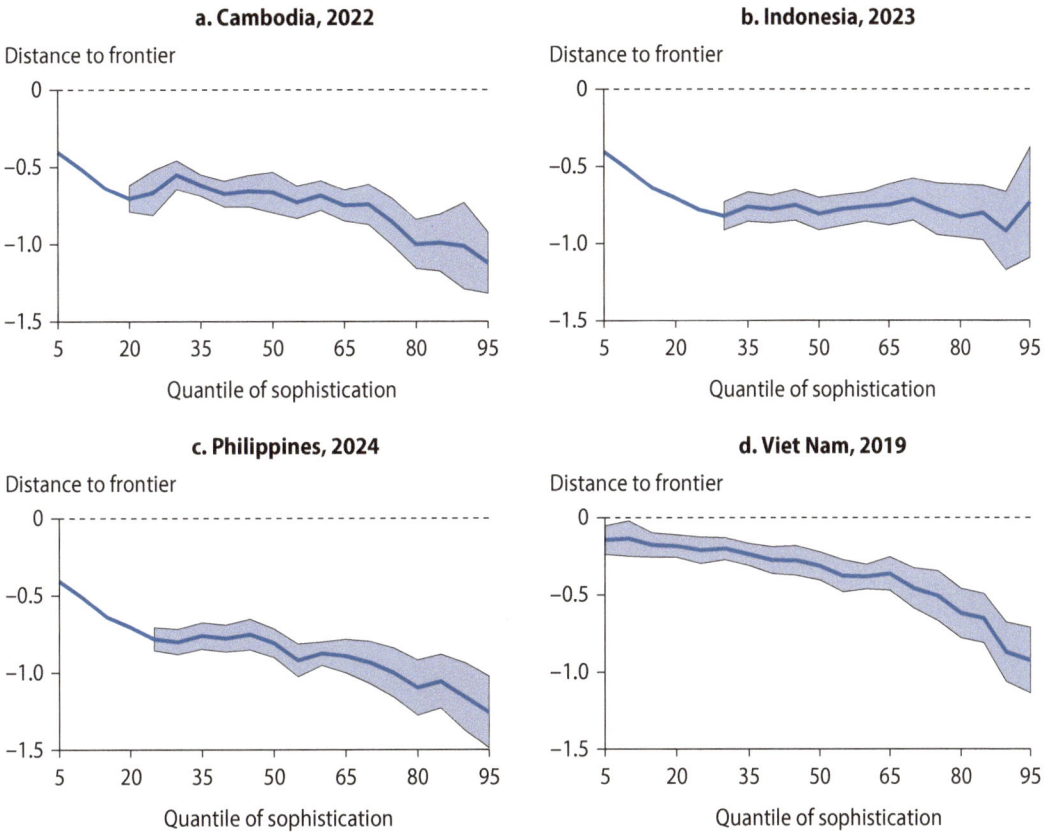

a. Cambodia, 2022

Distance to frontier

Quantile of sophistication

b. Indonesia, 2023

Distance to frontier

Quantile of sophistication

c. Philippines, 2024

Distance to frontier

Quantile of sophistication

d. Viet Nam, 2019

Distance to frontier

Quantile of sophistication

Source: Original figure for this publication based on the World Bank's FAT survey from Cirera et al. (forthcoming).
Note: The figure reflects the sophistication of the most-common general business function technology (intensive margin) for both manufacturing and services sectors. The distributions of firms in Cambodia, Indonesia, the Philippines, and Viet Nam are shown in a percentile-to-percentile comparison with the distribution of firms in the most-advanced country (Republic of Korea) in the FAT data. For example, "distance to frontier" at the 95th percentile compares the top 5 percent most-sophisticated firms in each country with the top 5 percent in Korea. More-negative numbers indicate larger technology gaps with Korean firms. Shaded areas represent the 95 percent confidence interval. FAT = Firm-level Adoption of Technology.

> The wide technological sophistication gaps between the best national firms and global firms is apparent in some countries in other regions.

FIGURE 3.10   **Technology gap between firms in select developing countries and the Republic of Korea, by sophistication level**

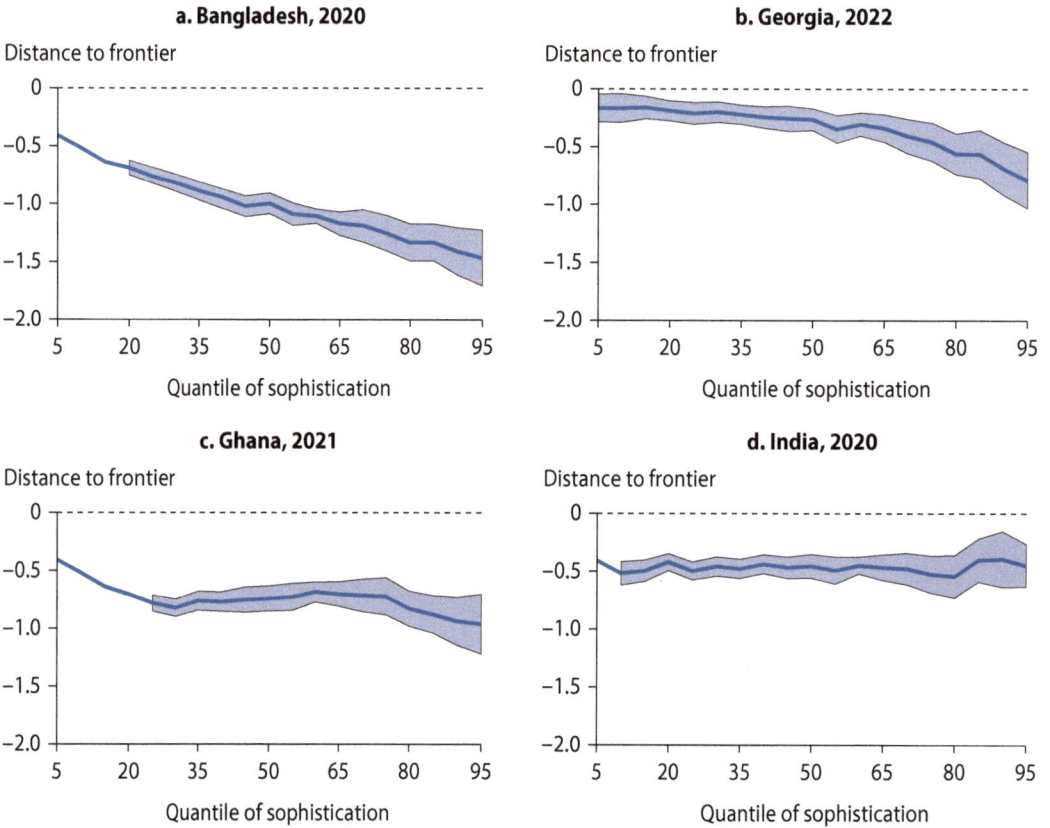

a. Bangladesh, 2020

Distance to frontier

b. Georgia, 2022

Distance to frontier

c. Ghana, 2021

Distance to frontier

d. India, 2020

Distance to frontier

Quantile of sophistication

Source: Original figure for this publication based on the World Bank's FAT survey from Cirera et al. (forthcoming).
Note: The figure reflects the sophistication of the most-common general business function technology (intensive margin) for both manufacturing and services sectors. The distribution of firms in each country is shown in a percentile-to-percentile comparison with the distribution of firms in the most-advanced country (Republic of Korea) in the FAT data. For example, data at the 95th percentile compares the top 5 percent most-sophisticated firms in each country with the top 5 percent in Korea. Shaded areas represent the 95 percent confidence interval. FAT = Firm-level Adoption of Technology.

Advanced digital technologies, such as data analytics, are also diffusing more slowly to EAP national leaders than to national leaders in other developing countries. Figure 3.9 compared firms in EAP to advanced-country benchmarks; here we compare EAP firms' technology use with that of firms in developing countries of similar incomes (refer to figure 3.11). Gaps in technology use are especially evident in the case of new technologies related to data analytics—technologies that have been strongly linked to the rising performance of the best firms globally.

Use of advanced data analytics software is limited in developing EAP.

FIGURE 3.11   Use of ERP data analytics software, by GDP per capita

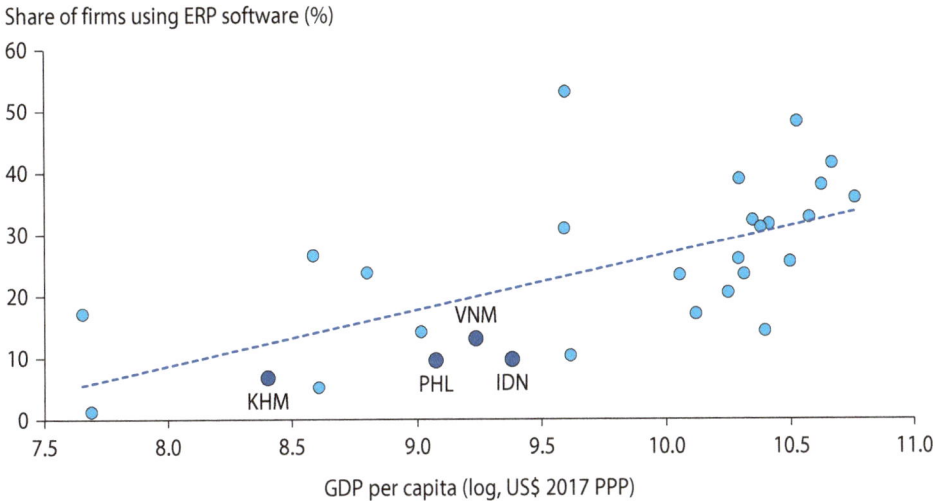

Share of firms using ERP software (%)

Source: Original figure for this publication using calculations based on data from the World Bank's FAT surveys 2019–24; Organisation for Economic Co-operation and Development ICT Access and Usage by Businesses database in 2019. *Note:* The figure reflects the share of manufacturing and services firms reporting they use ERP software. The scatterplot shows developing EAP countries in dark blue dots and other developing and high-income countries in light blue dots. ERP = enterprise resource planning; FAT = Firm-level Adoption of Technology; ICT = information and communication technology; IDN = Indonesia; KHM = Cambodia; PHL = the Philippines; PPP = purchasing power parity; VNM = Viet Nam.

A natural question is what has changed to cause the EAP national frontier to lag the global frontier. Data-driven business models are one candidate.[8] In advanced economies, the best firms have shifted their business models from investment in tangible assets like factories or machines to investment predominantly comprising intangibles like data or business processes (Corrado et al. 2018). Software alone is now responsible for 18 percent of total US corporate investment, up from 3 percent in 1980 (De Ridder 2024).

These data technologies require large fixed costs, in the form of the costs of acquiring and processing large volumes of data and reorganizing and retraining to embed data analytics within business operations. However, data intangibles can be duplicated and used throughout an organization at close to zero marginal cost, which can lead to substantial productivity gains (De Ridder 2024). The high fixed costs mean potential productivity gains are concentrated in a few firms that can deploy these technologies effectively—those with access to large international markets over which to spread the sunk costs, big data from customers and suppliers, and the necessary skills.

Investments in data appear to be growing slowly in EAP in contrast to the rapid growth in advanced economies (refer to figure 3.12). Measuring data investments is tricky, however. One common approach is bottom-up—reflecting the wages of all workers who perform data tasks, such as those related to the creation of databases, analysis of data, or creation of software to analyze data. We combine the Goodridge, Haskel, and Edquist (2022) classification of such occupations and the time each worker spends doing data tasks with information on the number of workers and their wages from Labor Force Survey data for the EAP region.[9] The results are likely to be an upper bound for EAP, because workers in EAP potentially spend less time creating or analyzing data than workers in the same occupations in the European Union (EU).

Investment in data (creating or analyzing data) as a share of gross domestic product in Indonesia, Malaysia, Thailand, and Viet Nam is less than one-third that of the EU and shows no obvious sign of increasing over time. Further, the limited data investment in EAP is concentrated in basic tasks such as data entry rather than more-advanced ones such as data analytics (refer to appendix B, figure B.3). Taken together, these findings indicate a significant gap with advanced economies, both in scope and depth of investment in data.

> **EAP investment in data is low and stagnant relative to advanced economies.**

FIGURE 3.12   **Data investment by firms in developing EAP countries versus EU countries, as a share of GDP, 2011 and 2018**

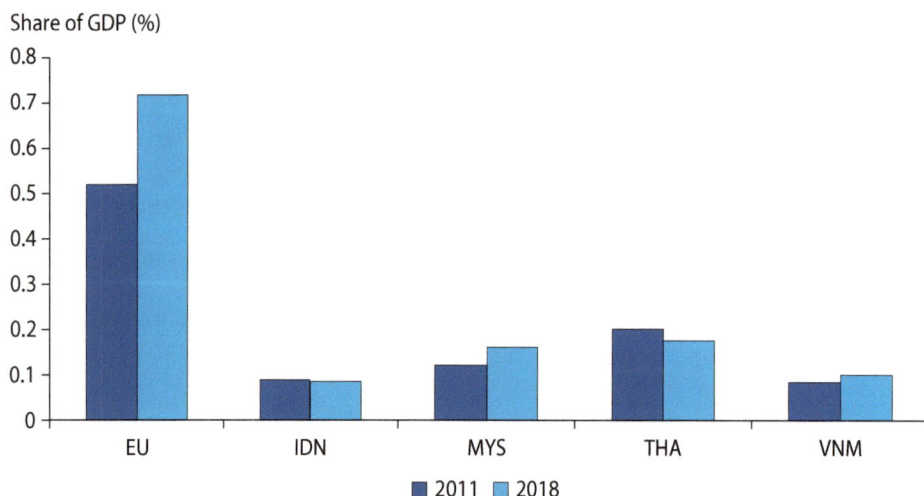

Share of GDP (%)

Sources: Original figure for this publication based on calculations using data from Goodridge, Haskel, and Edquist (2022) for the EU; also based on calculations using East Asia Pacific Labor Force Surveys.
Note: Because comparable estimates of data investment using Labor Force Surveys for the United States were unavailable, the EU serves as the benchmark for advanced economies. EU = European Union; IDN = Indonesia; MYS = Malaysia; THA = Thailand; VNM = Viet Nam.

Frontier East Asian firms are also falling behind their US counterparts in investments in fixed-cost technologies (refer to figure 3.13). In the literature, fixed-cost investments are often considered a proxy for innovation. For instance, in France and the United States, these estimates are strongly correlated with firm investments in software and research and development. De Ridder (2024) demonstrates that investments in fixed costs enable firms to reduce variable costs, thereby enhancing productivity. In the Philippines, fixed costs are strongly correlated with firm investments in information technology (IT), data, and software (refer to box 3.4). Using listed-firm data as a proxy for the frontier in each country allows us to estimate the fixed costs of frontier firms. EAP frontier firms are gradually increasing fixed-cost investments. However, this transition has been slow, with smaller increases in each EAP country than in the United States, which started with much higher fixed-cost levels. Out of the Box 2 explores how one multinational, STEER World, targets growth and technology diffusion.

Fixed-cost investments are low in EAP.

FIGURE 3.13 **Firms' fixed costs, as a share of total costs, in developing EAP countries versus the United States, 2005–23**

Share of total costs (%)

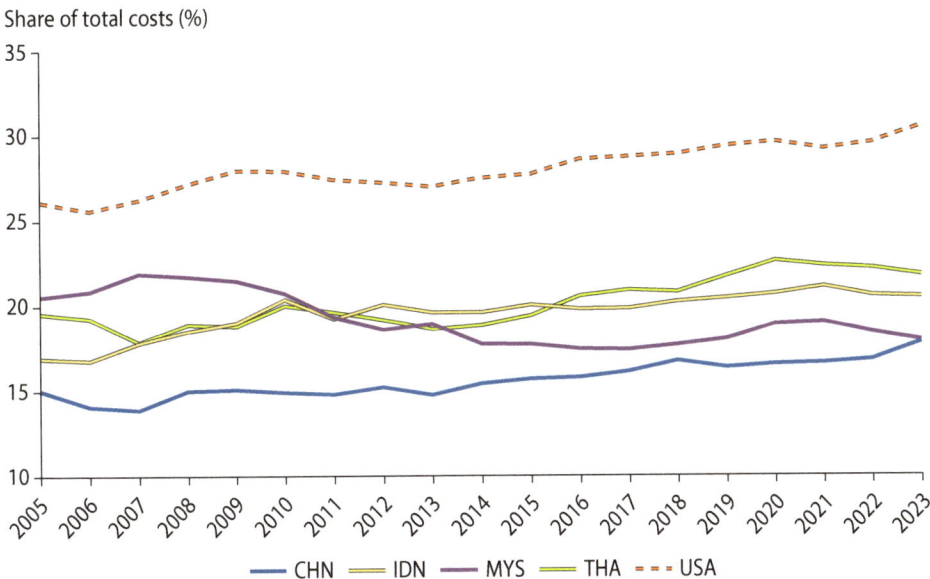

Source: Original figure for this publication using Worldscope listed firms, following De Ridder (2024).
Note: Markups used in the fixed-cost calculation are estimated following De Loecker, Eeckhout, and Unger (2020), using output elasticities from cost shares. Weighted average of firm-level fixed costs, using revenue weights. Following De Ridder (2024), we use the United States as a benchmark. CHN = China; IDN = Indonesia; MYS = Malaysia; THA = Thailand.

Box 3.4   Investments in fixed-cost technologies

Many technologies involve fixed costs. Adoption of information technologies, such as artificial intelligence and data analytics, require large investments in acquiring and storing prerequisite data as well as investments in the necessary skills and organizational capital to implement the technology throughout the organization. Technologies such as robots or drones incur fixed production costs to save on variable inputs such as labor or pesticides. As with information technologies, these fixed costs relate not only to the machines but also to prerequisite technologies (such as sensors) and the cost of reorganizing business processes, which can be four times as much as the robot itself (Zinser, Rose, and Sirkin 2015).[a]

Measuring fixed costs is not straightforward. Financial statements containing broad categories cannot readily be used to obtain measures of fixed costs. We measure fixed costs as the difference between marginal markups and the average profit per sale, following De Ridder (2024). Markups (the difference between price and marginal cost) can reflect market power and the extent of competition. However, markups

> **Markups are increasingly mostly in the United States and advanced economies, rather than in EAP.**

FIGURE B3.4.1   Markup rates in EAP, emerging markets, the United States, and other advanced economies, 2005–16

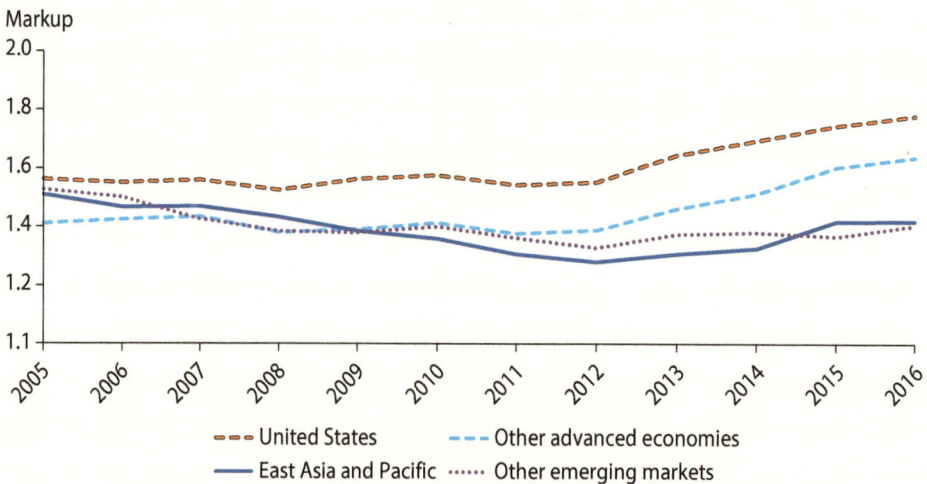

Source: Original figure for this publication using calculations based on data from Eeckhout (2021).
Note: The figure presents unweighted average of markups (the estimated ratio of price to marginal cost) across countries. East Asia and Pacific includes China, Indonesia, Malaysia, the Philippines, and Thailand. "Other emerging markets" reflects 11 economies (included in IMF [2019] classifications). "Other advanced economies" encompasses 22 high-income economies.

(continued)

Box 3.4   Investments in fixed-cost technologies *(Continued)*

are also necessary to recoup fixed investment costs, so changes in markups may instead reflect production technologies. East Asia exhibits largely stagnant markups, in contrast to the rapid rise in advanced economies (refer to figure B3.4.1), which is consistent with evidence of slower diffusion of fixed-cost technologies (as also shown in figure B3.4.1).

Some technologies can allow firms to mitigate fixed costs. For instance, e-commerce and labor market platforms can affect productivity by reducing fixed search costs and expanding market access. Instead of establishing their own e-commerce websites, firms can pay a variable fee to e-commerce platforms, which bear some of the fixed costs related to searching, matching, and transacting with consumers. Cloud computing can allow firms to avoid many of the fixed costs of investing in their own information technology (IT) infrastructure and IT departments, accessing these services as a variable expense instead (DeStefano et al. 2024).

Our firm-level measures of fixed costs are strongly related to productivity-enhancing technologies in the Philippines, such as investments in data and software (refer to figure B3.4.2). Fixed costs are positively related to investment in overall IT capital, data, and software as well as to other sophisticated uses of IT such as managing supply chains or customer relationships. In contrast, there is a more-limited link between fixed costs and cloud computing and no evidence of a link with e-commerce technologies. Increases in investment in overall IT capital or data and software are strongly related to improvements in firm productivity (as shown in chapter 1, figure 1.7). We see weaker evidence for e-commerce and no clear productivity link for adopting e-commerce via platforms specifically.

To leverage fixed-cost technologies requires sufficient scale, but in many developing countries, firms face challenges in scaling up. To profitably make fixed investments, firms require sufficient sales to spread these costs. Data from the Philippines show that larger firms are much more likely than smaller ones to invest in IT capital or data and software and are also more likely to use IT in managing supply chains or customer relationships. Yet in many developing countries, including Indonesia and Viet Nam, firms struggle to scale up, and there are too few large firms (Ciani et al. 2020). This book similarly observes that the most-productive firms are not increasing their market shares. Later sections examine why this is the case.

(continued)

Box 3.4   Investments in fixed-cost technologies *(Continued)*

Firm fixed costs are strongly related to IT and data in the Philippines.

FIGURE B3.4.2   **Fixed costs (as a share of total costs) for various technologies in the Philippines**

Share of total costs (%)

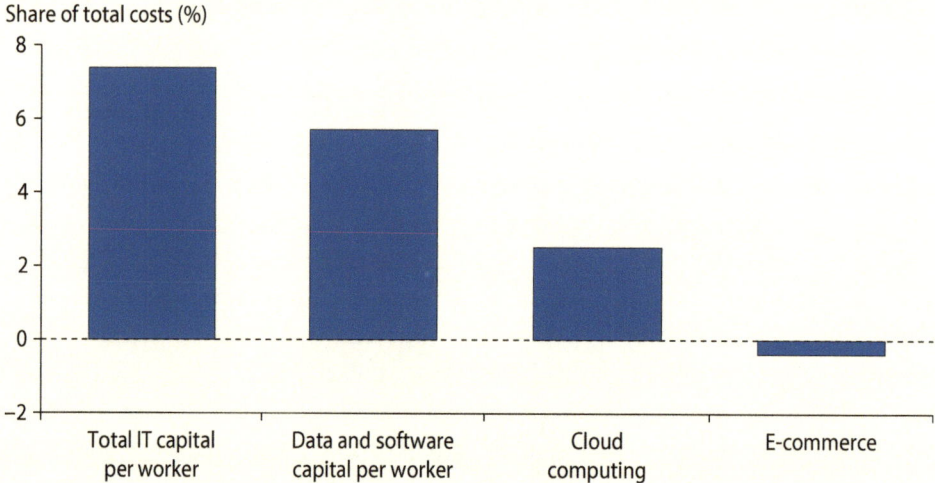

Source: Original figure for this publication using calculations based on microdata from the Annual Survey of Philippine Business and Industry and Census of Philippine Business and Industry databases of the Philippines Statistics Authority, 2010–21.

Note: The figure measures a 1 standard deviation increase in each technology (to account for different units across the technologies) from regressions controlling for two-digit industry and year fixed effects. IT = information technology.

a. Improvements in the labor-saving capabilities of robots, coupled with declines in the relative price of robots (versus worker wages), explain a large part of the rapid diffusion of robots in global manufacturing (Arias et al. 2025).

Out of the Box 2   How one multinational, STEER World, achieves growth and technology diffusion

STEER World, founded in 1993, is an advanced manufacturing firm that specializes in materials transformation in plastics, polymers, pharmaceuticals, nutraceuticals, food, biomaterials, and biorefining. Headquartered in Bangalore, India, the company's global presence spans locations including China, Japan, and the United States. This box summarizes an interview with STEER World for this report.

(continued)

Out of the Box 2   How one multinational, STEER World, achieves growth and technology diffusion *(Continued)*

How does STEER World target growth?

STEER World's strategy has evolved from its initial focus as a batch manufacturing firm to continuous processing and more recently to becoming a manufacturing services solutions company. To do so, STEER acquired firms in China, Japan, and the United States to expand into new applications for its technologies. For example, STEER acquired a Chinese pipe manufacturing company, which it upgraded to produce fiber-reinforced pipes using STEER technology. And in Germany, Japan, and the United States, new types of materials are really blossoming, enabling new applications of STEER technology. For example, STEER's acquisition of a US firm enabled it to produce new film and sheet materials and to finish them into various forms.

STEER also emphasizes the necessity of scaling for long-term impact. To achieve long-term growth, it focuses first on building market presence in terms of revenue and patent portfolios and has been willing to incur a short-term hit to profitability to achieve this. The shift to being a global manufacturing services solutions firm implies high sunk costs before the profitability benefits are realized. STEER's experience mirrors the more-general findings of Brynjolfsson, Rock, and Syverson (2021) about the shift to general-purpose technologies such as artificial intelligence. These technologies require significant complementary up-front investments (in training and organizational change), and the productivity benefits can take several years to materialize, leading to a so-called productivity J-curve.

How are technology adoption decisions made at STEER World?

The COVID-19 pandemic accelerated a transition toward a more-centralized business model. At STEER World, technology adoption decisions were decentralized, leaving discretion to each local team. Enterprise resource management tools, for instance, had been adopted since 2006 and chosen based on a common framework, but local teams had flexibility to make their own decisions. With the disruption of COVID-19, STEER realized there was a lot of disparity in how it could respond across its business. It didn't have the kind of controls, reporting, and information it needed across the organization and has since transitioned to more-structured, more-decision-making. To this end, it has shifted away from being family-run and toward professional senior management.

(continued)

Out of the Box 2   How one multinational, STEER World, achieves growth and technology diffusion *(Continued)*

What are STEER World's biggest barriers to innovation?

STEER's research and development investments span industries such as pharmaceuticals, food, and plastic waste transformation. Given the long time required to bring innovations to market, the company also spends significant amounts on setting up basic infrastructure. Beyond funding issues, human resources pose another major challenge because innovation requires fresh perspectives beyond traditional problem solving. Successfully commercializing innovations requires a workforce that not only understands the technology but also has the enthusiasm and belief to drive it forward.

Source: Box original for this publication based on an interview with STEER World.

Multinational affiliates also lag behind in advanced technology use

In addition to spurring domestic competition, openness to foreign investment can provide access to new foreign technologies, skills, and expertise. Advanced technologies often diffuse first to the subsidiaries of multinationals and then to their domestic suppliers, their local competitors, and so on. But is openness to foreign investment sufficient to ensure technology diffusion, or is technology diffusion imperfect even within these foreign firms? To assess this, we use novel firm survey data from Spiceworks that captures technology diffusion within multinational firms in 7 emerging and 22 advanced economies.[10] As explained later, the global data on multinational affiliates allow us to examine the role of country, industry, and affiliate firm characteristics that predict diffusion—going beyond foreign ownership alone. We focus on data analytics technologies, especially artificial intelligence (AI), because they are likely to have disruptive and wide-ranging impacts upon productivity. The potential impact of the spread of AI on productivity is discussed in box 3.5.

Use of advanced data analytics is far more prevalent in subsidiaries of multinationals than in other medium and large firms within the same country and industry, and this is especially true within emerging markets (refer to figure 3.14). In China and Thailand, multinational subsidiaries are four to six times more likely than other medium and large firms to use advanced data analytics.

Box 3.5 AI and productivity

Artificial intelligence (AI) has improved rapidly in recent years. It can now outperform human capabilities across a number of tasks, including image recognition, reading comprehension, and visual reasoning (Maslej et al. 2024). New large language models (LLMs)—such as OpenAI's ChatGPT 4, Google's Gemini, and Anthropic's Claude, all launched during 2023—can now both use and create a variety of different media, including text in many languages, realistic images, and audio products such as interactive podcasts. Use of these improved tools appears to be increasing rapidly: For example, despite only launching in November 2022, Open AI's ChatGPT.com had 3.7 billion website visits in October 2024 (Carr 2024).

The AI implications for productivity are hard to predict. Some authors envisage that large productivity gains of up to 18 percent over the next decade are possible, whereas others predict less than 1 percent (Baily, Brynjolffson, and Korinek 2023; Acemoglu 2025). The productivity impact depends upon how widely AI is used, how much AI outperforms human-only productivity in the tasks where it is used (via automating or augmenting humans), and the extent of new innovations through AI. Experimental evidence has shown large productivity gains of using AI in particular tasks such as coding, customer services, taxi driving, or professional writing (Brynjolfsson, Li, and Raymond 2025; Noy and Zhang 2023; Kanazawa et al. 2022). Innovation is harder to measure, but randomly assigning AI assistance in one research and development (R&D) lab led researchers to discover 44 percent more materials and 39 percent more patents (Toner-Rodgers 2024), and the 2024 Nobel Prize in Chemistry was awarded for the development of AI algorithms to discover new proteins. If earlier major technological changes like electricity are a useful guide, the full impact may take many years to be realized, often requiring a new generation of business practices.

How widely AI will diffuse is a hotly debated question and accounts for the bulk of the variation in productivity forecasts. Some authors suggest AI will be profitably used in about 5 percent of tasks; others suggest more than 50 percent could be affected (Acemoglu 2025; Baily, Brynjolfsson, and Korinek; 2023). The potential diffusion of AI in East Asia and Pacific countries, with their smaller services sectors, appears to be somewhat lower than in higher-income countries (World Bank 2024). These future diffusion patterns have been predicted based on the number of jobs exposed to the types of tasks AI does, but hard data on actual AI use across countries have been lacking, especially for developing economies. One common source, online job postings, is typically available only for rich, English-speaking countries.

Advanced data analytics are used predominantly within multinationals.

FIGURE 3.14   Share of medium and large firms in emerging markets and advanced economies using ERP software, MNEs versus non-MNEs, 2022

Share of firms using ERP software (%)

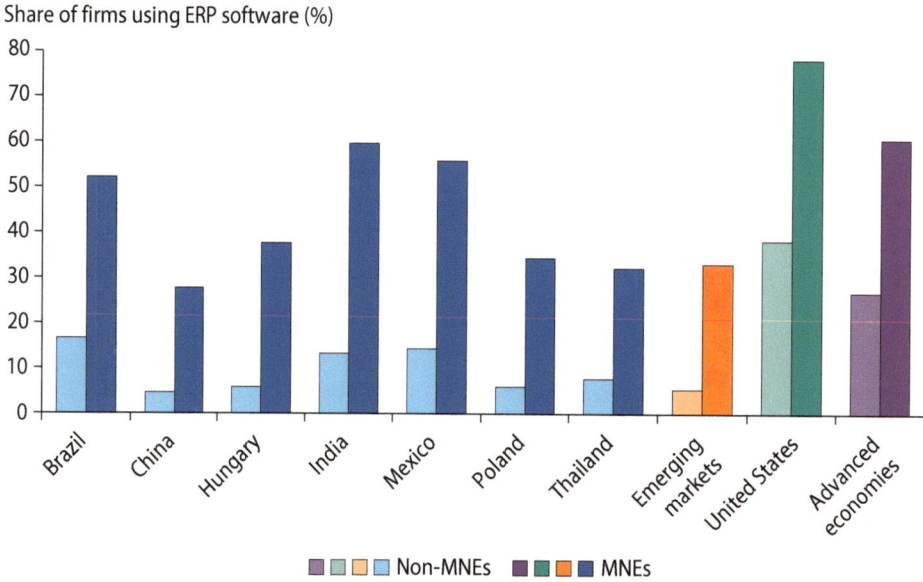

Non-MNEs ▪▪▪   MNEs ▪▪▪

Source: Original figure for this publication based on calculations using Spiceworks Computer Intelligence Technology Database data for 2022.
Note: The figure reflects the use of ERP database software by medium and large firms (defined as having at least 50 employees). "Emerging markets" (which include the subset of 7 countries) are defined according to IMF (2019). "Advanced economies" include Australia, Austria, Belgium, the Czech Republic, Denmark, Finland, France, Italy, the Netherlands, New Zealand, Norway, Portugal, the Slovak Republic, Spain, Sweden, Switzerland, the United Kingdom, and the United States. ERP = enterprise resource planning; MNEs = multinational enterprises.

Although multinational subsidiaries in EAP tend to use more-advanced technologies than other national firms, they lag behind the subsidiaries in advanced economies in that regard. AI is spreading rapidly around the world although diffusion remains incomplete and lags far behind the United States (a global leader in AI diffusion). Multinational enterprises (MNEs) also account for most AI use in our data. They are much more likely than other medium and large firms to have adopted AI by 2022 in both emerging and advanced economies (refer to figure 3.15).[11] In China, for example, MNEs are more than five times more likely to use AI than other medium and large firms, and in Thailand nearly four times more likely. In the United States, more than one-third of MNEs use AI and are four times more likely to use AI than other firms.

AI is used predominantly within multinationals.

FIGURE 3.15 Share of medium and large firms in emerging markets and advanced economies using AI, MNEs versus non-MNEs, 2022

Share of firms using ML (%)

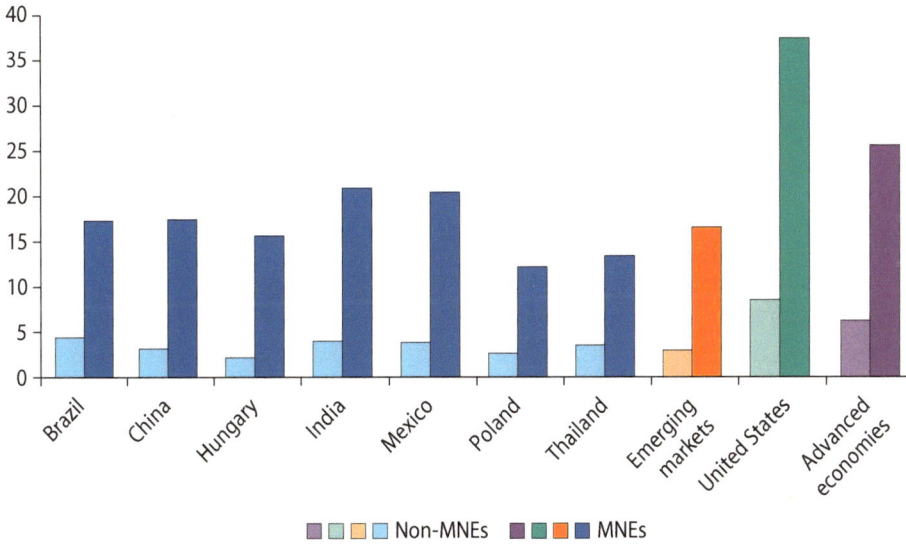

Non-MNEs ■ ■ ■ ■   MNEs ■ ■ ■ ■

Source: Original figure for this publication based on calculations using Spiceworks Computer Intelligence Technology Database data for 2022.
Note: "AI" reflects the use of machine learning, a subset of all AI use, by medium and large firms (defined as having at least 50 employees). "Emerging markets" (including the 7-country subset) are defined according to IMF (2019). "Advanced economies" include Australia, Austria, Belgium, the Czech Republic, Denmark, Finland, France, Italy, the Netherlands, New Zealand, Norway, Portugal, the Slovak Republic, Spain, Sweden, Switzerland, the United Kingdom, and the United States. AI = artificial intelligence; ML = machine learning; MNEs = multinational enterprises.

The disparity in adoption is so large that MNEs and their subsidiaries account for the bulk of AI users (despite MNEs representing a minority of firms) and outnumber domestic-owned AI users two to one. Looking beyond AI, job postings data for 29 technologies across 17 advanced economies shows that MNEs and their supply chains account for around one-third of all technology-related job advertisements (Bastos et al. 2024). However, comparing MNEs across countries shows that AI adoption in EAP lags far behind the United States: 13–17 percent of MNE subsidiaries in China and Thailand use AI, compared with 37 percent in the United States.

Why are MNE affiliates in developing countries lagging behind?

That even MNE performance falls below the global frontier could be for at least two reasons: First, MNEs that invest in developing countries are often not the most-sophisticated global firms—reducing the scope for spillovers of technology or productivity. Second, a given MNE's affiliates in developing countries may lack the prerequisite capabilities to enable them to adopt their parent firm's advanced technology or business practices. We examine each of these reasons in turn.

Foreign affiliates in poorer countries tend to be part of less-productive, less technologically advanced MNEs than affiliates in richer countries. For example, the parent MNEs of affiliates in emerging economies tend to have nearly 11 percent lower labor productivity (refer to figure 3.16). These parent firms are also 10 percentage points less likely to use cloud computing, 22 percentage points less likely to use advanced data analytics, and around 14 percentage points less likely to use AI—that is, nearly half as likely to use AI as parents in advanced economies. More generally, the sophistication of parent MNEs seems to matter for the productivity gains of their affiliates abroad. For example, increased patenting by US MNEs in their home market led to increases in productivity of their subsidiaries in China and spillovers to domestic firms in close proximity (Gong 2023).

> **Affiliates in emerging economies tend to be part of less-productive and less technologically advanced multinationals.**

FIGURE 3.16 **Technology and labor productivity gaps between MNE affiliates in advanced and emerging economies, 2022**

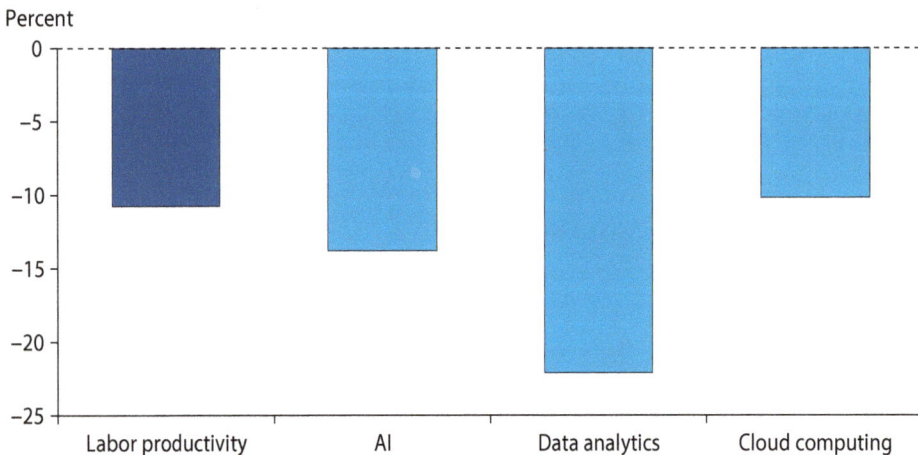

Source: Original figure for this publication using Spiceworks Computer Intelligence Technology Database data.
Note: The figure reflects 2022 data for 22 high-income economies and 7 emerging economies ("emerging" is according to IMF [2019] classifications). Regressions control for the country of origin of the parent MNE and reflect foreign affiliates of MNEs (that is, affiliates in countries other than the parent firm's). "Labor productivity" reflects multinational group revenue (in US dollars) per worker in 2020. "AI" reflects the use of machine learning. "Data analytics" reflects the use of enterprise resource planning software. "Cloud computing" reflects using Infrastructure as a Service (for example, servers, storage, networking, and virtualization). AI = artificial intelligence; MNE = multinational enterprise.

Moreover, technology diffusion within MNEs is often rapid but incomplete. In our data, more than three-quarters of affiliates adopt AI in the same year as the headquarters. Yet about half of MNE subsidiaries have not adopted it, even when the headquarters did so. Only 13 percent of AI-using MNEs have completely diffused AI to all their subsidiaries (refer to figure 3.17, panel a).

Other older data technologies are similarly partially diffused beyond the headquarters, such as using business data processing or ERP databases, suggesting the partial diffusion is not due to the newness of AI. In contrast, cloud computing appears to be somewhat different, with nearly half of MNEs using cloud computing in every subsidiary (refer to figure 3.17, panel b). This difference may be because cloud computing is a flexible, variable expense compared with most other IT that requires substantial software and hardware fixed costs (DeStefano et al. 2024).

FIGURE 3.17   **Share of MNE subsidiaries using AI or cloud computing, by usage level, 2022**

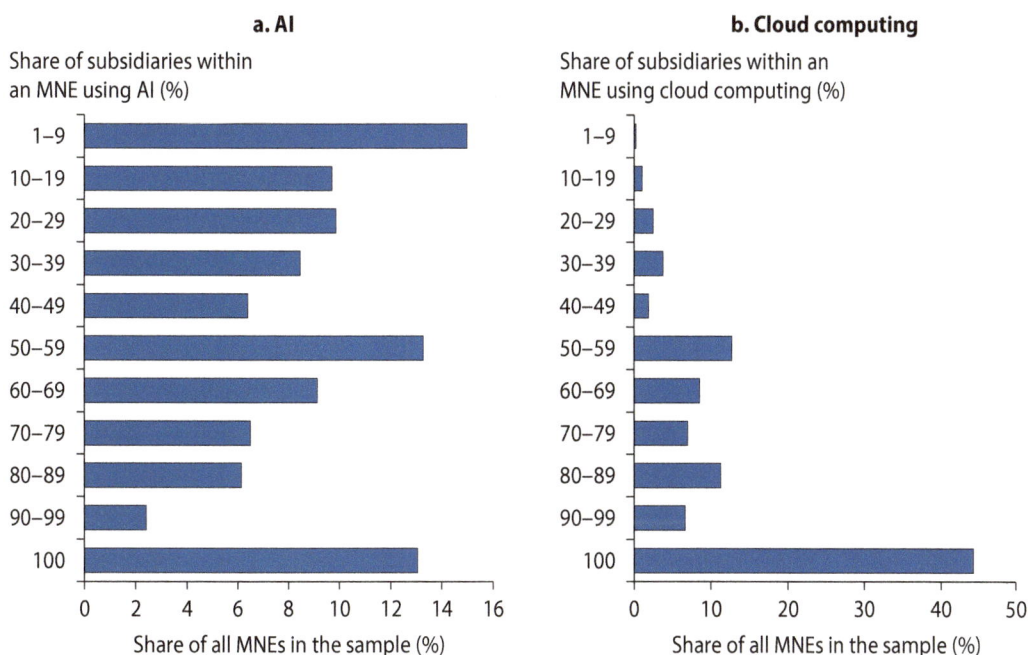

a. AI

Share of subsidiaries within an MNE using AI (%)

b. Cloud computing

Share of subsidiaries within an MNE using cloud computing (%)

Source: Original figure for this publication using Spiceworks Computer Intelligence Technology Database data.
Note: The figure reflects 2022 data for 22 high-income economies and 7 emerging economies ("emerging" is according to IMF [2019] classifications). The figure also reflects MNEs with at least 1 subsidiary using AI or cloud computing (that is, excluding 0 percent share of subsidiaries). For example (panel a), in about 15 percent of the MNEs, only 1–9 percent of the subsidiaries use AI. Panel a reflects 4,229 MNEs, and panel b, 27,204 MNEs. "AI" reflects the use of machine learning. "Cloud computing" reflects using Infrastructure as a Service (for example, servers, storage, networking, and virtualization). AI = artificial intelligence; MNE = multinational enterprise.

MNE affiliates in developing countries lack capabilities to adopt sophisticated technologies

What determines whether AI diffuses to subsidiaries or not? Country and industry characteristics play a role in determining technology diffusion within an MNE, but what matters most is that the subsidiaries have the prerequisite technologies in place. Once the headquarters has adopted AI, AI is less likely to diffuse to subsidiaries in lower-income countries than to those in richer countries. But country income may reflect several underlying differences, including access to markets, skills, or the prerequisite data technologies (such as cloud computing or ERP software).

We do not find a robust role for subsidiary labor productivity or size or for country income, country skills, or intellectual property restrictions. We find that AI is more likely to diffuse to service sector subsidiaries and those operating in more skill-intensive sectors or sectors that are more open to trade (with a higher share of trade in value added) (refer to figure 3.18).

Preexisting use of both ERP software and cloud computing has the largest impact for the diffusion of AI—dominating the use of either of these technologies individually or the role of distance. One reason is that the MNE affiliates in developing countries may lack the capabilities to adopt advanced technology or business practices of their parent firm, which we discuss in the next chapter. Out of the Box 3 discusses the challenges of implementing new technologies in complex production processes in a multinational company in the EAP region.

AI has been widely labeled a disruptive technology, with potentially widespread impacts that raise hopes of allowing firms in developing countries to leapfrog to the frontier. However, the evidence in this chapter suggests that prerequisites matter: New technologies often build on earlier ones. Earlier evidence from the FAT surveys (Cirera et al., forthcoming) showed that EAP firms had been falling behind in adopting frontier technologies such as ERP software—exactly those technologies that appear to matter most for next-generation technologies like AI. Here we find, similarly, that subsidiaries within the same MNE in emerging economies are less likely than those in richer countries to have these prerequisites in place (such as data analytics and cloud computing). The ability to take advantage of AI's potential requires policy to fix the incentives and capabilities that also hold back the productive investments in technology more generally.

| Preexisting use of data technologies predicts subsidiary adoption of AI. |

FIGURE 3.18   **Factors determining AI diffusion within MNEs**

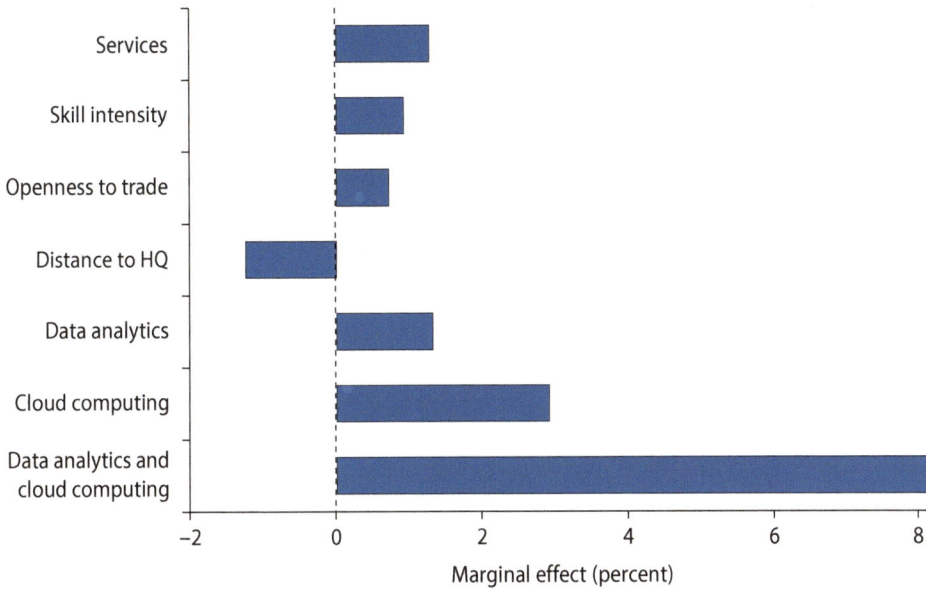

Source: Original figure for this publication based on calculations using Spiceworks Computer Intelligence Technology Database data.

Note: To aid comparisons across regressions, the figure presents the estimated percentage change in subsidiary AI adoption from a 1 standard deviation change of each factor. Regressions of subsidiary AI adoption during 2019–22 on the preexisting use of AI in the headquarters interacted with the factors listed above. Regressions include MNE dummies and examine diffusion within a given MNE. Sector skill intensity and openness to trade are defined using the United States as a frictionless benchmark. "Skill intensity" reflects the share of workers with tertiary education, and "openness to trade" is imports and exports as a share of value added, measured in 2019. Subsidiary preexisting use of data analytics or cloud computing is also measured in 2019. "Data analytics" reflects the use of enterprise resource planning software. AI = artificial intelligence; HQ = headquarters; MNE = multinational enterprise.

Out of the Box 3   How companies can automate complex production processes

This box summarizes an interview for this report with a manager of a global electronics multinational company with headquarters and subsidiaries based in the East Asia and Pacific (EAP) region.

(continued)

Out of the Box 3   How companies can automate complex production processes *(Continued)*

What processes are automated?

The company's headquarters establishes product designs and overall strategic direction, including manufacturing locations for each product. The regional branches have much autonomy to determine production methods, such as adoption of automation. This structure provides flexibility to adapt to local conditions, including worker skills, labor costs, and materials costs.

Before implementing new technologies, local branches conduct detailed feasibility assessments to evaluate cost-effectiveness and expected quality improvements and then compare the actual experience with the simulations to learn from any discrepancies. Saving on labor costs is a main motivation for automation, along with improving worker productivity, reducing materials waste, and increasing product quality. For example, the company recently automated the delivery of materials from the factory gate to the production line, requiring investment in technologies to scan the materials, identify their place in the line, and deliver these automatically using robots. This automation has sped up materials delivery and allowed the company to hold a smaller materials inventory.

However, not all processes are expected to be automated. Some tasks are better performed by humans, such as those requiring high levels of dexterity or judgment regarding fine adjustments. Some processes are undertaken infrequently and so are not worth incurring the fixed costs to automate. Finally, human workers are also preferred for the processes critical to determining overall product quality.

What are the challenges for automation?

One key challenge is ensuring that automation investments deliver expected performance improvements and integrate smoothly into existing workflows. To achieve this goal, automation is performed step-by-step and then evaluated after each step rather than redesigning production from scratch.

Supply chain constraints are a barrier to innovation. For example, certain countries in the region experience more-limited access to certain supplementary materials and equipment. These materials typically must be imported, whereas other regional branches have more domestic suppliers. In addition, meeting local regulatory

(continued)

Out of the Box 3   How companies can automate complex production processes *(Continued)*

requirements and obtaining quality certifications is a complex and time-intensive process, which can complicate the introduction of new production methods.

The transition to automation also presents challenges in workforce adaptation and training. Employees need training to operate advanced technologies safely and effectively, while the automation processes must be user-friendly to local employees to facilitate a smooth transition.

How are new technologies learned?

Structured knowledge-sharing programs are established across the company's global network. Experts from headquarters frequently visit regional branches for extended training programs and may stay to support local teams for several years. Local employees also travel to headquarters to gain exposure to new product models and production techniques. In addition, cross-country meetings can help teams exchange expertise and share best practices.

Source: Box original for this publication based on an interview with a multinational company in the EAP region.

Notes

1. "Productivity" refers to total factor productivity: The residual measure of improvements in technology and organization that cannot be explained by changes in capital or labor inputs. Where the report considers labor productivity, it is referred to as such. "Labor productivity" is defined as value added per worker.
2. "Advanced" economies are high-income countries according to World Bank income classifications. "Developing" countries are low- and middle-income countries according to World Bank income classifications.
3. Evidence for the United States is more mixed, with Ganapati (2021) and Covarrubias, Gutiérrez, and Philippon (2020) finding differing conclusions for the link between concentration and productivity.
4. Note that by allowing for composition changes, the cross-section distributions presented here are substantially different from examination of only surviving firms. For instance, the firm-level convergence literature commonly finds that laggard firms have faster growth rates than more-productive firms (Bartelsman, Haskel, and Martin 2008; Griffith, Redding, and Van Reenen 2004). But this convergence analysis is inherently conditional upon survival over the period—to be able to measure a firm's growth rates. Surviving laggards tend to be much more productive than laggards in general or new-entrant laggards. Therefore, convergence of surviving laggards may not imply changes in the cross-section distribution.

5. It is important to contrast the statistics presented on cross-sections of the productivity distribution with so-called firm-level convergence regressions (for example, Bartelsman, Haskel, and Martin 2008; Griffith, Redding, and Van Reenen 2004).
6. As noted in chapter 1, we focus on the productivity of medium and large firms to enable comparability across countries.
7. Note that the size of the technology gaps between the least-sophisticated firms in EAP and advanced countries may be partly due to a floor in technology use.
8. Other candidates—which, as noted earlier, may be related to data technologies—are the increasing importance of intangibles more generally, such as management skills, the network effects of platforms, and weakening competition or globalization (Van Reenen 2022).
9. Other authors have reached higher valuations on data. For example, Corrado et al. (2022) find that data output averages 6.6 percent of gross value added across six European economies. One key difference is that the value of the data output produced can be several times higher than the cost of the data workers used to produce these assets (that we capture here). A second difference is that Corrado et al. (2022) define the workers who perform data tasks more broadly than Goodridge, Haskel, and Edquist (2022).
10. "Emerging" economies are defined according to International Monetary Fund classifications (IMF 2019).
11. Whereas our data finish in 2022, AI diffusion appears to have only accelerated since then. For example, evidence from the EU finds the share of medium and large firms using AI nearly doubled between 2021 and 2024, from 15 percent to 25 percent (calculations based on OECD 2025).

References

Acemoglu, D. 2025. "The Simple Macroeconomics of AI." *Economic Policy* 40 (121): 13–58.

Andrews, D., C. Criscuolo, and P. N. Gal. 2016. "The Best versus the Rest: The Global Productivity Slowdown, Divergence across Firms and the Role of Public Policy." OECD Productivity Working Papers No. 5, Organisation for Economic Co-operation and Development, Paris.

Araujo, J. T., E. Vostroknutova, K. M. Wacker, and M. Clavijo. 2016. *Understanding the Income and Efficiency Gap in Latin America and the Caribbean.* Directions in Development Series. Washington, DC: World Bank.

Autor, D., D. Dorn, L. F. Katz, C. Patterson, and J. Van Reenen. 2020. "The Fall of the Labor Share and the Rise of Superstar Firms." *Quarterly Journal of Economics* 135 (2): 645–709.

Baily, M. N., E. Brynjolfsson, and A. Korinek. 2023. "Machines of Mind: The Case for an AI-Powered Productivity Boom." Research report, Brookings Institution, Washington, DC.

Bajgar, M., G. Berlingieri, S. Calligaris, C. Criscuolo, and J. Timmis. 2023. "Industry Concentration in Europe and North America." *Industrial and Corporate Change*: dtac059.

Bajgar, M., C. Criscuolo, and J. Timmis. 2025. "Intangibles and Industry Concentration: A Cross-Country Analysis." *Oxford Bulletin of Economics and Statistics.* https://doi .org/10.1111/obes.12659.

Bartelsman, E., J. Haskel, and R. Martin. 2008. "Distance to Which Frontier?: Evidence on Productivity Convergence from International Firm-level Data." Working Paper No. 7032, Centre for Economic Policy Research, London.

Bastos, P., K. Stapleton, D. Taglioni, and H. Y. Wei. 2024. "Firm Networks and Global Technology Diffusion." Policy Research Working Paper 10905, World Bank, Washington, DC.

Bighelli, T., F. Di Mauro, M. J. Melitz, and M. Mertens. 2023. "European Firm Concentration and Aggregate Productivity." *Journal of the European Economic Association* 21 (2): 455–83.

Bloom, N., R. Sadun, and J. Van Reenen. 2012. "Americans Do IT Better: US Multinationals and the Productivity Miracle." *American Economic Review* 102 (1): 167–201.

Brynjolfsson, E., D. Li, and L. Raymond. 2025. "Generative AI at Work." *Quarterly Journal of Economics* 140 (2): 889–942.

Brynjolfsson, E., A. McAfee, M. Sorell, and F. Zhu. 2008. "Scale without Mass: Business Process Replication and Industry Dynamics." Harvard Business School Technology & Operations Management Unit Research Paper No. 07-016, Cambridge, MA.

Brynjolfsson, E., D. Rock, and C. Syverson. 2021. "The Productivity J-Curve: How Intangibles Complement General Purpose Technologies." *American Economic Journal: Macroeconomics* 13 (1): 333–72.

Calvino, F., C. Criscuolo, L. Marcolin, and M. Squicciarini. 2018. "A Taxonomy of Digital Intensive Sectors." OECD Science, Technology and Industry Working Papers No. 2018/14, Organisation for Economic Co-operation and Development, Paris.

Carr, D. F. 2024. "Rapid Growth Continues for ChatGPT, Google's NotebookLM." Similarweb Blog, November 6, 2024. https://www.similarweb.com/blog/insights/ai-news/chatgpt-notebooklm/.

Ciani, A., M. C. Hyland, N. Karalashvili, J. L. Keller, A. Ragoussis, and T. T. Tran. 2020. *Making It Big: Why Developing Countries Need More Large Firms.* Washington, DC: World Bank.

Cirera, X., D. Comin, M. Cruz, K. M. Lee, and A. Soares Martins Neto. Forthcoming. "Distance and Convergence to the Technology Frontier." Research paper, World Bank, Washington, DC.

Cirera, X., A. D. Mason, F. de Nicola, S. Kuriakose, D. S. Mare, and T. T. Tran. 2021. *The Innovation Imperative for Developing East Asia.* Washington, DC: World Bank.

Comin, D. A., M. Cruz, X. Cirera, K. M. Lee, and J. Torres. 2022. "Technology and Resilience." Working Paper 29644, National Bureau of Economic Research, Cambridge, MA.

Corrado, C., C. Criscuolo, J. Haskel, A. Himbert, and C. Jona-Lasinio. 2021. "New Evidence on Intangibles, Diffusion and Productivity." OECD Science, Technology and Industry Working Papers No. 2021/10, Organisation for Economic Co-operation and Development, Paris.

Corrado, C., J. Haskel, C. Jona-Lasinio, and I. Massimiliano. 2018. "Intangible Investment in the EU and US before and since the Great Recession and Its Contribution to Productivity Growth." *Journal of Infrastructure, Policy and Development* 2 (1): article 205.

Corrado, C., J. Haskel, C. Jona-Lasinio, and I. Massimiliano. 2022. "The Value of Data in Digital-Based Business Models: Measurement and Economic Policy Implications." OECD Economics Department Working Papers No. 1723, Organisation for Economic Co-operation and Development, Paris.

Covarrubias, M., G. Gutiérrez, and T. Philippon. 2020. "From Good to Bad Concentration? US Industries over the Past 30 Years." *NBER Macroeconomics Annual* 34 (1): 1–46.

Criscuolo, C. 2023. "Productivity Growth and Structural Change in the Era of Global Shocks." PowerPoint, KDI–Brookings Joint Seminar: Productivity in a Time of Change, April 11. https://www.brookings.edu/wp-content/uploads/2023/04/2.1-KDI-Brookings-Jointt -Seminar-revised-ppt_Chiara-Criscuolo.pdf.

Crouzet, N., and J. Eberley. 2019. "Understanding Weak Capital Investment: The Role of Market Concentration and Intangibles." Working Paper 25869, National Bureau of Economic Research, Cambridge, MA.

De Loecker, J., J. Eeckhout, and G. Unger. 2020. "The Rise of Market Power and the Macroeconomic Implications." *Quarterly Journal of Economics* 135 (2): 561–644.

Eeckhout, J. 2021. *The Profit Paradox: How Thriving Firms Threaten the Future of Work.* Princeton, NJ: Princeton University Press.

De Ridder, M. 2024. "Market Power and Innovation in the Intangible Economy." *American Economic Review* 114 (1): 199–251.

DeStefano, T., N. Johnstone, R. Kneller, and J. Timmis. 2024. "Do Capital Incentives Distort Technology Diffusion? Evidence on Cloud, Big Data and AI." Research Paper 2024/04, Centre for Research on Globalisation and Economic Policy, University of Nottingham, UK.

Ganapati, S. 2021. "Growing Oligopolies, Prices, Output, and Productivity." *American Economic Journal: Microeconomics* 13 (3): 309–27.

Gong, R. K. 2023. "The Local Technology Spillovers of Multinational Firms." *Journal of International Economics* 144: 103790.

Goodridge, P., J. Haskel, and H. Edquist. 2022. "We See Data Everywhere Except in the Productivity Statistics." *Review of Income and Wealth* 68 (4): 862–94.

Griffith, R., S. Redding, and J. Van Reenen. 2004. "Mapping the Two Faces of R&D: Productivity Growth in a Panel of OECD Industries." *Review of Economics and Statistics* 86 (4): 883–95.

Haskel, J., and S. Westlake. 2018. *Capitalism without Capital: The Rise of the Intangible Economy.* Princeton, NJ: Princeton University Press.

IMF (International Monetary Fund). 2019. *World Economic Outlook 2019: Global Manufacturing Downturn, Rising Trade Barriers.* Washington, DC: IMF.

Kanazawa, K., D. Kawaguchi, H. Shigeoka, and Y. Watanabe. 2022. "AI, Skill, and Productivity: The Case of Taxi Drivers." Working Paper 30612, National Bureau of Economic Research, Cambridge, MA.

Maslej, N., L. Fattorini, R. Perrault, et al. 2024. "Artificial Intelligence Index Report 2024." AI Index Steering Committee, Institute for Human-Centered AI, Stanford University, Stanford, CA.

Noy, S., and W. Zhang. 2023. "Experimental Evidence on the Productivity Effects of Generative Artificial Intelligence." *Science* 381 (6654): 187–92.

OECD (Organisation for Economic Co-operation and Development). 2025. ICT Access and Usage by Businesses (database), OECD, Paris. https://prosperitydata360.worldbank.org/en /dataset/OECD+ICT_BUS.

Toner-Rodgers, A. 2024. "Artificial Intelligence, Scientific Discovery, and Product Innovation." Paper, Department of Economics, Massachusetts Institute of Technology, Cambridge, MA. https://doi.org/10.48550/arXiv.2412.17866.

Van Reenen, J. 2022. "The Rise of Superstar Firms: Causes and Consequences." Online presentation, Digital Economics Conference, Toulouse School of Economics, Toulouse, France. January 14. https://www.tse-fr.eu/publications/rise-superstar-firms -causes-and-consequences.

World Bank. 2022. *World Bank East Asia and the Pacific Economic Update April 2022: Braving the Storms.* Washington, DC: World Bank.

World Bank. 2024. *World Bank East Asia and the Pacific Economic Update October 2024: Jobs and Technology.* Washington, DC: World Bank.

Zinser, M., J. Rose, and H. Sirkin. 2015. "The Robotics Revolution: The Next Great Leap in Manufacturing." BCG article, September 23. Boston Consulting Group, Boston.

Why Are the Leaders Not Leading?

4

Key messages

Frontier firms' productivity is stagnating, and their market shares are falling; both these factors dampen aggregate productivity growth. What is behind the East Asia and Pacific (EAP) region's relative inertia?

- Impediments to competition are inhibiting the incentive to innovate, especially for frontier firms, and are preventing the reallocation of resources toward more-productive firms.
- Although manufacturing tariffs are relatively low in EAP countries, nontariff measures in manufacturing and restrictions on services trade limit competition.
- Weaknesses in human capital and infrastructure are limiting the capacity to innovate.
- The adoption of sophisticated technologies and productivity growth require a broad range of skills and high-quality digital infrastructure, which are unevenly available in the EAP region.

Firms require incentives from competition

Low levels of competition could explain the relatively low productivity growth of frontier firms in EAP. Higher competition (or the threat of competition), which can come from openness to trade and investment, increases the incentives for frontier firms to innovate and grow (refer to figure 4.1). Firms in Indonesia and Viet Nam report competitive pressures as the most-important driver of technology adoption, and in the Philippines, as the second most-important (Cirera et al., forthcoming).

However, these pressures can have heterogeneous effects. Firms that are close to the technology frontier innovate to stay ahead of their competitors, whereas laggard firms are discouraged and innovate less (Aghion 2017; Aghion et al. 2005, 2009). For example, competition from Chinese firms has been found to increase the innovation of leading firms but to depress it among nonleading firms in other parts of the world (Cusolito, Garcia-Marin, and Maloney 2023; Iacovone 2012). In Portugal, increased import competition led the most-productive firms to increase investments in automation technologies to compete, whereas the least-productive firms reduced their investments (Bastos, Flach, and Keller 2023).

Low levels of competition can reduce productivity growth of frontier firms.

FIGURE 4.1 Illustration of the relationship between competition and productivity growth of frontier and laggard firms

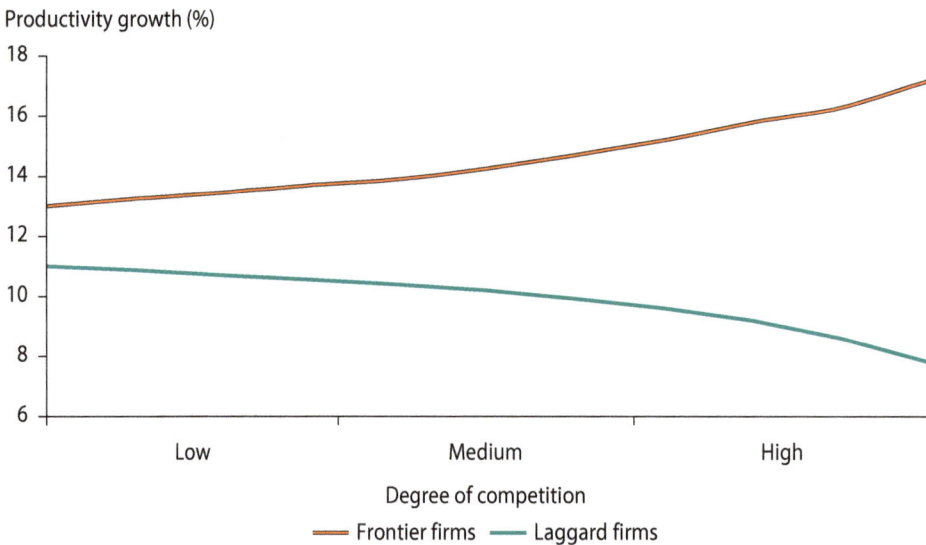

Source: The figure is reprinted from Aghion (2017), Figure 3, using the Creative Commons Attribution 4.0 International License (http://creativecommons.org/licenses/by/4.0/). The following changes were made to the figure: The title was changed from "Competition, growth, and distance to frontier," the colors of the data lines were changed, the x-axis was changed from "Competition," and the y-axis was changed from "Growth of firms."
Note: The figure illustrates the relationship between firms' productivity growth and competition. "Frontier firms" refer to the most-productive 90 percent of firms within a country and industry and "laggard firms" to the least-productive 10 percent. Frontier firms grow more slowly and laggard firms more quickly in low-competition environments.

Competition-limiting effects of state-owned enterprises

The dynamism of frontier firms depends on the threat of competition from both other incumbents and entrants. The existence of larger state-owned enterprises (SOEs) can discourage the entry of new firms and increase market concentration in those same sectors (refer to figure 4.2). When capital and labor are trapped in less-productive SOEs, it is harder for start-ups to attract the resources needed to enter, and it is harder for productive incumbents to scale up and grow.[1] For example, in Chinese prefectures, SOEs' adverse impact on entry reduces productivity through greater misallocation of capital, with capital remaining trapped in less-productive incumbents (Brandt, Kambourov, and Storesletten 2020). Conversely, the disruption of politically connected firms following the fall of the Suharto regime in Indonesia led to improvements in measures of competition in these industries (Hallward-Driemeier, Kochanova, and Rijkers 2021).

> Higher SOE presence is associated with lower firm entry and greater market concentration.

FIGURE 4.2   Changes in firm entry and market concentration from a doubling of state ownership in a sector

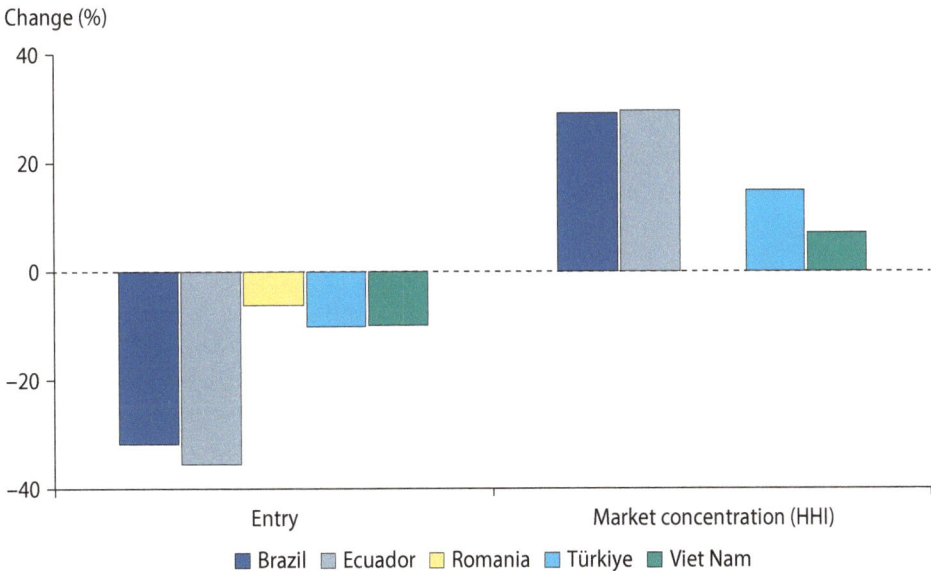

Source: Reprinted from World Bank (2023).
Note: The figure shows that in Brazil, for example, doubling the state's share in a sector is associated with 30 percent less entry. "Entry" refers to the entry rate of new firms in Romania and Türkiye and to the share of revenue accounted for by young firms (less than 5 years old) in Brazil, Ecuador, and Viet Nam. "Market concentration" is measured using the HHI. The years covered vary by country: 2016–19 for Brazil, 2011–19 for Ecuador and Romania, 2015–19 for Türkiye, and 2007–19 for Viet Nam. All effects are statistically significant except for market concentration in Romania. HHI = Herfindahl-Hirschman Index; SOE = state-owned enterprise.

In addition, labor market restrictions can make hiring qualified workers harder, such that labor flows more slowly to the most-productive firms. During the COVID-19 pandemic, countries with a stronger competitive environment showed more reallocation of employment toward more-productive firms (Bruhn, Demirgüç-Kunt, and Singer 2023). Box 4.1 reviews the empirical evidence on the sources of misallocation and the related productivity losses.

Box 4.1   Drivers of misallocation and productivity loss in the East Asia and Pacific region

By distorting the allocation of resources across producers, policy interventions may give rise to misallocation and lower productivity growth. This box provides an overview of the sources of misallocation and their estimated productivity impact in the East Asia and Pacific region. Importantly, each channel considered by itself cannot explain the overall amount of misallocation. However, empirical evidence sheds light on distortionary policies that harm productivity growth.

Regulation

Preferential access to resources for state-owned enterprises (SOEs) is associated with sizable productivity losses that tend to increase (Song, Storesletten, and Zilibotti 2011). Studying 1985–2007 data in China, Brandt, Tombe, and Zhu (2013) find that within-province misallocation of capital between state and nonstate sectors reduced the nonagricultural total factor productivity (TFP) growth rate by 0.5 percent per year. The costs of misallocation appear to have sharply increased during the latest period they analyzed, 1997–2007.

Regulatory restrictions on movements across space are also associated with considerable misallocation. Bryan and Morten (2019) leveraged detailed data from Indonesia to estimate the aggregate productivity gains from reducing barriers to internal labor migration, accounting for worker selection and spatial differences in human capital. They found that removing all barriers would increase labor productivity by 22 percent. The estimate hides substantial heterogeneity, with gains exceeding 100 percent in some more-constrained localities.

Misallocation due to migration costs is also sizable in China. Tombe and Zhu (2019) studied the impact of frictions in goods markets and labor markets using a general equilibrium model calibrated with Chinese data. They found that the reduction in

(continued)

Box 4.1 Drivers of misallocation and productivity loss in the East Asia and Pacific region *(Continued)*

the cost of internal trade and migration accounted for 28 percent of aggregate labor productivity growth in 2000–05, while the reduction of the costs of international trade accounted for only 8 percent of labor productivity growth. Despite reductions in internal trade and migration costs during the period studied, these costs remain high. The quantitative model indicates that gains from further liberalization could be large, especially with respect to land reform.

Trade and competition

Trade policy influences the allocation of resources across heterogeneous producers and consequently affects aggregate productivity. Two approaches are used to quantitatively assess the impact of tariffs or other distortionary forms of protection. One approach is to gather evidence from model-based estimates. For example, Edmond, Midrigan, and Xu (2015) (building on Arkolakis, Costinot, and Rodríguez-Clare 2012) studied the impact of moving from autarky to free trade by calibrating a model to Taiwanese manufacturing data. Opening to trade leads to greater competitive pressure and substantially reduces markup distortions. Consequently, it reduces misallocation and improves TFP by more than 12 percent.

Another approach is to examine specific trade policy changes for causal inference. Khandelwal, Schott, and Wei (2013) study the elimination of externally imposed quotas on Chinese textile and clothing exports. Interestingly, the distortionary effects of the quotas imposed by Canada, the European Union, and the United States were compounded by the effects of government-imposed quotas allocated in favor of (less-productive) SOEs. The authors find that 71 percent of the productivity gains derived from the empirical analysis are due to the elimination of misallocated quota licenses, whereas the remaining 29 percent are explained by the removal of misallocation due to the quota itself.

Financial and information frictions

There is an established literature on the positive correlation between financial market development and growth. (For an overview, see Buera, Kaboski and Shin [2015].) Credit constraints may lead to misallocation, potentially magnifying the persistence of low productivity, as more-productive firms take a longer time to overcome financial constraints. This empirical question has been tested in multiple frameworks, and

(continued)

Box 4.1   Drivers of misallocation and productivity loss in the East Asia and Pacific region *(Continued)*

the resulting estimates tend to vary substantially across studies. On the conservative side are the results by Midrigan and Xu (2014). They calibrate a model with plant-level data from the Republic of Korea and find that losses from misallocation in an environment with borrowing constraints amount to 4.7 percent of the TFP decline (accounting for over one-fourth of the TFP decline). Borrowing constraints harm growth more through the selection (into a sector) channel rather than through the misallocation (within the sector) channel.

A complementary analysis is proposed by David, Hopenhayn, and Venkateswaran (2016), who focus on informational frictions. Under their framework, firms have limited knowledge about the demand conditions in their own markets when choosing inputs. The authors estimate a structural model with 2012 data on firm-level production variables and stock returns for three countries: China, India, and the United States. Informational frictions for investment but not labor decisions lead to losses in productivity (of 4 percent, 7 percent, and 10 percent) and output (of 5 percent, 10 percent, and 14 percent) for the United States, China, and India, respectively. Those authors show that financial markets have limited ability to overcome these frictions given the high level of noise in market prices. Conversely, valuable information can be inferred from private (internal to the firm) sources.

Competition-limiting effects of tariffs and regulations

Trade policy could explain the low levels of competition slowing frontier growth, as noted earlier. Although tariffs on imports are relatively low in EAP countries, agricultural tariffs and nontariff measures in manufacturing still limit competition. Furthermore, competition-inhibiting product market regulations, such as restrictions on foreign ownership, are 50 percent more restrictive in China and Indonesia than in the United States (OECD 2023). Some EAP markets, for example in Viet Nam, are dominated by SOEs (refer to figure 4.3). As for labor markets, the Organisation for Economic Co-operation and Development (OECD) employment protection index shows around 40 percent more restriction in Malaysia and Thailand, and around twice the restriction in Indonesia, as in OECD economies (OECD 2022).

SOEs account for a large share of GDP in some EAP countries.

FIGURE 4.3   State-owned enterprise revenue as a share of GDP, 2019

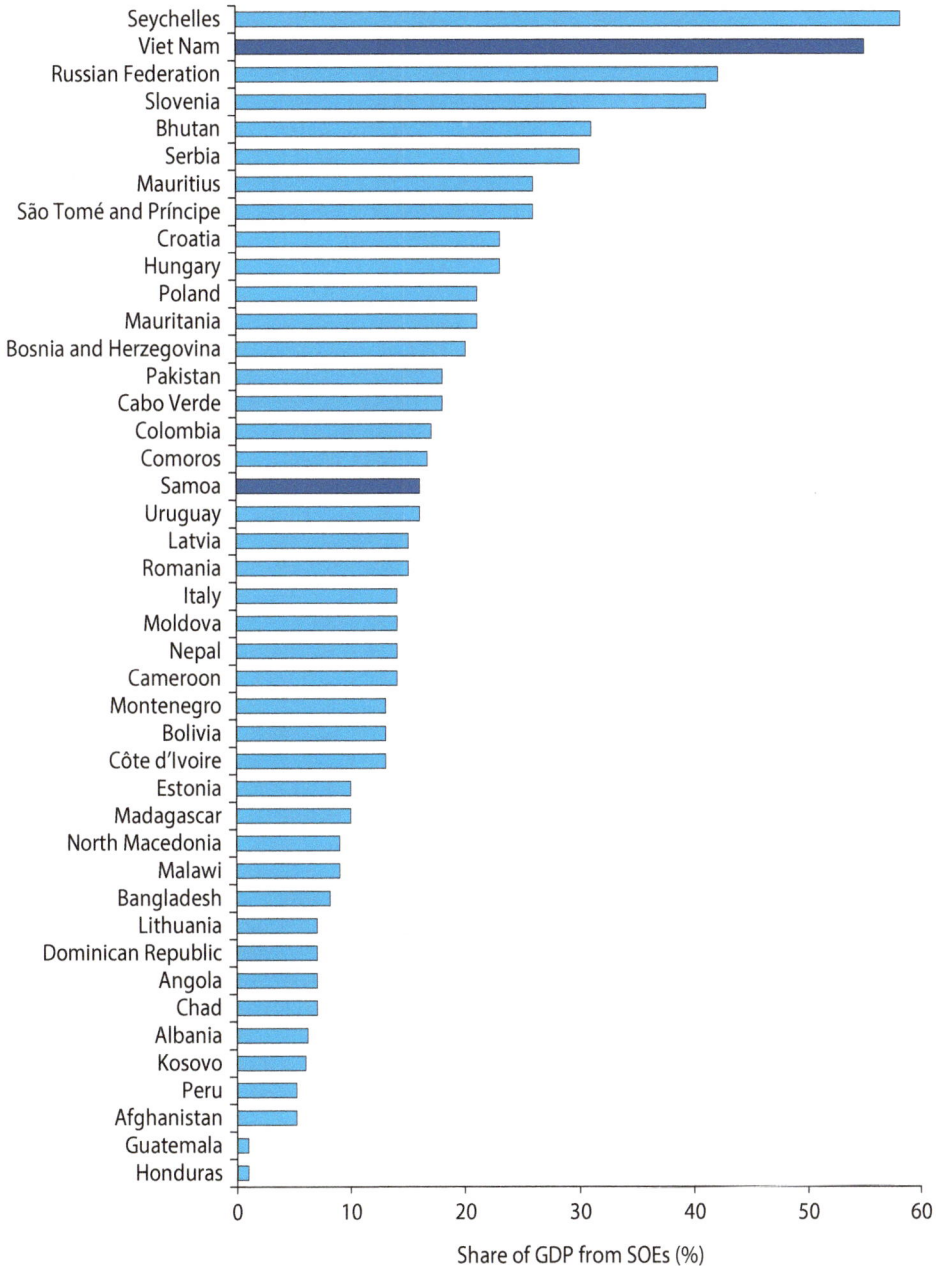

Share of GDP from SOEs (%)

Source: Reprinted from World Bank (2023).
Note: Dark blue bars designate East Asia and Pacific countries. GDP = gross domestic product; SOEs = state-owned enterprises.

Importance of start-ups to domestic competitiveness

Competition from start-ups has fallen dramatically in recent decades, especially in digital-intensive sectors. One way of measuring the importance of start-ups in an economy is by their share of employment. Employment shares from young firms (less than 5 years old) have fallen dramatically in all EAP economies for which we have firm-level data, and this is especially the case in digital-intensive sectors (refer to figure 4.4).[2] For example, in Viet Nam's digital sectors, the share of young firms declined from around one-half of industry employment in 2011 to less than one-third in 2021. In digital services sectors in the Philippines, the share of young firms fell from more than 20 percent of employment in 2010 to less than 10 percent in 2021.

> **Firm entry has slowed in EAP countries, especially in digital sectors.**

FIGURE 4.4   Young firms' share of industry employment in selected EAP countries, by sector digital intensity

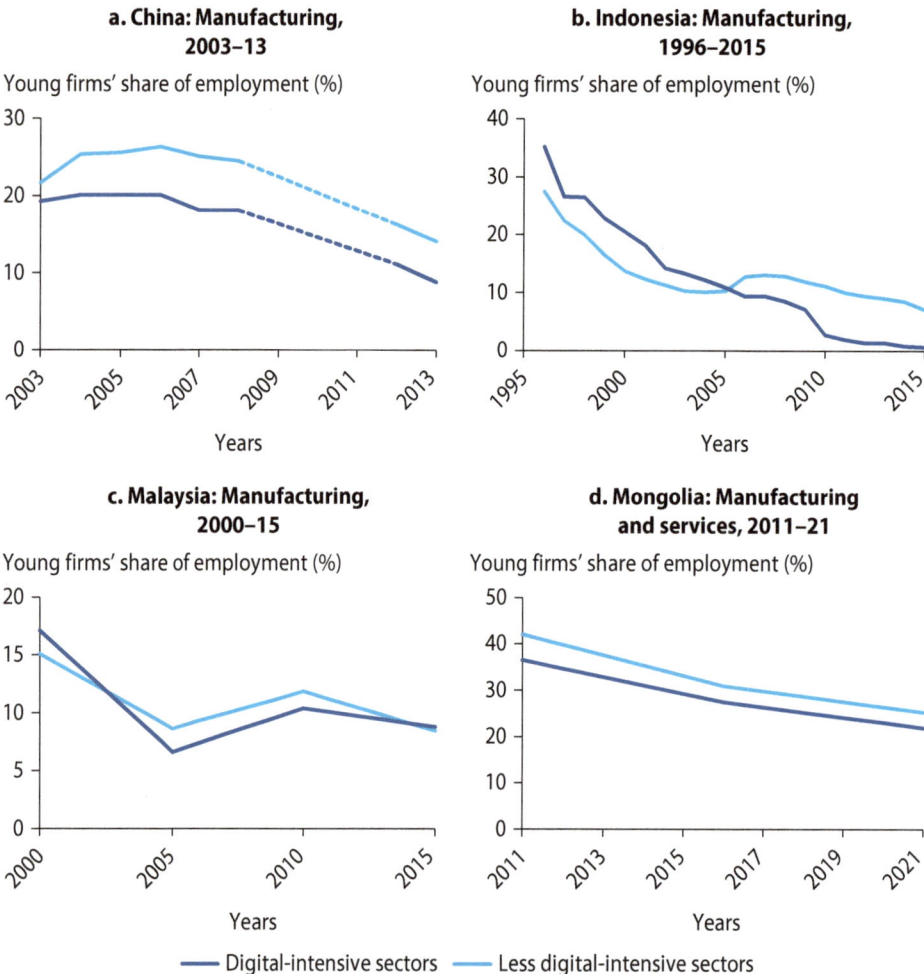

(continued)

FIGURE 4.4 **Young firms' share of industry employment in selected EAP countries, by sector digital intensity** *(Continued)*

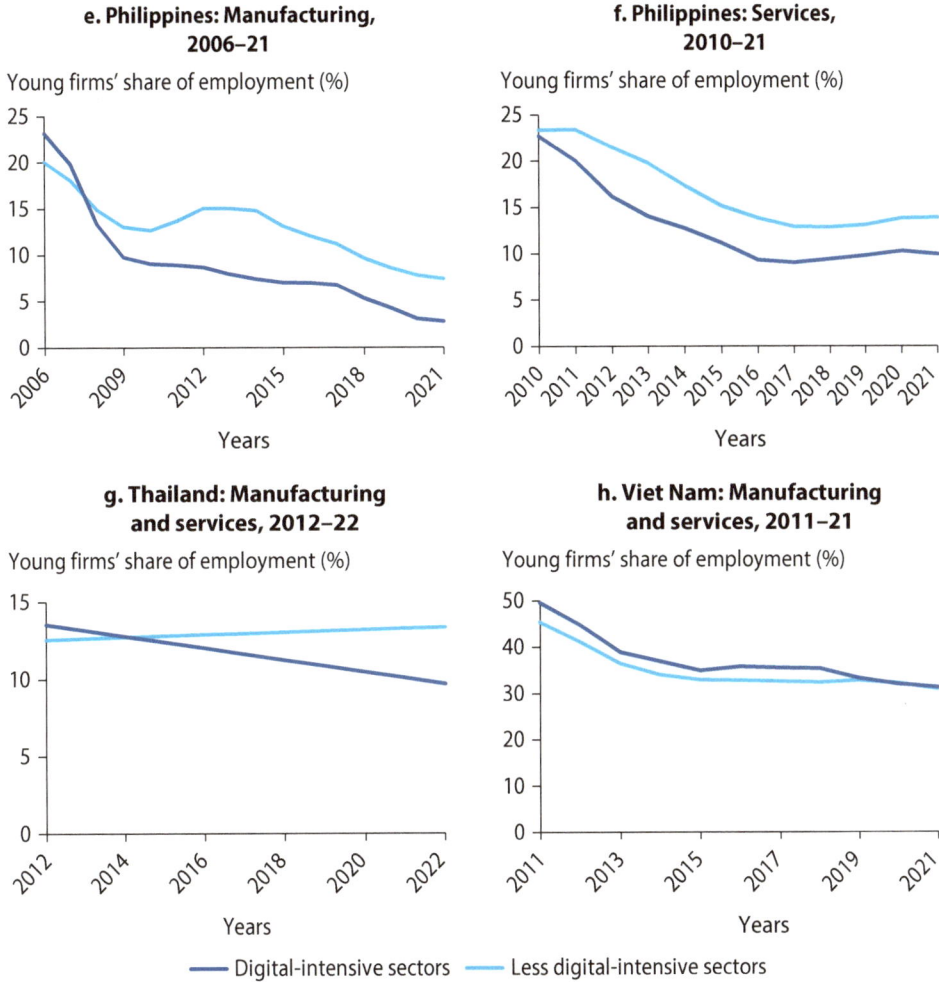

e. Philippines: Manufacturing, 2006–21

f. Philippines: Services, 2010–21

g. Thailand: Manufacturing and services, 2012–22

h. Viet Nam: Manufacturing and services, 2011–21

— Digital-intensive sectors — Less digital-intensive sectors

Source: Original figure for this publication using calculations based on statistical office microdata.
Note: The vertical axis shows the unweighted average of the employment share of young firms (5 years old or less) within each two-digit industry by digital intensity. "Digital intensity" is defined according to Eurostat's Digital Intensity Index. Thailand data are available only for the years 2012 and 2022 and Mongolia data are available for 2011, 2016, and 2021. In panel a, dotted lines for China reflect a linear interpolation between time periods observed in the data.

World Bank Enterprise Surveys provide similar evidence of declining entry rates in a broader range of EAP countries. In addition, the *quality* of entrants appears to have not increased in China and Indonesia—with new entrants being less productive than incumbents in recent years. The region is increasingly full of aging incumbents.

Importance of foreign-owned competition to frontier productivity

Frontier firms in EAP that are more exposed to international competition show faster productivity growth (refer to figure 4.5). Firms at the national frontier are more likely to be foreign-owned or exporters, but foreign firms and exporters remain in the minority, even within the frontier (as noted earlier). The national frontier comprises a mix of firm types, so unsurprisingly not all frontier firms are stagnating. Foreign-owned frontier firms show 3.4 percent faster annual productivity growth than other frontier firms, whereas state-owned firms have 3.5 percent slower productivity growth.[3]

To maintain pace with the global frontier, the national frontier would need to grow more than 4 percent faster in digital sectors. Moreover, competition from foreign-owned or state-owned firms within their sector can have important spillovers on the growth of domestically or privately owned firms. A 10 percent increase in the share of foreign ownership is associated with a 1.3 percent higher productivity growth

---

Higher SOE presence in EAP is associated with lower TFP growth of frontier firms, and higher foreign-firm presence is associated with higher TFP growth.

FIGURE 4.5   **Correlation between productivity growth of EAP frontier firms and the presence of state-owned or foreign-owned firms**

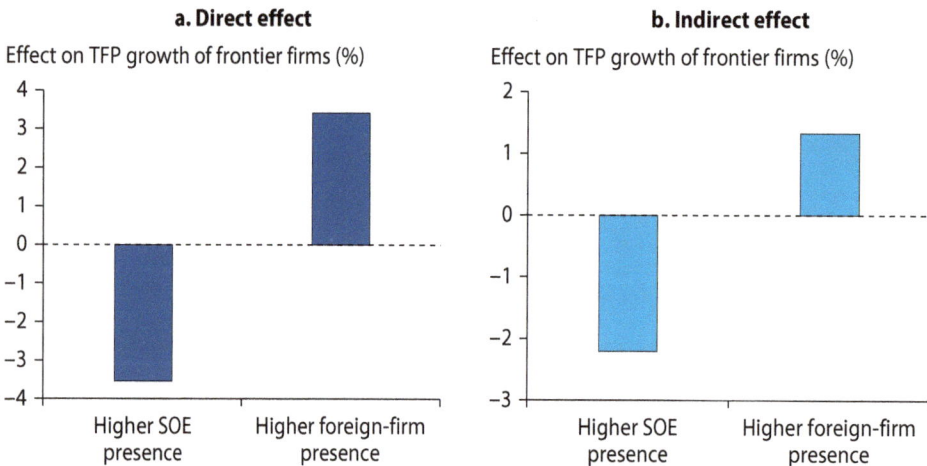

Source: Original figure for this publication using calculations based on statistical office microdata for China, Indonesia, the Philippines, and Viet Nam. Refer to box 1.1 for years of data.

Note: State ownership data are available only for China and Indonesia; foreign ownership data are available for all four countries. "Direct effect" of foreign ownership (panel a) reflects the difference in annual TFP growth between foreign-owned and domestic-owned frontier firms. "Frontier firms" are the most-productive 10 percent of firms within a country and industry. "Indirect effect" (panel b) represents the differential annual TFP growth for domestic-owned frontier firms in industries with 10 percent higher foreign ownership (measured as the share of industry sales due to foreign-owned firms). The direct and indirect effects of higher state ownership are defined similarly. The figure reflects an unweighted average across countries. All estimated effects are statistically significant at the 95 percent level. SOE = state-owned enterprise; TFP = total factor productivity.

of domestic-owned frontier firms. Conversely, 10 percent higher state ownership shares is correlated with 2.2 percent lower productivity growth of privately owned frontier firms.

Importance of incentives to invest in new technologies

Better access to international markets can also increase incentives for frontier firms to adopt modern technologies that drive productivity growth (refer to figure 4.6). Access to large markets increases the returns to adopting technologies and can spur adoption. Modern data technologies have high fixed costs, but these technologies are scalable and can, therefore, lead to productivity gains throughout the organization.

Firm incentives to invest in these high fixed-cost technologies depend on access to large international markets (in goods and services), which makes it possible to spread the cost of adoption over a larger output. However, the restrictions on foreign entry

---

Openness to foreign investment is positively associated with technology diffusion and productivity.

FIGURE 4.6 **Correlation between foreign ownership and technology diffusion and productivity in EAP countries**

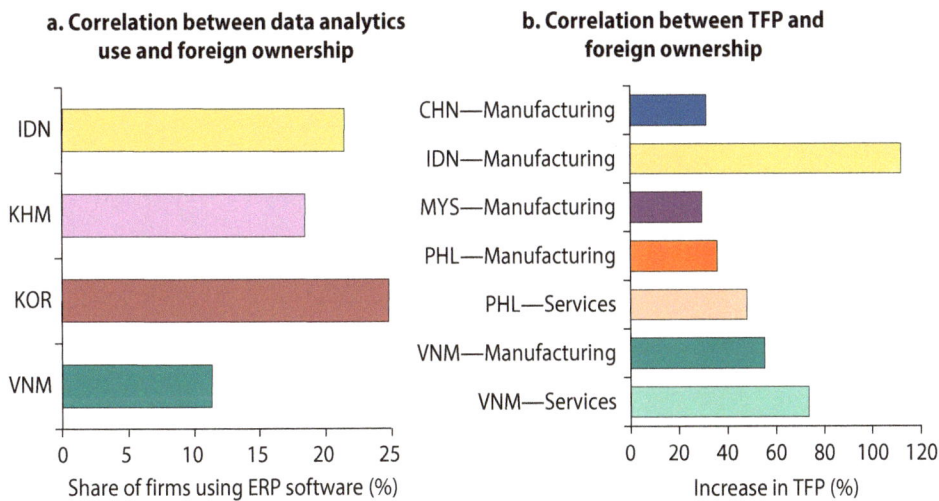

a. Correlation between data analytics use and foreign ownership

b. Correlation between TFP and foreign ownership

Sources: Original figure for this publication using the World Bank's FAT survey from Cirera et al. (forthcoming) (panel a); calculations using statistical office microdata (panel b).

Note: "Foreign ownership" is a dummy variable that reflects at least 50 percent foreign ownership of a firm. Panel a reflects the percentage difference in the use of ERP database software between foreign-owned and domestic-owned firms. Data reflect medium and large manufacturing firms (with more than 20 employees) for the following years: Cambodia 2022, Indonesia 2023, Republic of Korea 2020–21, and Viet Nam 2019. Panel b reflects the percentage difference in TFP between foreign-owned and domestic-owned firms. Data reflect medium and large firms for the following years: China 1998–2007, Indonesia 1996-2015, Malaysia 2000-15, the Philippines 2006–21, and Viet Nam 2001–15. CHN = China; ERP = enterprise resource planning; FAT = Firm-level Adoption of Technology; IDN = Indonesia; KHM = Cambodia; KOR = Republic of Korea; MYS = Malaysia; PHL = the Philippines; TFP = total factor productivity; VNM = Viet Nam.

in EAP markets, especially in the services sectors, have the effect of segmenting regional markets and depriving firms of the innovation incentives stemming from large-scale production.

Effects of restrictions on foreign investment and services trade

EAP countries have more restrictions on foreign investment than other countries at a similar level of development (refer to figure 4.7). The OECD's Foreign Direct Investment (FDI) Regulatory Restrictiveness Index measures restrictions on foreign direct investment such as foreign equity limits, screening and approval requirements, restrictions on key foreign personnel, regulatory transparency, and state monopolies. Some EAP countries have made substantial improvements in removing restrictions on foreign investment, such as in many sectors in Indonesia (Presidential Regulation No. 10 of 2021) and in the public sector in the Philippines (New Public Services Act or Republic Act No. 11659 of 2022). Despite these improvements, foreign investment restrictions remain high in EAP. Another book in the EAP Development Studies Series, *Green Technologies: Decarbonizing Development in East Asia and Pacific* (de Nicola,

> Most EAP countries have higher foreign investment restrictions than other economies at comparable levels of development.

FIGURE 4.7   FDI restrictiveness in EAP countries and GDP per capita, 2023

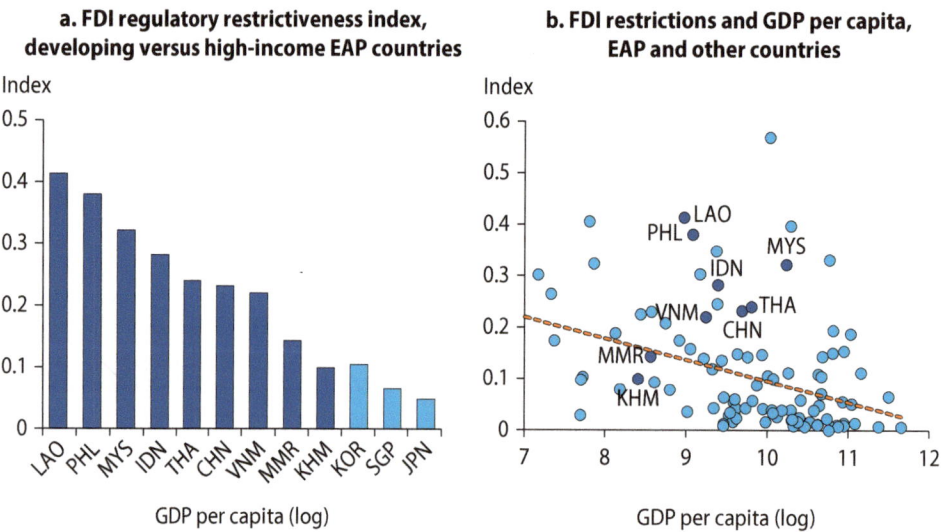

a. FDI regulatory restrictiveness index, developing versus high-income EAP countries

b. FDI restrictions and GDP per capita, EAP and other countries

Source: Original figure for this publication using 2023 FDI Regulatory Restrictiveness Index data, OECD.
Note: Indexes in both panels show the average OECD FDI Regulatory Restrictiveness Index per country (0–1 scale). Panels shows developing EAP countries in dark blue bars or dots and high-income EAP countries in light blue. CHN = China; FDI = foreign direct investment; GDP = gross domestic product; IDN = Indonesia; JPN = Japan; KHM = Cambodia; KOR = Republic of Korea; LAO = Lao PDR; MMR = Myanmar; MYS = Malaysia; OECD = Organisation for Economic Co-operation and Development; PHL = Philippines; SGP = Singapore; THA = Thailand; VNM = Viet Nam.

Mattoo, and Tran, forthcoming), shows how trade restrictions, such as minimum local content requirements, have curtailed the diffusion of green technologies in the region.

Services Unbound (World Bank 2024) unveiled new evidence from the Services Trade Restrictions Index (STRI) produced by the World Bank and the World Trade Organization (WTO). The STRI measures the restrictiveness of an economy's regulatory and policy framework regarding trade in services, computed from the Services Trade Policy Database (of the World Bank and WTO), which includes a broad set of measures affecting services trade both by sectors and mode of delivery. These indicators belong to four distinct areas of policy measures: conditions of market entry, conditions of operation, measures affecting competition, and administrative procedures.

Services liberalization remains an unfinished business. The STRI reflects services trade barriers across the sectors of commercial banking, telecommunications, life insurance, and maritime transportation. Figure 4.8 (panel a) reports the STRI in the larger EAP region as well as two Asian advanced economies: Japan and the Republic

> Most EAP countries restrict services trade more than other economies at comparable levels of development.

FIGURE 4.8 Services trade restrictiveness in EAP countries and correlation with GDP per capita, 2022

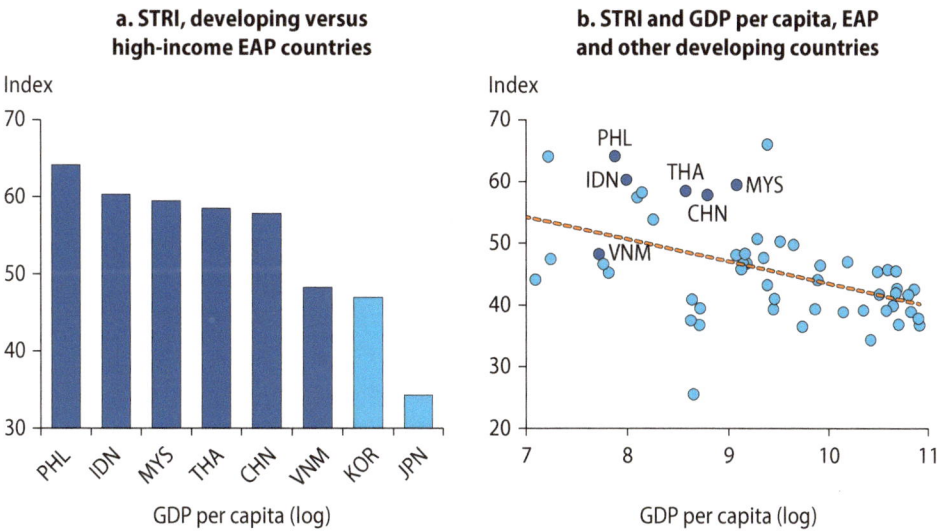

Source: Original figure for this publication using data from World Bank (2024).
Note: Indexes in both panels show the average STRI per country. Panels shows developing EAP countries in dark blue bars or dots and high-income EAP countries in light blue. CHN = China; FDI = foreign direct investment; GDP = gross domestic product; IDN = Indonesia; JPN = Japan; KOR = Republic of Korea; MYS = Malasia; PHL = the Philippines; STRI = Services Trade Restrictions Index; THA = Thailand; VNM = Viet Nam.

of Korea. Scatterplots are also presented (refer to figure 4.8, panel b) for the STRI against the level of development, measured as the logarithm of gross domestic product per capita. As of 2022, EAP countries are still characterized by relatively restrictive regimes for services trade in most of the sectors. Moreover, compared with other economies, this restrictiveness is higher than what would be expected based on the level of development.

Effects of tariffs and nontariff measures

Turning to the trade in goods, whereas the applied tariff rates have declined drastically over the past few years (with the notable exception of the increase in tariffs due to the US-China trade tensions), nontariff measures (NTMs) have increased substantially in the EAP region. These measures can be classified as either technical measures (such as technical barriers to trade and sanitary and phytosanitary measures) or nontechnical measures (such as quantity controls and licensing requirements).

According to a recent survey, 55 percent of the exporters in the EAP region mention NTMs as a burden and as barriers that limit their ability to expand into new markets (ITS 2023). Map 4.1 reports the average difference between the number of border NTMs applied by a given economy in each product and the average number of measures applied to that product in the world in 2021. Some EAP economies display an incidence of border NTMs higher than other regions.

Firms must have the necessary capabilities

Skills and digital infrastructure

Productivity growth and adoption of sophisticated technologies require a broad range of skills and high-quality digital infrastructure. Some technologies are relatively straightforward to adopt, such as off-the-shelf e-commerce websites, and require only basic mobile broadband and workers with foundational skills. In contrast, modern data technologies (such as data analytics or cloud computing) require high-speed fiber broadband to send and receive data, as well as the right combination of digital and management skills to embed data-driven decision-making within business models.

The most-productive EAP firms are more likely to identify barriers to trade, paucity of skills, and weakness in the transport and telecommunications infrastructure as key constraints to growth (refer to figure 4.9). Policy barriers that can prevent firms from entering markets (or scaling up if they do) include formalization costs or business

China, Lao PDR, the Philippines, and Viet Nam have border nontariff measures higher than the world average.

MAP 4.1   Number of border NTMs, by country, relative to global averages, 2021

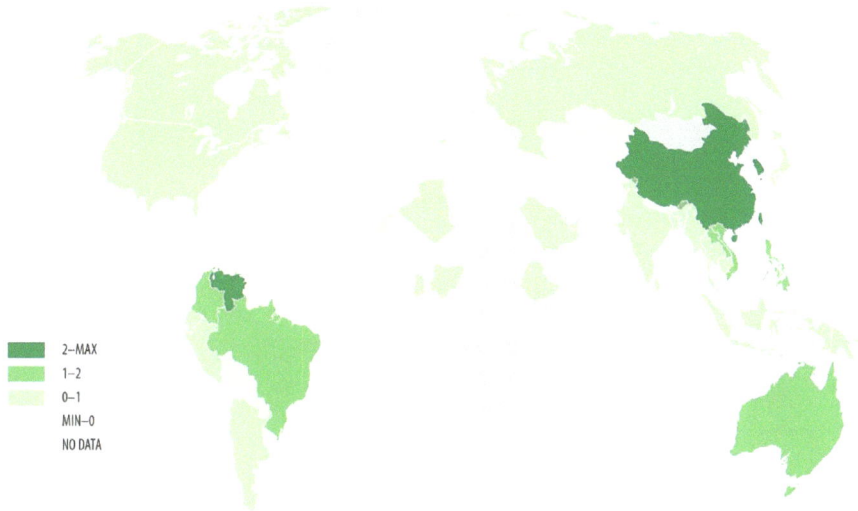

2–MAX
1–2
0–1
MIN–0
NO DATA

IBRD 47927 |
MARCH 2024

Source: World Bank IBRD 47927, March 2024, using Trade Analysis and Information System data, United Nations Conference on Trade and Development.
Note: The map shows the average difference between the number of border NTMs applied by an economy in each product and the average number of measures applied to that product based on TRAINS NTM data in 2021. Averages are computed by weighing each product by its importance in world trade. Following Ederington and Ruta (2016), border NTMs cover all price and quantity control measures (for example, quotas, bans, prohibitions, and nonautomatic licenses); preshipment inspections; and port of entry or direct consignment requirements, as well as other customs monitoring and surveillance requirements, customs inspection, processing and servicing fees, additional taxes, and charges levied in connection to services provided by the government (for example, stamp tax and statistical tax). Border NTMs also cover sanitary and phytosanitary measures registration, testing, certification, inspection, traceability, quarantine requirements, and conformity assessments, as well as technical barriers to trade registration, testing, certification, inspection, traceability requirements, and conformity assessments. NTMs = nontariff measures; TRAINS = Trade Analysis Information System.

licensing regulations, enforcement of labor market policies, limited access to finance, or size-dependent tax enforcement (Bachas, Fattal-Jaef, and Jensen 2019; Didier and Cusolito, 2024; Fattal-Jaef 2022).

These policies typically affect new or small firms the most. For instance, in the EAP region, business licensing requirements, corruption or court inefficiency, inadequate electricity infrastructure, or high tax rates are key constraints to the business operations of lower-productivity firms but are less of an obstacle to the most-productive firms (refer to figure 4.10). In contrast, less is known about the barriers that apply differentially to the most-productive firms. The most-productive EAP firms are more likely to report barriers relating to accessing markets (transportation or trade regulations), telecommunications infrastructure, or skills.

More-productive firms report trade regulations, weak workforce skills, and inadequate transport or telecommunication infrastructure as important constraints to business operations.

FIGURE 4.9   Most-severe constraints to business operations of EAP's most-productive firms, by labor productivity quartile (versus bottom quartile)

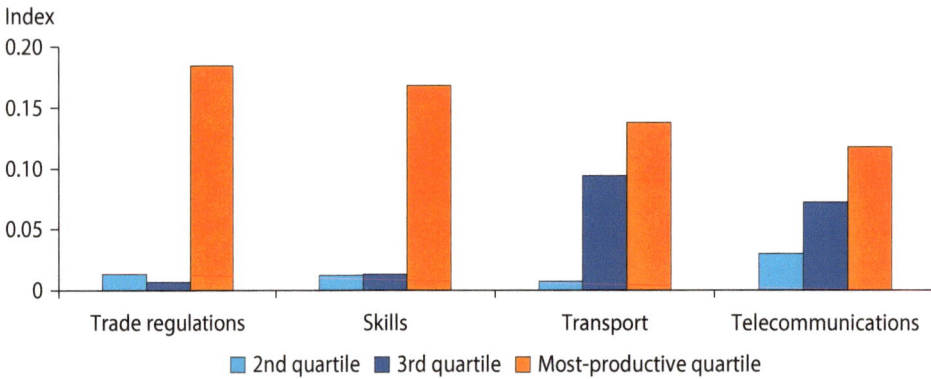

Source: Original figure for this publication using calculations based on World Bank Enterprise Surveys.
Note: The figure reflects data for 11 low- and middle-income EAP countries from Enterprise Surveys between 2009 and 2023. Labor productivity quartiles of manufacturing firms are calculated within each country and year (applying sampling weights). Scores reflect the severity of constraint reported by firms (on a 0–4 scale) within each quartile relative to the bottom quartile (least-productive firms). The figure presents the results of firm-level regressions of reported constraints on labor productivity quartiles, controlling for firm size and country and year fixed effects.

However, the most-productive firms report fewer constraints relating to business licensing, corruption and the courts, electricity infrastructure, or taxes.

FIGURE 4.10   Least-severe constraints to business operations of EAP's most-productive firms, by labor productivity quartile (versus bottom quartile)

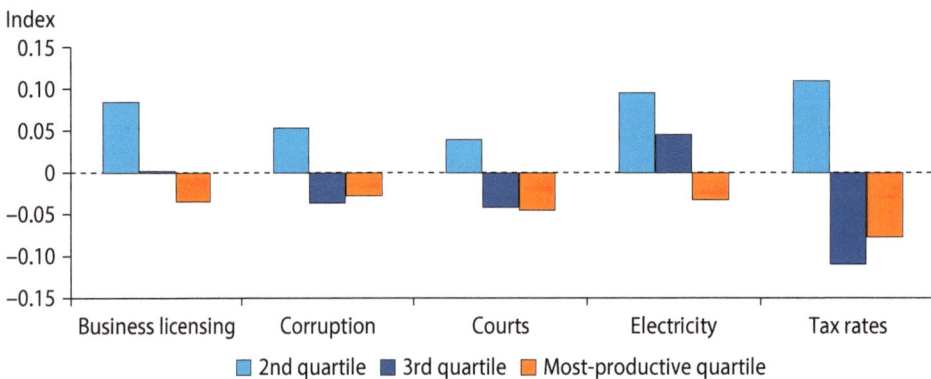

Source: Original figure for this publication using calculations based on World Bank Enterprise Surveys.
Note: The figure reflects data for 11 low- and middle-income EAP countries from Enterprise Surveys between 2009 and 2023. Labor productivity quartiles of manufacturing firms are calculated within each country and year (applying sampling weights). Scores reflect the severity of constraint reported by firms (on a 0–4 scale) within each quartile relative to the bottom quartile (least-productive firms). The figure presents the results of firm-level regressions of reported constraints on labor productivity quartiles, controlling for firm size and country and year fixed effects.

An uneven data infrastructure

Access to modern data infrastructure is uneven in the EAP region and needs to go beyond only access considerations to focus on integrated, high-quality digital public infrastructure. Whereas access to mobile broadband is widespread in EAP, high-speed fiber is unevenly available across and within countries (refer to map 4.2).

The region also shows wide variations in the availability of data centers needed to store, share, and process data via the cloud (refer to figure 4.11). Data centers are much more widely available in richer countries: on average, every 10 percent gain in a country's wealth yields around 20 percent more data center capacity per person (World Bank, forthcoming). Data localization and variations in data privacy laws limit access to cross-border data and cloud computing.

High-speed broadband is unevenly available within and across EAP countries.

MAP 4.2   Fixed broadband speeds in EAP countries, 2023

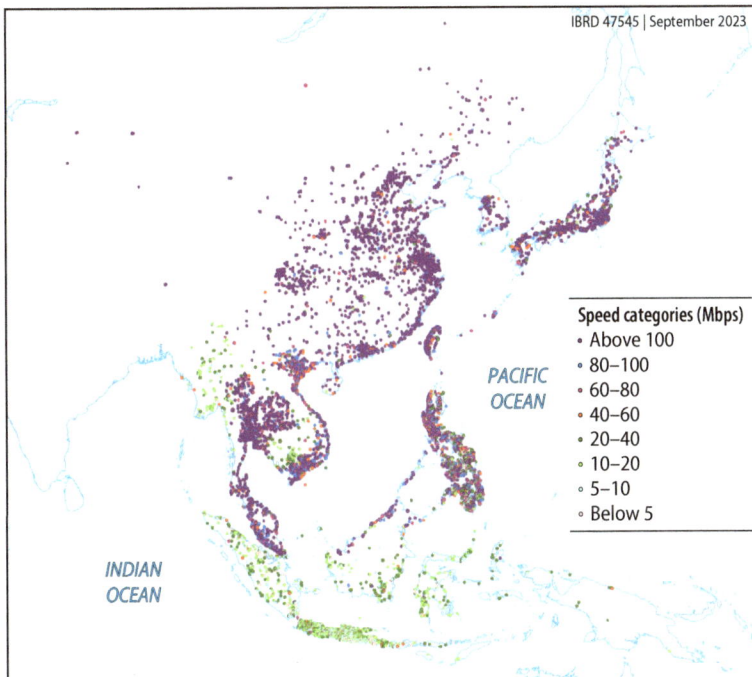

Source: World Bank IBRD 47545, December 2023, using Ookla fixed broadband speedtest data from 2023-Q2.
Note: Mbps = megabits per second.

Cloud computing data centers are not widely available in developing countries.

FIGURE 4.11   **Correlation between data center availability and GDP per capita in EAP and other countries**

Data centers (log, m² per capita)

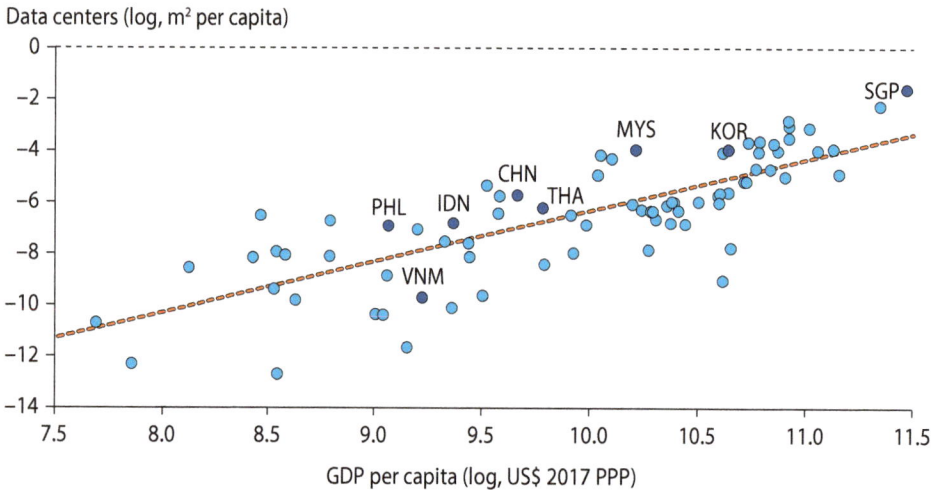

GDP per capita (log, US$ 2017 PPP)

Source: Original figure for this publication based on World Bank (forthcoming) calculations using TeleGeography data.
Note: CHN = China; GDP = gross domestic product; IDN = Indonesia; KOR = Republic of Korea; MYS = Malaysia; PHL = Philippines; PPP = purchasing power parity; SGP = Singapore; THA = Thailand; VNM = Viet Nam. The size of data centers in square meters reflects a common proxy for data center capacity (Greenstein and Fang 2021).

Needs for system integration and interoperability

Governments need to go beyond piecemeal access to focus on whole-of-government integration of digital stacks. So-called digital stacks refer to the integration and interoperability of systems, including digital identity, digital payment systems, data exchange, and information systems such as those relating to health or education (World Bank 2022). The interoperability of these digital systems facilitates digital services and can lead to innovation in both the public and private sector—which allows Thailand, for instance, to link digital IDs with financial accounts to facilitate online payments. However, many countries within the EAP region have struggled with the challenge of shifting toward electronic health records and integrated digital health systems (Raghavan 2023).

The worker skills shortage

The right skills to leverage technology productively are not widely available in EAP. In 14 of the region's 22 middle-income countries, more than half of 10-year-olds cannot read and understand an age-appropriate text (Afkar et al. 2023). Countries must invest in basic education in tandem with teaching the more-sophisticated skills required for new technology adaptation and innovation.

Digital occupations also demand different skills from nondigital jobs (Cunningham et al. 2022). Another book in the EAP Development Studies Series, *Jobs and Technology in East Asia and Pacific* (Arias et al. 2025), highlights how the diffusion of robots has increased both employment and wages of more-skilled workers. But even basic digital skills are not widely available in EAP, with less than one-fourth of workers in Cambodia, Mongolia, the Philippines, Thailand, and Viet Nam able to use the "copy and paste" function in a document (refer to figure 4.12, panel a). Far fewer can write a computer program (figure 4.12, panel b). Ensuring universal foundational skills through basic education in the region is essential.

The management skills shortage

An often-overlooked dimension of the skills gap is the lack of managerial capabilities needed to take advantage of technologies and reap the productivity gains. Management skills and organizational capital have been shown to be strongly correlated with technology adoption and productivity (Bloom, Sadun, and Van Reenen 2012). Data from the World Bank Firm-level Adoption of Technology

---

Digital skills are unevenly available in EAP.

FIGURE 4.12 **Share of workers with selected digital skills in developing versus advanced EAP countries**

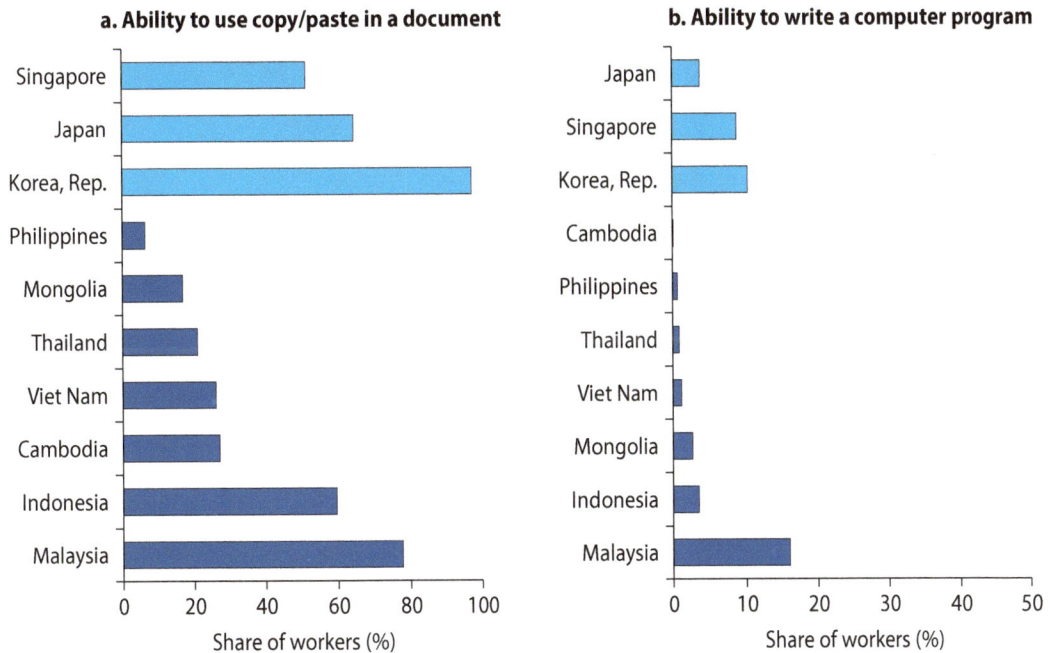

a. Ability to use copy/paste in a document

b. Ability to write a computer program

Source: Original figure for this publication using calculations based on International Telecommunication Union data.
Note: Dark blue bars designate developing EAP countries and light blue bars, advanced (high-income) EAP countries.

(FAT) survey show that, in the Philippines, managers who have studied abroad and have experience with large companies are likelier to adopt and use more-sophisticated technologies (Cirera et al., forthcoming).

Firms in both advanced and developing EAP countries are, on average, less well managed than US firms (refer to figure 4.13). Notably, the best-managed firms in developing EAP countries are further behind the best-managed firms in advanced EAP and far behind the best-managed in the United States. Securing the best managers appears to be a challenge for the best firms in developing EAP. The lack of high-quality CEOs could be due to the lack of high-quality business education in developing countries, and the mismatch between firms and the quality of their CEOs can lead to substantial productivity losses (Dahlstrand et al. 2025). The challenges of local skills for innovation are discussed in Out of the Box 4.

> The best-managed firms in developing EAP countries have management skills far below the best in advanced economies.

FIGURE 4.13   **Management skill gaps between EAP firms and US firms, by level of management sophistication**

Management score gap

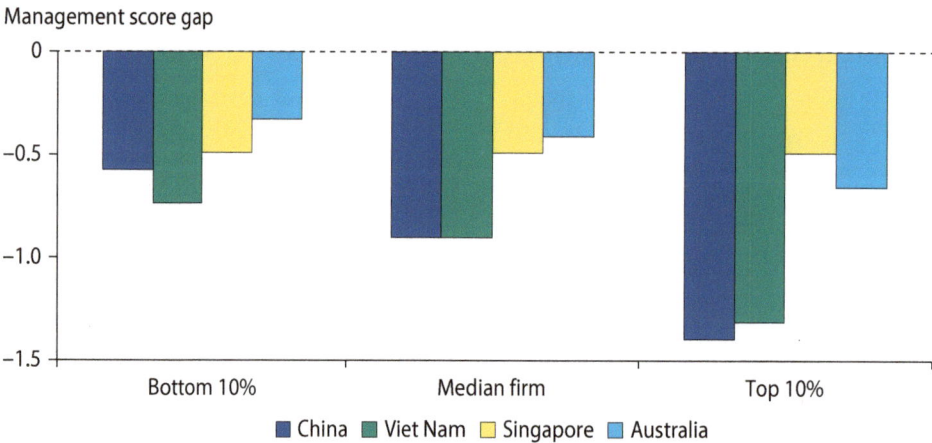

China   Viet Nam   Singapore   Australia

Source: Original figure for this publication based on the regression coefficients reported in Table 1 of Maloney and Sarris (2017).
Note: The figure reflects the gap in management scores between the best-managed firms (top 10 percent) in selected EAP countries and those in the United States. The bottom 10 percent and median are defined similarly.

Out of the Box 4   How skills and local regulations matter for innovation at one food and beverage multinational

This box summarizes an interview for this report with a manager of a global food and beverage multinational, which has both research and development (R&D) centers and manufacturing locations in the East Asia and the Pacific (EAP) region.

How does your firm target growth in the EAP region?

Our firm's approach is centered on expanding market share through continuous innovation. This innovation takes two main forms: the introduction of new products that cater to evolving consumer preferences and the reformulation of existing products to align with changing market demand. For example, our company has observed increasing demand for healthier product options and so is reducing the sugar, fat, and salt content of its products.

What innovation decisions are made globally as opposed to locally?

Our firm typically uses the same production technologies throughout its organization but customizes the products toward local demand. Its innovation and operational strategies balance the need for global economies of scale with the benefits of local customization. Decisions on broad product categories and innovation priorities are made at the global level. However, most product R&D is regional rather than global.

The regional R&D centers enable local teams to select and modify products to better align with local taste preferences. However, product customization is not completely country-specific and are grouped into sub-regions for economies of scale.

What barriers to innovation does your firm face in the region?

Regulatory inconsistencies and workforce capabilities both pose challenges to innovation. One key barrier is the lack of harmonized food and drug regulations across countries. Differences in approval processes for new ingredients create inefficiencies, making it difficult to transfer products across markets. Even if a product or ingredient has been approved in one jurisdiction, local safety approval in another can take years because of capacity constraints at the national laboratories. As a result, our firm often chooses to focus on a smaller set of products in each location.

(continued)

Out of the Box 4   How skills and local regulations matter for innovation at one food and beverage multinational *(Continued)*

In addition, regulations vary significantly between countries for setting up advanced production facilities. Obtaining the necessary licenses and permits for state-of-the-art technology can be a lengthy and complex process.

Finally, the availability of skilled labor is another crucial factor because facilities are mostly operated by local workers. When starting up new production facilities, we often incur the costs of bringing workers from abroad, especially managers. Over time, local workers need to replace these foreign workers.

Source: Box original for this publication based on an interview with a multinational company in the EAP region.

Are technologies appropriate for developing-county skills?

Evidence of technology appropriateness in the literature

New technologies are mostly developed in advanced economies and are designed to be appropriate for advanced-economy conditions.[4] Because capital and skills are relatively abundant, the technologies will tend to be capital-intensive and skill-biased, improving the productivity of capital-intensive or skill-intensive production (Acemoglu and Zilibotti 2001; Atkinson and Stiglitz 1969). Examples of such technologies include automation (such as robotics in manufacturing and artificial intelligence in service sectors) or precision agriculture instruments (such as GPS-guided tractors or drones for monitoring crop health). These technologies may lead to lower productivity gains in developing countries where capital and skills are relatively scarce. Thus, even with complete technology diffusion, productivity in developing countries could still lag behind rich countries, simply because the technology is less suitable for developing-country conditions.

There have been few empirical tests of the appropriateness of technology, and the emerging firm-level evidence is mixed. Firms adopt technologies because of the expected net gains of doing so—that is, if the productivity gain exceeds the cost. Inappropriate technologies are less likely to be adopted or deliver lower productivity gains for adopters. The existing research has largely focused on the former. For example, the high relative cost of management in developing countries can discourage the adoption of management-intensive modern business structures (Hjort, Malmberg, and Schoellman 2022).

The more-convincing evidence of inappropriate technology adoption is from agriculture. Crops are mostly bred in advanced economies and to be productive in the face of specific pests. Moscona and Sastry (2025) have created a measure of how vulnerable crops are to each pest and combine this with data on the distribution of these pests around the world. They found that crops mismatched to local pests are less likely to diffuse, and this issue especially slows diffusion from more- to less-innovative countries. In contrast, Comin, Cirera, and Cruz (2025) did not find support for inappropriate technology, because more-sophisticated technology is similarly correlated with firm productivity across advanced and developing countries, using World Bank FAT survey data.

Evidence of technology appropriateness from Viet Nam

To assess the appropriate technology hypothesis, we use novel data on Vietnamese manufacturing firms that contain information on the country of origin of their primary manufacturing technology in 2010–18. Surveys of firms' technology use typically do not capture the technology's origin, and customs data (while capturing origin) misreport technology use. For example, they often miss the firms that use domestically made technology, are indirectly importing it via wholesalers or retailers, or are using second-hand or rented machinery (Bassi et al. 2022; Mas 2008).

We capture potential inappropriateness as the mismatch between the capital- or skill-intensity of the firm and the capital- or skill-abundance of the country from which they source their technology. If the "appropriate technology" hypothesis is true, we would expect higher productivity gains when the mismatch is low—that is, when more-skill-intensive firms source from more-skill-abundant countries or, conversely, when less-skill-intensive firms source from less-skill-abundant countries.

Vietnamese firms are roughly evenly divided regarding the country of origin of their primary technology: China, Viet Nam, or one of several high-income countries (HICs).[5] However, because technology from HICs is more expensive, 65 percent of total technology spending is on technologies sourced from HICs, compared with only 6 percent on Vietnamese technology and 26 percent on Chinese technology. Spending on high-income and Chinese technologies has been growing, in contrast to largely stagnant investment in home-grown technologies (refer to figure 4.14).

Appropriateness may affect the adoption decision as well as the productivity gains for those that adopt. We consider these two aspects in turn.[6] To ensure comparability, all estimations contrast firms within the same two-digit manufacturing sector.

> **Vietnamese firms are increasingly investing in technologies from high-income countries and China.**

FIGURE 4.14   **Investment by Vietnamese firms in technologies from China, Viet Nam, and HICs, 2010–18**

Technology capital investment (log US$ PPP)

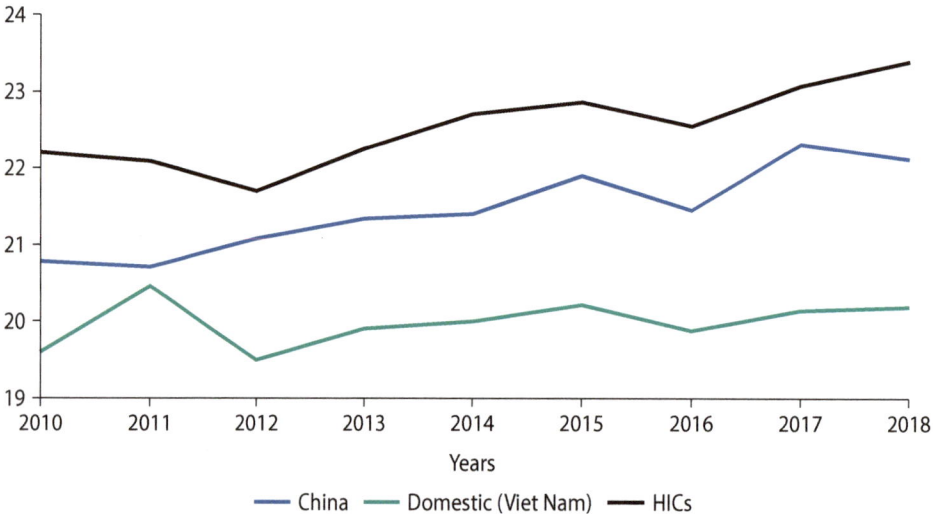

— China   — Domestic (Viet Nam)   — HICs

Source: Original figure for this publication using calculations based on data from Viet Nam's General Statistics Office.
Note: Data reflect 34 HICs, including Australia, European countries, Japan, the Republic of Korea, and the United States. HICs = high-income countries; PPP = purchasing power parity.

Technology adoption decision. In Viet Nam, a firm's initial skills matter for their technology sourcing decisions. Firms whose employees are initially more skilled—defined by the share of employees with university degrees—are more likely to either use or adopt new technologies from more skill-abundant, more capital-abundant, or more-advanced economies (for the former, refer to figure 4.15). (A source country's "skill abundance" is defined by its share of employees with master's degrees.) Although statistically significant, these impacts are economically small. Increasing the share of workers with a university degree from the level of the median firm to the level in the top 10 percent—implying that 17 percent more of their workers have a degree (a huge increase)—is associated with switching sourcing to a country with only 0.6 percent more master's degrees. This is the equivalent of switching from Italy to Ireland.

The evidence that Vietnamese firms' capital intensity or productivity matters for their technology sourcing is much less robust than the evidence that skills matter. Firm initial capital intensity and productivity are correlated with *using* technology from more capital-abundant or higher-income countries, but those factors have no correlation with *adoption* (that is, switching to new country sources).

Firms with higher initial skills source technology from more skill-abundant countries.

FIGURE 4.15   Skill abundance of country technology sources for Vietnamese firms, by firm skill quintile

Country skill level (%, 3rd quintile = 0)

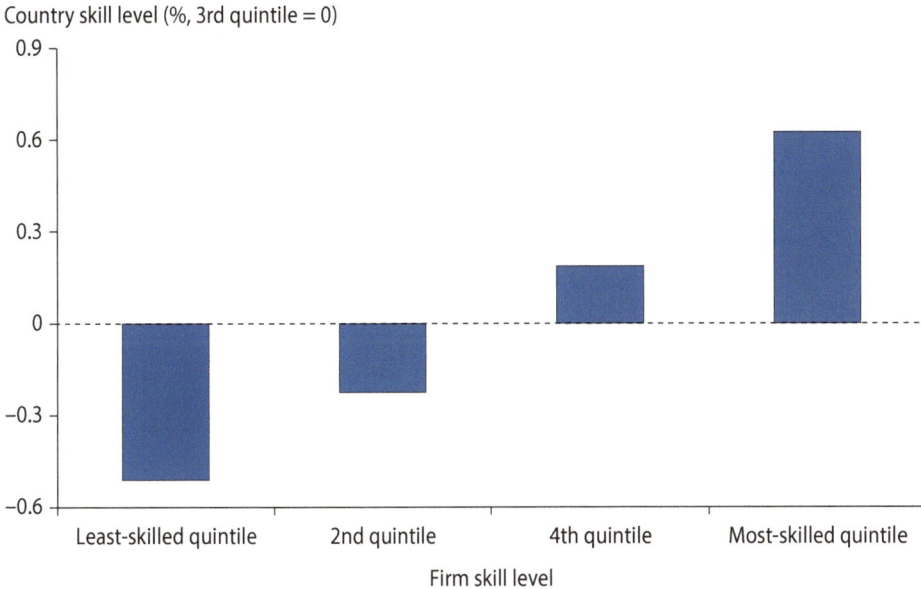

Firm skill level

Source: Original figure for this publication using calculations based on 2010–18 data from Viet Nam's General Statistics Office.

Note: "Firm skill" quintiles are defined according to the firms' share of workers with a university degree. Skill levels, by quintile, are relative to 3rd quintile firm skills (= 0) within the same two-digit industry and year. "Country skill" refers to the skill abundance of the technology origin country, comprising 71 countries including China, Viet Nam, 34 high-income countries, and 35 developing countries. Country skill abundance reflects the share of the population with a master's degree. Similar but more noisy results are obtained using a university degree. All estimated effects are statistically significant at the 90 percent level or more.

In sum, appropriateness affects technology sourcing decisions only at the margin. If firm skills predicted technology sourcing decisions perfectly, one would expect all the firms to be along the diagonal in table 4.1. However, many Vietnamese firms use technologies from countries that have a very different skill mix compared with the firm itself. In table 4.2, only 26 percent of firms are along the diagonal. This is clearly far from perfect prediction. Firms of all skill levels source technologies from the least-skill-abundant countries, namely China and Viet Nam (refer to the top row of table 4.2). Conversely, even the least-skilled manufacturing firms in Viet Nam source technologies from the most-skilled countries (refer to the bottom row of table 4.2).

TABLE 4.1   Classification of the mismatch between skills in Vietnamese firms and those in technology origin countries

Country skill	Firm skill				
	Least-skilled	2nd quintile	Middle quintile	4th quintile	Most-skilled
Least-skilled					
2nd quintile					
Middle quintile					
4th quintile					
Most-skilled					

Source: Original table for this publication.
Note: Country and firm skill levels, by quintile, are within the same two-digit industry and year. "Firm skill" quintiles are defined according to the share of workers with a university degree. "Country skill" quintiles refer to "skill abundance" of the technology origin country, comprising 71 countries including China, Viet Nam, 34 high-income countries, and 35 developing countries. Skill abundance of origin countries reflects the share of the population with a master's degree. Similar but more noisy results are obtained using a university degree. Blue shades represent underskilled firms relative to the technology origin country; red shades represent overskilled firms relative to the technology origin country.

> **Firm skills are only weakly associated with technology sourcing from skill-abundant countries.**

TABLE 4.2   Relationship between skills in Vietnamese firms and those in technology origin countries

Percentage of Vietnamese firms (by firm skill quintile) buying technology from origin countries (by country skill abundance quintile)

Country skill	Firm skill				
	Least-skilled	2nd quintile	Middle quintile	4th quintile	Most-skilled
Least-skilled	14%	25%	19%	20%	22%
2nd quintile	9%	39%	19%	17%	15%
Middle quintile	12%	21%	22%	23%	22%
4th quintile	13%	25%	21%	20%	22%
Most-skilled	6%	15%	21%	24%	35%

Source: Original table for this publication using calculations based on 2010–18 data from Viet Nam's General Statistics Office.
Note: Percentages sum to 100 percent by row. One would expect there to be 20 percent along the diagonal if firms were randomly assigned to technology, and 100 percent of firms would be on the diagonal if the skill-level matching were perfect. "Firm skill" quintiles are defined according to the share of workers with a university degree. "Country" refers to the technology origin country, comprising 71 countries including China, Viet Nam, 34 high-income countries, and 35 developing countries. The origin country's "skill abundance" is defined as the share of the population with a master's degree. Similar but more noisy results are obtained using a university degree.

Productivity gains from adoption. What matters most for the productivity gains from technology is the skills of a firm's workforce (refer to figure 4.16). Where these technologies are *sourced* from seems to be less consequential. Increasing technology capital per worker is correlated with increasing TFP of Vietnamese firms. But if the "appropriateness" hypothesis holds true, then technology adoption should have stronger productivity gains where there are smaller mismatches between the skills of firms and those of countries from which they source technology. In our data, the degree of mismatch does not appear to robustly affect the productivity gains from technology adoption. The most-skilled firms have similarly large productivity gains from sourcing technology from either more- or less-skill-abundant countries. In contrast, the least-skilled firms do not seem to experience productivity gains, no matter which countries they source technology from. Firms need the necessary skills and organizational capital to implement technologies effectively and translate them into productivity gains.[7]

Overall, we find limited support for the appropriate-technology hypothesis when looking at firm adoption decisions but no evidence of inappropriateness when looking at the productivity gains from technology adoption. Thus, the impact of inappropriateness appears to be small.

> **Productivity gains from technology adoption accrue only to firms with more-skilled workers.**

FIGURE 4.16   **Increase in Vietnamese firms' TFP from a doubling of technology capital per worker, by firm skill quartile**

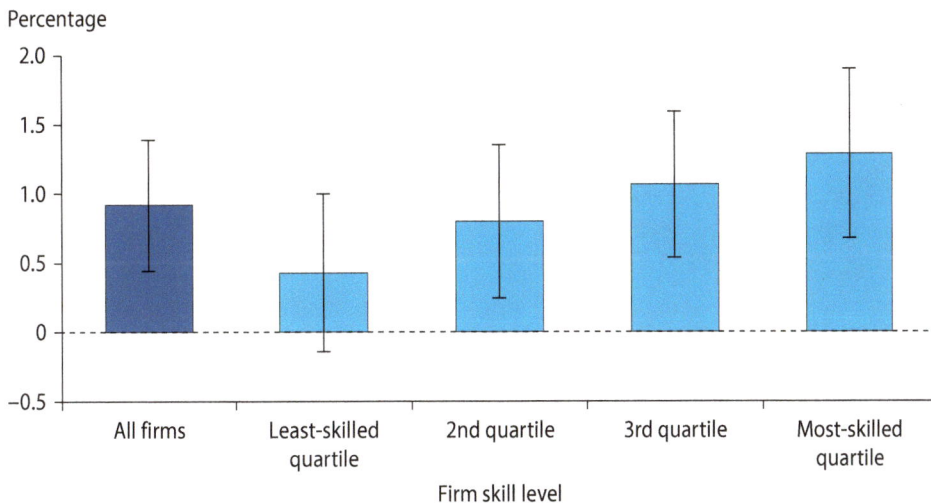

Percentage

Source: Original figure for this publication using calculations based on 2010–18 data from Viet Nam's General Statistics Office.
Note: The figure presents results from an estimation of within-firm changes in TFP on changes in the (log) value of a firm's primary technology capital per worker, interacted with a skills quartile dummy. Skills are measured in the initial period and reflect the share of workers with a university degree, and quartiles are calculated within a two-digit industry. Error bars denote 90 percent confidence intervals; hence, the coefficients on the bottom skill quartile are not significantly different from 0. TFP = total factor productivity.

Notes

1. Informality can be a challenge for productivity growth, but this largely affects growth at the bottom of the productivity distribution. Barriers to entry into the formal sector or size-dependent distortions (such as taxes or employment regulations), can lead to a missing middle if too many firms remain small and informal. Competition from informal firms can also reduce the ability of formal sector firms to grow (for example, refer to Amin 2021). In EAP, smaller firms are more likely to report competition from informal firms being a problem, according to World Bank Enterprise Surveys.
2. The high share of young firms in Viet Nam relative to other countries is also noted by Pimhidzai and Cunningham (2018).
3. We do not find a robust role for exports and frontier firm growth.
4. Note that this hypothesis, therefore, precludes tech firms from being able to perfectly segment markets and design distinct products appropriate to each destination market.
5. Only 3 percent of firms source technologies from other developing (low- and middle-income) countries (excluding China and Viet Nam).
6. We also control for the firm's cost of technology (from any source) in all estimations.
7. Of course, one unresolved question is why these underqualified firms are adopting these technologies at all—a puzzle for future research to solve.

References

Acemoglu, D., and F. Zilibotti. 2001. "Productivity Differences." *Quarterly Journal of Economics* 116 (2): 563–606.

Afkar, R., T. Beteille, M. E. Breeding, et al. 2023. *Fixing the Foundation: Teachers and Basic Education in East Asia and Pacific*. Washington, DC: World Bank.

Aghion, P. 2017. "Entrepreneurship and Growth: Lessons from an Intellectual Journey." *Small Business Economics* 48: 9–24.

Aghion, P., N. Bloom, R. Blundell, R. Griffith, and P. Howitt. 2005. "Competition and Innovation: An Inverted-U Relationship." *Quarterly Journal of Economics* 120 (2): 701–28.

Aghion, P., R. Blundell, R. Griffith, P. Howitt, and S. Prantl. 2009. "The Effects of Entry on Incumbent Innovation and Productivity." *Review of Economics and Statistics* 91 (1): 20–32.

Amin, M. 2021. "Does Competition from Informal Firms Hurt Job Creation by Formal Firms? Evidence Using Firm-Level Survey Data." Policy Research Working Paper 9515, World Bank, Washington, DC.

Arias, O., D. Fukuzawa, D. T. Le, and A. Mattoo. 2025. *Jobs and Technology in East Asia and Pacific*. East Asia and Pacific Development Series. Washington, DC: World Bank.

Arkolakis, C., A. Costinot, and A. Rodríguez-Clare. 2012. "New Trade Models, Same Old Gains?" *American Economic Review* 102 (1): 94–130.

Atkinson, A. B., and J. E. Stiglitz. 1969. "A New View of Technological Change." *Economic Journal* 79 (315): 573–78.

Bachas, P., R. N. Fattal Jaef, and A. Jensen. 2019. "Size-Dependent Tax Enforcement and Compliance: Global Evidence and Aggregate Implications." *Journal of Development Economics* 140: 203–22.

Bassi, V., R. Muoio, T. Porzio, R. Sen, and E. Tugume. 2022. "Achieving Scale Collectively." *Econometrica* 90 (6): 2937–78.

Bastos, P., L. Flach, and K. Keller. 2023. "Robotizing to Compete? Firm-level Evidence." Max Planck Institute for Innovation and Competition Research Paper, November 28, 2023.

Bloom, N., R. Sadun, and J. Van Reenen. 2012. "Americans Do IT Better: US Multinationals and the Productivity Miracle." *American Economic Review* 102 (1): 167–201.

Brandt, L., G. Kambourov, and K. Storesletten. 2020. "Barriers to Entry and Regional Economic Growth in China." Discussion Paper No. DP14965, Centre for Economic Policy Research, London.

Brandt, L., T. Tombe, and X. Zhu. 2013. "Factor Market Distortions Across Time, Space and Sectors in China." *Review of Economic Dynamics* 16 (1): 39–58.

Bruhn, M., A. Demirgüç-Kunt, and D. Singer. 2023. "Competition and Firm Recovery Post-COVID-19." *Small Business Economics* 61 (4): 1555–86.

Bryan, G., and M. Morten. 2019. "The Aggregate Productivity Effects of Internal Migration: Evidence from Indonesia." *Journal of Political Economy* 127 (5): 2229–68.

Buera, F. J., J. P. Kaboski, and Y. Shin. 2015. "Entrepreneurship and Financial Frictions: A Macrodevelopment Perspective." *Annual Review of Economics* 7 (1): 409–36.

Cirera, X., D. Comin, M. Cruz, K. M. Lee, and A. Soares Martins Neto. Forthcoming. "Distance and Convergence to the Technology Frontier." Research paper, World Bank, Washington, DC.

Comin, D. A., X. Cirera, and M. Cruz. 2025. "Technology Sophistication Across Establishments." Working Paper 33358, National Bureau of Economic Research, Cambridge, MA.

Cunningham, W., H. E. Moroz, N. Muller, and A. V. Solatorio. 2022. "The Demand for Digital and Complementary Skills in Southeast Asia." Policy Research Working Paper 10070, World Bank, Washington, DC.

Cusolito, A. P., A. Garcia-Marin, and W. F. Maloney. 2023. "Proximity to the Frontier, Markups, and the Response of Innovation to Foreign Competition: Evidence from Matched Production-Innovation Surveys in Chile." *American Economic Review: Insights* 5 (1): 35–54.

Dahlstrand, A., D. László, H. Schweiger, O. Bandiera, A. Prat, and R. Sadun. 2025. "CEO-Firm Matches and Productivity in 42 Countries." Working Paper 3324, National Bureau of Economic Research, Cambridge, MA.

David, J. M., H. A. Hopenhayn, and V. Venkateswaran. 2016. "Information, Misallocation, and Aggregate Productivity." *Quarterly Journal of Economics* 131 (2): 943–1005.

de Nicola, F., A. Mattoo, and T. T. Tran. Forthcoming. *Green Technologies: Decarbonizing Development in East Asia and Pacific.* East Asia and Pacific Development Studies Series. Washington, DC: World Bank.

Didier, T., and A. P. Cusolito. 2024. *Unleashing Productivity through Firm Financing.* Washington, DC: World Bank.

Ederington, J., and M. Ruta. 2016. "Non-Tariff Measures and the World Trading System." Policy Research Working Paper Series 7661, World Bank, Washington, DC.

Edmond, C., V. Midrigan, and D. Y. Xu. 2015. "Competition, Markups, and the Gains from International Trade." *American Economic Review* 105 (10): 3183–221.

Fattal Jaef, R. N. 2022. "Entry Barriers, Idiosyncratic Distortions, and the Firm Size Distribution." *American Economic Journal: Macroeconomics* 14 (2): 416–68.

Greenstein, S., and T. P. Fang. 2021. "Where the Cloud Rests: The Location Strategies of Data Centers." Harvard Business School Working Paper No. 21-042, Cambridge, MA.

Hallward-Driemeier, M., A. Kochanova, and B. Rijkers. 2021. "Does Democratisation Promote Competition? Evidence from Indonesia." *The Economic Journal* 131 (640): 3296–321.

Hjort, J., H. Malmberg, and T. Schoellman. 2022. "The Missing Middle Managers: Labor Costs, Firm Structure, and Development." Working Paper 30592, National Bureau of Economic Research, Cambridge, MA.

Iacovone, L. 2012. "The Better You Are, The Stronger It Makes You: Evidence on the Asymmetric Impact of Liberalization." *Journal of Development Economics* 99 (2): 474–85.

ITS (International Trade Centre). 2003. "Making Regional Integration Work: Company Perspectives on Non-Tariff Measures in Asia-Pacific." Report, ITS, United Nations Economic and Social Commission for Asia and the Pacific, Geneva.

Khandelwal, A. K., P. K. Schott, and S. J. Wei. 2013. "Trade Liberalization and Embedded Institutional Reform: Evidence from Chinese Exporters." *American Economic Review* 103 (6): 2169–95.

Maloney, W. F., and M. Sarrias. 2017. "Convergence to the Managerial Frontier." *Journal of Economic Behavior and Organization* 134: 284–306.

Mas, A. 2008. "Labour Unrest and the Quality of Production: Evidence from the Construction Equipment Resale Market." *Review of Economic Studies* 75 (1): 229–58.

Midrigan, V., and D. Y. Xu. 2014. "Finance and Misallocation: Evidence from Plant-Level Data." *American Economic Review* 104 (2): 422–58.

Moscona, J., and K. A. Sastry. 2025. "Inappropriate Technology: Evidence from Global Agriculture." Working Paper 33500, National Bureau of Economic Research, Cambridge, MA.

OECD (Organisation for Economic Co-operation and Development). 2022. OECD Indicators of Employment Protection (database), OECD, Paris, https://www.oecd.org/en/data/datasets/oecd-indicators-of-employment-protection.html.

OECD (Organisation for Economic Co-operation and Development). 2023. Product Market Regulation Indicators (database), OECD, Paris, https://www.oecd.org/en/topics/sub-issues/product-market-regulation.html.

Pimhidzai, O., and W. Cunningham. 2018. "Vietnam's Future Jobs: Leveraging Mega-Trends for Greater Prosperity." World Bank, Washington, DC.

Raghavan, A. 2023. "Asia's Digital Health Innovations: The Role of Cross-Border Health Data Sharing." Research Brief, Asia House, London.

Song, Z., K. Storesletten, and F. Zilibotti. 2011. "Growing Like China." *American Economic Review* 101 (1): 196–233.

Tombe, T., and X. Zhu. 2019. "Trade, Migration, and Productivity: A Quantitative Analysis of China." *American Economic Review* 109 (5): 1843–72.

World Bank. 2022. "A Digital Stack for Transforming Service Delivery: ID, Payments, and Data Sharing." Identification for Development (ID4D) Practitioner's Note, Report 170268, World Bank, Washington, DC.

World Bank. 2023. *The Business of the State*. Washington, DC: World Bank.

World Bank. 2024. *Services Unbound: Digital Technologies and Policy Reform in East Asia and Pacific*. East Asia and Pacific Development Series. Washington, DC: World Bank.

World Bank. Forthcoming. "Data Policy Landscape in the Philippines." Report, World Bank, Washington, DC.

How Can Policy Boost Technology Adoption and Productivity Growth?

5

Key messages

Policy reforms need to help generate both the incentives to increase productivity and the capabilities to do so. What must governments do to boost productivity and support the adoption of productivity-improving technologies?

- *Stop doing harm:* Eliminate the impediments to competition. Reforms to boost competition in goods and services markets can accelerate productivity growth.
- *Support the general good:* Invest in human capital and high-quality infrastructure. Fix the foundation of basic skills, equip workers with skills that complement new technologies, and enhance the abilities of managers.
- *Synchronize reforms:* Exploit the synergies between enhanced human capital, infrastructure, and competition.

Although policies to enhance competition, digital infrastructure, and skills are already recognized as drivers of growth more generally, this chapter shows how these policies can help reignite the productivity of firms in general and of frontier firms specifically.

Reforms to spur competition

Reform of tariffs and nontariff measures

Eliminating impediments to entry and competition in goods and services markets can accelerate productivity growth. Reform of both tariffs and nontariff measures could increase the exposure of goods markets to foreign competition. Viet Nam's tariff reductions since the 2000s are associated with direct productivity increases in the affected sectors (refer to figure 5.1, panel a). Vietnamese import tariffs fell substantially over the 2000s following its accession to the Association of Southeast Asian Nations (ASEAN) and the World Trade Organization (WTO) as well as trade agreements between ASEAN and China and Japan (McCaig, Pavcnik, and Wong 2023). Productivity increases are observed for both frontier firms and other firms in the same sectors.

There are even larger indirect productivity gains in sectors that use the products of these sectors as inputs (refer to figure 5.1, panel b). Although manufacturing tariffs tend to be low, many nontariff barriers behind the border persist, and their elimination could produce even larger benefits than those from tariff reductions.

Services liberalization

As for services firms, elimination of restrictions on entry and operation could have a pro-competitive impact not just on the services sectors themselves but also on the manufacturing firms that use these services (Arnold et al. 2016). Evidence for East Asia and Pacific (EAP) and other countries confirms that services liberalization leads to higher productivity growth in services sectors as well as in the manufacturing sectors that use these services.

Following Viet Nam's accession to the WTO in 2007, the Services Trade Restrictions Index (STRI), developed by the World Bank and the WTO, declined sharply in sectors such as finance, transport, and professional services (refer to figure 5.2, panel a). The liberalization led to a 2.9 percent annualized increase in labor productivity in these services sectors and a 3.1 percent increase in labor productivity in downstream manufacturing that used these services inputs (refer to figure 5.2, panel b). The STRI reveals that services trade liberalization is still unfinished business in the EAP region.

Structural regulatory or tax reform

Recent years have seen few structural reforms in the EAP region, which may explain the relatively limited role of reallocation between firms (World Bank 2024a). EAP economies still face distortions that prevent larger and more-productive firms

> **Opening goods to competition can increase productivity in these sectors and downstream sectors that use these inputs.**

FIGURE 5.1   Correlation between firm productivity and tariff reform in Viet Nam

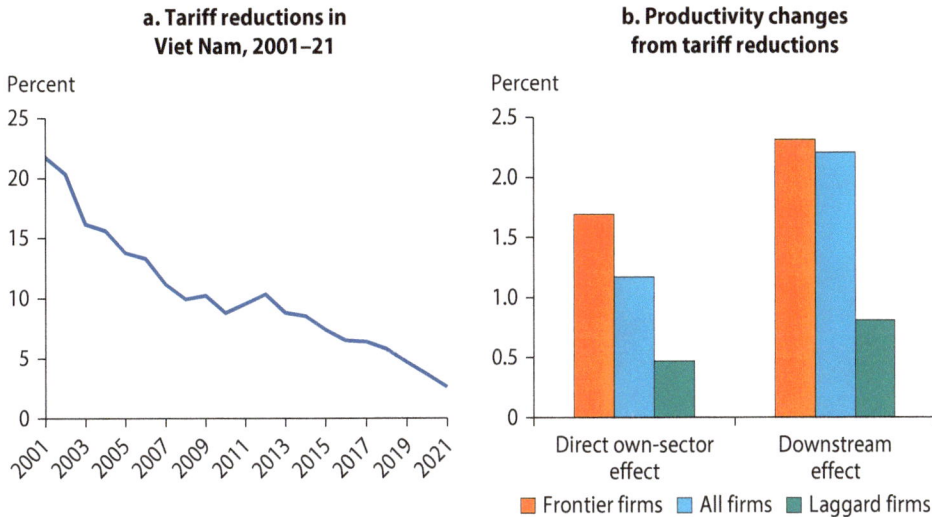

a. Tariff reductions in Viet Nam, 2001–21

b. Productivity changes from tariff reductions

■ Frontier firms ■ All firms ■ Laggard firms

Sources: Original figure for this publication using calculations based on enterprise surveys for manufacturing firms, General Statistics Office of Viet Nam; tariff data from McCaig, Pavcnik, and Wong (2023).
Note: "Frontier firms" are defined as the top 10 percent in TFP within an industry and "laggard firms" as the bottom 10 percent. Coefficients reflect the estimated increase in productivity for a 1 standard deviation decrease in tariffs. The coefficients on laggard firms are not statistically different from 0, all other coefficients are statistically significant at the 99 percent level. Panel a shows the effectively applied tariff rates over time; unweighted average by two-digit industry. Panel b presents the within-firm changes in TFP as a result of output tariff changes (labeled "direct own-sector effect") or input tariff changes (labeled "downstream effect"). The input tariffs have been calculated using the tariffs for each two-digit manufacturing sector, weighted by the corresponding share of inputs purchased from these sectors. The inputs are taken from the 2002 input-output tables for Viet Nam from the 2023 Organisation for Economic Co-operation and Development Inter-Country Input-Output tables. TFP = total factor productivity.

from investing in scale or productivity, such as the de jure or de facto exemption of smaller firms from regulation or taxation. For example, size-dependent public policies—which favor small and medium enterprises because of their size and not their potential productivity contribution—discourage the movement of capital and workers toward more-innovative, higher-productivity firms (World Bank 2024c).

Diffusion of new technologies

The diffusion of certain new technologies also presents new avenues for competition-induced growth. For example, the diffusion of digital platforms in the Philippines presents a competition shock. E-commerce platforms affect traditional wholesalers and retailers by offering customers new ways of connecting with suppliers—such as through online matching, review, and rating systems (Rivares et al. 2019).

> **Opening services to competition in Viet Nam increased productivity in these services sectors as well as in downstream manufacturing sectors that use services inputs.**

FIGURE 5.2   **Correlation between firm productivity and services reform in Viet Nam**

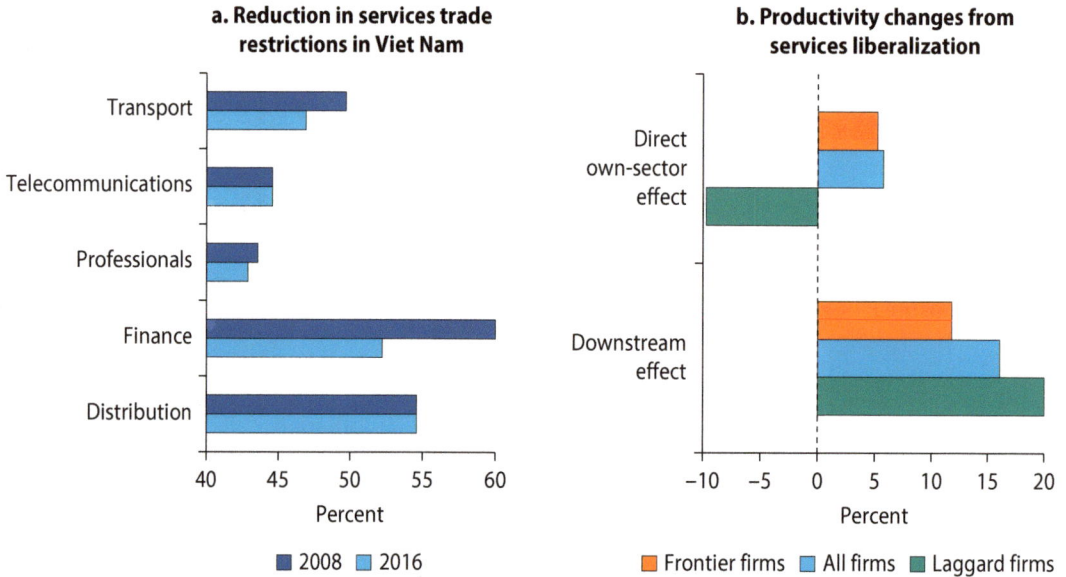

a. Reduction in services trade restrictions in Viet Nam

b. Productivity changes from services liberalization

■ 2008   ■ 2016

■ Frontier firms   ■ All firms   ■ Laggard firms

Source: Original figure for this publication using estimations based on data from 2008 and 2016 enterprise surveys, General Statistics Office of Viet Nam.

Note: The figure presents within-firms estimates of changes in total factor productivity between 2008 and 2016 and changes in the STRI of the World Bank and World Trade Organization. Coefficients reflect the estimated increase in productivity for a 1 standard deviation decrease in STRI. All coefficients are statistically significant at the 95 percent level. "Frontier firms" are defined as the top 10 percent most-productive firms within an industry, and "laggard firms" are the bottom 10 percent. The main explanatory variable is the change in STRI values in the trade, transport, finance, professionals, and telecommunications sectors between 2016 and 2008 in the "direct own-sector effect," and the change in the "downstream" STRI for manufacturing sectors in "downstream effect." The downstream STRI is a sector-specific measure for each two-digit manufacturing sector, calculated by the average STRI of the 5 services sectors, weighted by the corresponding purchasing value from each manufacturing sector. The regression sample in "direct own-sector effect" consists of all enterprises operating in the trade, transport, finance, professionals, and telecommunications sectors, and all manufacturing enterprises in "downstream effect," in 2008 and 2016. STRI = Services Trade Restrictions Index.

Following Rivares et al. (2019), we proxy the diffusion of platforms in the Philippines using Google Trends data for major platforms (refer to figure 5.3, panel a). There is a particularly rapid explosion in wholesale and retail (with major e-commerce platforms such as Grab, Lazada, and Shopee appearing in 2012–15) and, to a lesser degree, in transport and accommodation and travel (pre–COVID-19). Platform diffusion increases not only the wages and productivity of incumbents in the same sectors but also wages and productivity in downstream firms that use these services (refer to figure 5.3, panel b).

> **Diffusion of online platforms in the Philippines can be seen as a competition shock that increases firm productivity.**

FIGURE 5.3   **Trends in diffusion of online platforms in the Philippines and correlation with TFP and wages, 2010–20**

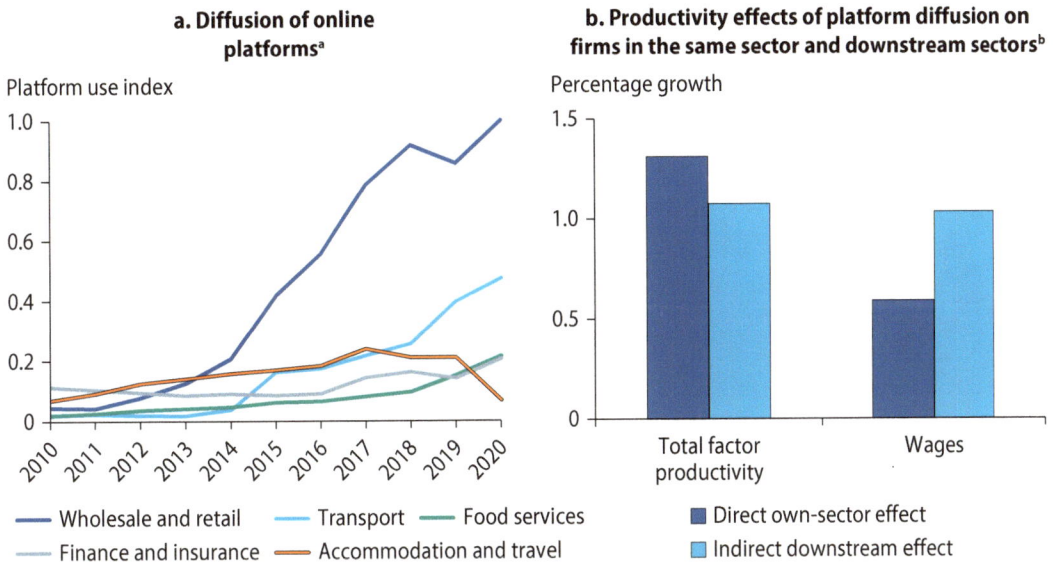

a. Diffusion of online platforms[a]

Platform use index

Legend:
- Wholesale and retail
- Finance and insurance
- Transport
- Accommodation and travel
- Food services

b. Productivity effects of platform diffusion on firms in the same sector and downstream sectors[b]

Percentage growth

Categories: Total factor productivity, Wages

Legend:
- Direct own-sector effect
- Indirect downstream effect

Sources: Original figure for this publication using calculations based on Google Trends data (panel a) and the Annual Survey of Philippine Business and Industry and Census of Philippine Business and Industry databases of the Philippines Statistics Authority (panel b).
a. Platform use is proxied using the frequency of Google searches, following Rivares et al. (2019). The figure reflects 42 platforms (9 retail, 11 transport, 8 food service, 7 finance, and 7 travel and accommodation). Platform use index is normalized relative to retail platform use in 2020.
b. The figure presents results from regressions of firm performance metrics on measures of platform diffusion, including firm and year fixed effects. To aid comparisons across regressions, it presents the estimated percentage change in firm performance from a 1 standard deviation change in online platform diffusion—roughly equivalent to going from the median to the 90th percentile of change. "Direct own-sector effect" reflects the correlations between firm performance and platform diffusion in 4 sectors: accommodation and travel, food services, transport, and wholesale and retail. "Indirect downstream effect" reflects a weighted sum of upstream platform diffusion, with the weights reflecting intermediate input shares taken from the Philippines Statistics Authority input-output table. Indirect downstream effects are representative of the manufacturing and services sectors (ISIC rev 4 divisions 10–33 and 45–82) for 2010–20. All coefficients are significant at the 90 percent level or more.

Reforms to enhance human capital

Skills alone may not be sufficient for EAP firms to avoid falling behind the global frontier, but they can help. For example, the region's frontier firms with a higher share of educated workers showed faster productivity growth than other frontier firms (refer to figure 5.4). Human capital matters a lot for productivity, but measuring skills is challenging, as discussed in appendix box A.1.

Employing more-skilled workers is positively correlated with faster productivity growth among frontier firms.

FIGURE 5.4 **Correlation of productivity growth and higher shares of educated workers in frontier firms, by education level**

Annual TFP growth (%)

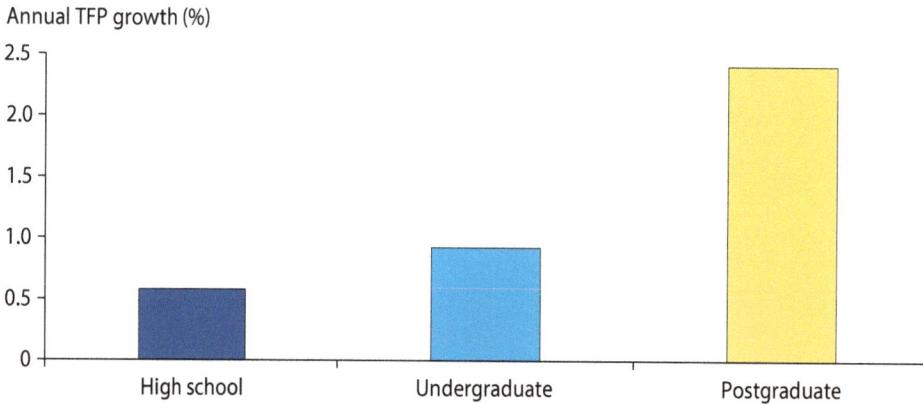

Source: Original figure for this publication using calculations based on statistical office microdata for Indonesia (1996–2015), Malaysia (2009–15), and Viet Nam (2010–15).

Note: The figure reflects the additional annual TFP growth of frontier firms (initially top 10 percent most productive within an industry) with initially 10 percent more workers with high school, undergraduate, or postgraduate education. Regressions control for country, two-digit industry, and year fixed effects. Represents an unweighted average across countries. All coefficients are significant at the 99 percent level. TFP = total factor productivity.

Firms with 10 percentage points more workers with an undergraduate university degree—equivalent to going from a least-skilled frontier firm (bottom 25 percent of the frontier) to a most-skilled firm (top 25 percent)—could achieve almost 1 percent faster productivity growth per year. To maintain pace with the global frontier in digital sectors, annual productivity growth would need to be more than 4 percent faster (refer to chapter 3), and the required skill base must be much stronger.

Strengthen basic skills and invest in advanced skills

Improving human capital has at least three dimensions. First is completing the unfinished agenda of fixing the foundation of basic skills on which more-advanced skills can be built (Afkar et al. 2023). Teachers' knowledge of content and teaching practices have been identified as key problems. Ensuring meritocratic teacher recruitment and investing in teacher training, motivation, and support are imperative and are estimated to produce benefits in terms of discounted lifetime earnings that are 10 times larger than the costs. Another book in the East Asia and Pacific Economic Outlook Series, *Jobs and Technology*, highlights examples of how countries can bring development of digital and socioeconomic skills into school curricula (Arias et al. 2025).

Second, individuals must be equipped with the skills to work with new technologies and the ability to innovate. That requires investments in tertiary education to develop workers' advanced cognitive, technical, and socioemotional skills. A significant proportion of innovative firms in Indonesia, Malaysia, Myanmar, the Philippines, Thailand, and Viet Nam cite the scarcity of interpersonal and communication, foreign language, computer and information technology (IT) skills, or technical (non-IT) skills as critical challenges when it comes to hiring (Cirera et al. 2021). In China and Viet Nam, innovation-intensive firms have higher demand for analytical and interpersonal skills (refer to figure 5.5). Links between classroom learning and

---

More-innovative firms have higher demand for analytical or interpersonal skills.

FIGURE 5.5   Demand for analytical, interpersonal, or routine tasks in China and Viet Nam, by firm's innovation intensity (regression coefficient)

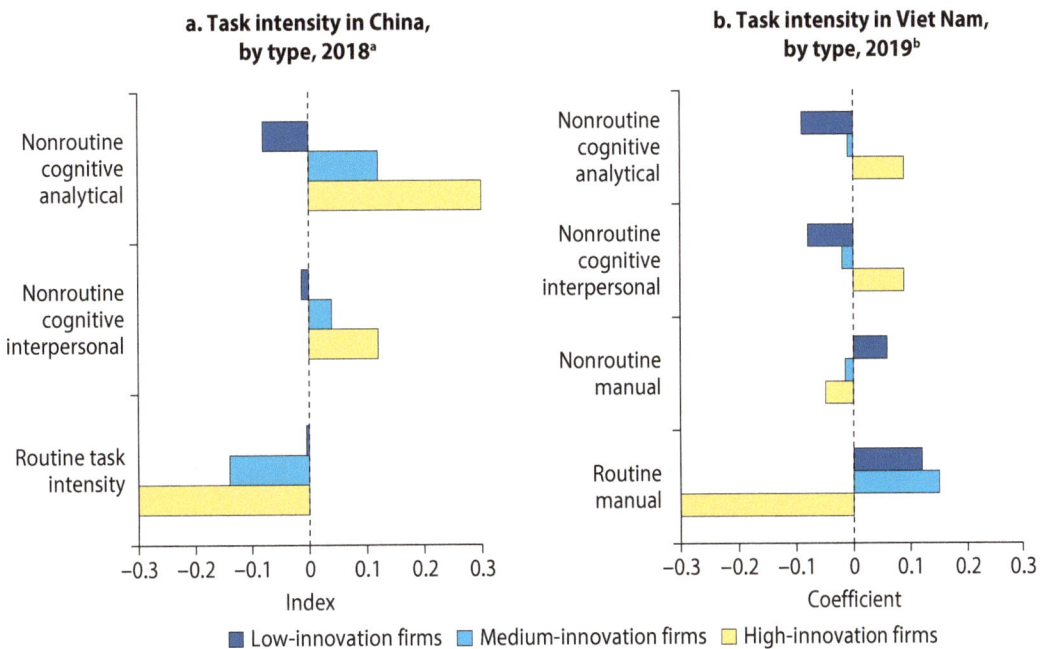

a. Task intensity in China, by type, 2018[a]

b. Task intensity in Viet Nam, by type, 2019[b]

■ Low-innovation firms   ■ Medium-innovation firms   ☐ High-innovation firms

Sources: Original figure for this publication using calculations from de Nicola et al. (2021), based on Park and Xuan (2020) and Miyamoto and Sarzosa (2020), using, respectively, the 2018 China Employer-Employee Survey (CEES) and the 2019 Enterprise Survey on Innovation and Skills (ESIS) for Viet Nam.

Note: Firms are categorized by "innovation intensity," measured by the number of innovation activities undertaken, as captured in the respective surveys. Scaled from 0–5, low-, medium-, and high-innovation are defined, respectively, as those undertaking 0–1, 2–3, and 4–5 innovation activities. The Viet Nam analysis does not include an aggregated measure of "routine task intensity"; therefore, panel b shows instead an individual measure of "routine manual" tasks. No information was included in either panel on routine cognitive tasks because none of the related regression coefficients were statistically significant.

a. The CEES collected responses of 2,001 manufacturing firms and 16,379 workers from 5 Chinese provinces: Guangdong, Jiangsu, Jilin, Hubei, and Sichuan.

b. The ESIS collected responses from 201 manufacturing and information and communication technology services firms and 849 staff in 5 Vietnamese provinces: Bac Ninh, Binh Duong, Da Nang, Hanoi, and Ho Chi Minh City.

exposure to tasks from the factory floor to the research and development center can help. Today, links between research institutions and firms, including incentives for research institution–industry collaboration, are weak in the region and need to be strengthened.

Technology is simply a tool by itself and requires complementary skills training for productivity gains to materialize. For instance, in historical examples of technology transfer to China and Italy, advanced machinery had a small and temporary impact on productivity, but when accompanied by skills training there were permanent increases in firm productivity (Giorcelli 2019; Giorcelli and Li 2024).

Advancing along the parallel tracks of ensuring universal strong foundations and more-advanced skills is a balancing act. The extent of prioritization varies with a country's demographic and institutional context and development level. A key challenge is determining the different roles for the public and private sectors in financing, provision, and regulation of education services. Governments must ensure equitable access through direct provision, financing, and other targeted policies to remedy market failures and align the supply of skills to the demand.

Enhance management capabilities

The third dimension of improving human capital is enhancing the abilities of managers, whether they are new graduates or already in the workforce. Differences in management quality are an important contributor to productivity differences across countries. Recent research suggests that management quality can be improved through interventions. For example, firms receiving management consulting in Colombia improved their management practices and increased employment (Iacovone, Maloney, and McKenzie 2022). Another example comes from business training in Kenya, which helped firms figure out new products to sell. The training had little adverse impact on their rivals, so overall (market) sales volume has grown (McKenzie and Puerto 2021). Such targeted support can be especially effective when combined with fostering competition, which further motivates managers to upgrade their skills.

Improving management capabilities is likely to be especially important for laggard firms because increased competition magnifies their limited capabilities. Laggard firms are heterogeneous: some are simply young and starting small; others are inefficient firms that should exit the market (Berlingieri et al. 2020). Therefore, support must both be targeted to firms with sufficient growth potential and be cost-effectively scalable (refer to box 5.1). In Colombia, intensive and expensive one-on-one consulting, as well as consulting in small groups of firms led to improvements in management practices of a similar magnitude (8–10 percentage points) and in firm sales, profits, and labor productivity (Iacovone, Maloney, and McKenzie 2022). But returns on group-based learning were higher and more robust, pointing to the potential of group-based approaches to scale up management improvements. Training microentrepreneurs in Chile found similar returns to individual and group training (Lafortune, Riutort, and Tessada 2018). In addition, group-based consulting is often less expensive and hence more scalable than one-on-one consulting (McKenzie et al. 2023).

There also appear to be important synergies between worker skills in general and management skills specifically. Regions in 19 countries (including China) with greater availability of skills and closer proximity to universities have firms with better management practices (Feng and Valero 2020). Other research, using data that followed rotations of managers within a large multinational firm over 10 years across 100 countries, shows that being allocated a good manager leads to persistent gains for other workers on their team, in terms of wages, promotion, and productivity (Minni 2023).

The benefits of improving skills are augmented by boosting competition incentives. Widening access to higher education in China led to increases in technology adoption and productivity, and these gains were especially large for foreign-owned firms (Che and Zhang 2018). Indonesia trade liberalization led to productivity-enhancing increases in foreign direct investment, and these gains were especially large for firms with more-skilled workforces (Blalock and Gertler 2009).

Box 5.1 Targeted support to firms

Industrial policy actions (that is, government interventions that target specific sectors) have surged in recent years, especially in Group of 20 (G-20) countries such as China, India, most European Union countries, and the United States. Domestic subsidies, financial grants, and tax breaks have become increasingly popular—for example, from the US Inflation Reduction Act of 2022 to promote the green transition in the United States, China's domestic subsidies to prop up manufacturing, and India's import licensing requirements on information and communication technology, to Germany's financial grants to compensate for higher fuel prices.

(continued)

Box 5.1   Targeted support to firms *(Continued)*

Industrial policy can be justified by the presence of externalities, coordination (or agglomeration) failures, and public input provision (Juhász, Lane, and Rodrik 2023). Externalities can take the form of learning-by-doing or research and development spillovers across producers, cost-discovery externalities (when costs and demand conditions are uncertain for new entrants [Hausmann and Rodrik 2003]), and national security motives. Coordination failures arise when an individual producer's profitability depends on the action undertaken by others. Facing budget and capacity constraints, governments need to prioritize investments in public goods.

In principle, industrial policy can boost sectoral growth-protecting, nascent domestic industries from external competition. The Republic of Korea offers an example of successful implementation of industrial policy: temporary subsidies had a large and statistically significant effect on firm sales as long as 30 years after subsidies ended (Choi and Levchenko 2021). China combined domestic subsidies with controls on foreign direct investment to boost and upgrade domestic production.

However, industrial policy interventions may misfire, and extensive investments may yield limited results at best. The Malaysian government's efforts to establish a national car company, Proton, have met with lackluster results. In contrast, Korean support for Hyundai succeeded in creating a global brand. China's investments in the shipbuilding industry echo patterns observed in other countries: entry subsidies were wasteful, attracting small and inefficient firms, and production subsidies yielded negative net returns (Barwick, Kalouptsidi, and Zahur 2024). Historically, industrial policy interventions were more likely to succeed when the policy support was conditioned on firm performance.

Political economy considerations are first-order, too. The success of industrial policy is predicated on implementing sound policies that are politically feasible and do not overstretch implementation capacity. Korea's political landscape in the 1960s and 1970s fostered outward-oriented industrial policies and the contentious reforms necessary to implement them. However, interventions that are driven by political capture or violate political economy constraints are likely to fail. The 1970s' Thai "export-oriented protectionism"—a contradictory mix of import substitution and export promotion—was largely unsuccessful, whereas the 1980s' more-coherent export promotion policy was more successful (Juhász and Lane 2024).

(continued)

Box 5.1   Targeted support to firms *(Continued)*

Diagnosing the economic and political environment is thus a critical first step to devise successful industrial policy interventions. The presence of the market failures discussed earlier requires state interventions in principle, but it would be important also to assess whether implementation is compatible with political and capacity constraints. Ideally, interventions would be transparent, credibly tied to performance outcomes, protected from political influence, and ensure openness to domestic—and ideally international— competition. Countries may also seek to negotiate deep trade agreements to avoid becoming victims of other countries' protectionist industrial policy. Such agreements have been shown to have a shielding effect and may even benefit trading partners when the agreements have deep disciplines on subsidies (Barattieri, Mattoo, and Taglioni 2024).

Infrastructure and the synergies between reforms

Widening access to infrastructure can accelerate the diffusion of technology. The rollout of the internet backbone to rural Philippine provinces (refer to figure 5.6, panel a) led to increased use of e-commerce, a relatively accessible technology that needs relatively slow broadband speeds, limited investment fixed costs, and limited skills. E-commerce use increased in places with all but the slowest internet speeds, and it was about twice as high in the most-skilled locations (refer to figure 5.6, panel b). The rural rollout did not, however, appear to increase the use of more-sophisticated technologies (such as data analytics or cloud computing) or investment in IT in general—technologies that have a more-robust link with firm productivity (refer to chapter 1, figure 1.7).

Access to fast and stable fiber broadband in the Philippines did lead to the adoption of more-sophisticated technologies, such as data analytics, and helped boost firm productivity (refer to figure 5.7). Complementing better infrastructure with openness to foreign competition, reflected in higher foreign ownership, doubled the extent of both technology adoption and productivity increase.

> **Rural rollout of internet backbone in the Philippines is associated with increased e-commerce use.**

FIGURE 5.6   **Change in Philippine firms' e-commerce use after 2012 arrival of internet backbone**

a. Provinces initially without internet backbone, 2012

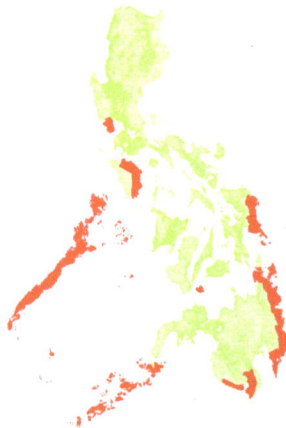

b. Correlation between internet backbone arrival and changes in e-commerce as a share of total sales, 2010–20

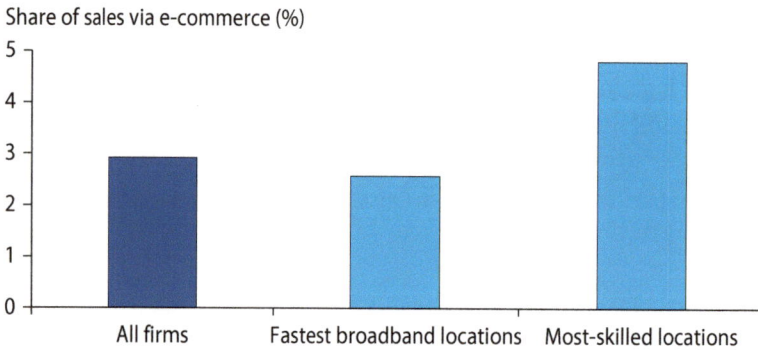

Share of sales via e-commerce (%)

Source: Original figure for this publication using calculations based on the Annual Survey of Philippine Business and Industry and Census of Philippine Business and Industry databases of the Philippines Statistical Authority.
Note: Panel a highlights in red the provinces without internet backbone in 2012. In panel b, the correlation between e-commerce and the timing of internet backbone arrival is estimated as within-firm changes, including firm and year fixed effects. "Most-skilled locations" reflect the top quartile most-skilled municipalities, where skill reflects the share of people who completed high school (the top quartile has a mean share of 50 percent) using 2010 Labor Force Survey data. "Fastest broadband locations" reflect the municipalities in the top quartile of proximity to the fiber backbone cable (specifically within 3 kilometers), so are most likely to have fastest speeds. All coefficients are significant at the 90 percent level or more.

> **Firm productivity or data analytics use is strongly associated with having both access to fiber broadband and foreign ownership.**

FIGURE 5.7   Comparisons of productivity or data analytics use in relation to foreign ownership or fiber broadband capability in the Philippines

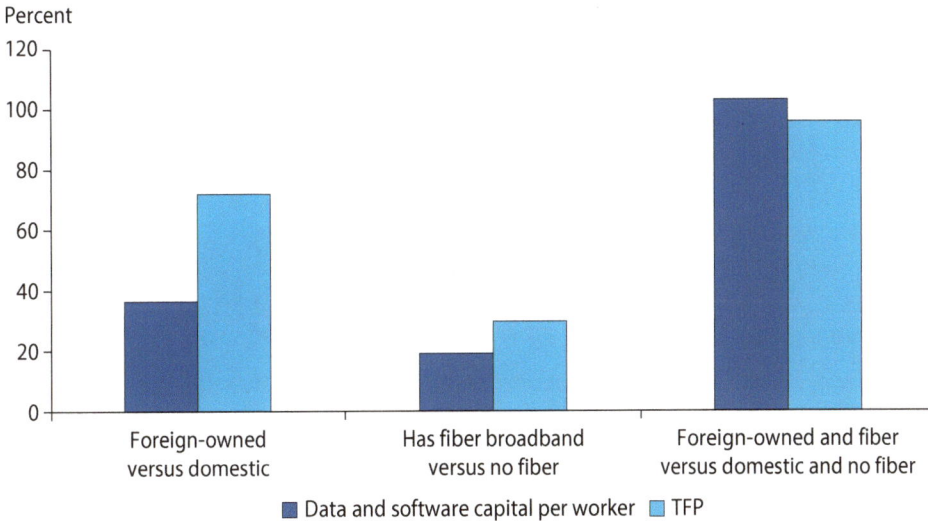

Source: Original figure for this publication using calculations based on the Annual Survey of Philippine Business and Industry and Census of Philippine Business and Industry databases of the Philippines Statistical Authority.
Note: The figure shows the percentage increase in firm TFP or in data and software capital per worker associated with foreign-owned firms compared with domestically owned firms; firms with fiber broadband compared with those without fiber; and foreign-owned firms with fiber broadband compared with domestic-owned firms without fiber. Regressions control for two-digit industry and year fixed effects. All coefficients are significant at the 95 percent level or more. TFP = total factor productivity.

References

Afkar, R., T. Beteille, M. E. Breeding, et al. 2023. *Fixing the Foundation: Teachers and Basic Education in East Asia and Pacific.* Washington, DC: World Bank.

Arias, O., D. Fukuzawa, D. T. Le, and A. Mattoo. 2025. *Jobs and Technology in East Asia and Pacific.* East Asia and Pacific Development Series. Washington, DC: World Bank.

Arnold, J. M., B. Javorcik, M. Lipscomb, and A. Mattoo. 2016. "Services Reform and Manufacturing Performance: Evidence from India." *Economic Journal* 126 (590): 1–39.

Barattieri, A., A. Mattoo, and D. Taglioni. 2024. "Trade Effects of Industrial Policies: Are Preferential Agreements a Shield?" Policy Research Working Paper 10806, World Bank, Washington, DC.

Barwick, P. J., M. Kalouptsidi, and N. B. Zahur. 2024. "Industrial Policy: Lessons from Shipbuilding." *Journal of Economic Perspectives* 38 (4): 55–80.

Berlingieri, G., S. Calligaris, C. Criscuolo, and R. Verlhac. 2020. "Laggard Firms, Technology Diffusion and Its Structural and Policy Determinants." OECD Science, Technology and Industry Policy Papers No. 86, Organisation for Economic Co-operation and Development, Paris.

Blalock, G., and P. J. Gertler. 2009. "How Firm Capabilities Affect Who Benefits from Foreign Technology." *Journal of Development Economics* 90 (2): 192–99.

Che, Y., and L. Zhang. 2018. "Human Capital, Technology Adoption and Firm Performance: Impacts of China's Higher Education Expansion in the Late 1990s." *The Economic Journal* 128 (614): 2282–2320.

Choi, J., and A. A. Levchenko. 2021. "The Long-Term Effects of Industrial Policy." Working Paper 29263, National Bureau of Economic Research, Cambridge, MA.

de Nicola, F., X. Cirera, A. D. Mason, F. de Nicola, S. Kuriakose, D. S. Mare, and T. Tran. 2021. *The Innovation Imperative for Developing East Asia*. Washington, DC: World Bank.

Feng, A., and A. Valero. 2020. "Skill-Biased Management: Evidence from Manufacturing Firms." *Economic Journal* 130 (628): 1057–80.

Giorcelli, M. 2019. "The Long-Term Effects of Management and Technology Transfers." *American Economic Review* 109 (1): 121–52.

Giorcelli, M., and B. Li. 2024. "Technology Transfer and Early Industrial Development: Evidence from the Sino-Soviet Alliance." Working Paper 29455, National Bureau of Economic Research, Cambridge, MA.

Hausmann, R., and D. Rodrik. 2003. "Economic Development as Self-Discovery." *Journal of Development Economics* 72 (2): 603–33.

Iacovone, L., W. Maloney, and D. McKenzie. 2022. "Improving Management with Individual and Group-Based Consulting: Results from a Randomized Experiment in Colombia." *Review of Economic Studies* 89 (1): 346–71.

Juhász, R., and N. Lane. 2024. "The Political Economy of Industrial Policy." *Journal of Economic Perspectives* 38 (4): 27–54.

Juhász, R., N. J. Lane, and D. Rodrik. 2023. "The New Economics of Industrial Policy." Working Paper 31538, National Bureau of Economic Research, Cambridge, MA.

Lafortune, J., J. Riutort, and J. Tessada. 2018. "Role Models or Individual Consulting: The Impact of Personalizing Micro-Entrepreneurship Training." *American Economic Journal: Applied Economics* 10 (4): 222–45.

McCaig, B., N. Pavcnik, and W. F. Wong. 2023. "Foreign and Domestic Firms: Long Run Employment Effects of Export Opportunities." Working Paper No. 10168, CESifo, Munich.

McKenzie, D., and S. Puerto. 2021. "Growing Markets Through Business Training for Female Entrepreneurs: A Market-Level Randomized Experiment in Kenya." *American Economic Journal: Applied Economics* 13 (2): 297–332.

McKenzie, D., C. Woodruff, K. Bjorvatn, et al. 2023. "Training Entrepreneurs." *VoxDevLit* 1 (1): 3.

Minni, V. 2023. "Making the Invisible Hand Visible: Managers and the Allocation of Workers to Jobs." Discussion Paper No. 1948, Centre for Economic Performance, London School of Economics and Political Science, London.

Miyamoto, K., and M. Sarzosa. 2020. "Workforce Skills and Firm Innovation: Evidence from an Employer-Employee Linked Survey Data in Vietnam." Unpublished manuscript, World Bank, Washington, DC.

Nayyar, G., M. Hallward-Driemeier, and E. Davies. 2021. *At Your Service? The Promise of Services-Led Development.* Washington, DC: World Bank. http://hdl.handle .net/10986/35599.

Park, A., and W. Xuan. 2020. "Skills for Innovation in China." Background paper for this report, Hong Kong University of Science and Technology, Hong Kong SAR, China.

Rivares, A. B., P. Gal, V. Millot, and S. Sorbe. 2019. "Like It or Not? The Impact of Online Platforms on the Productivity of Incumbent Service Providers." Economics Department Working Papers No. 1548, Organisation for Economic Co-operation and Development, Paris.

World Bank. 2024a. *World Bank East Asia and the Pacific Economic Update April 2024: Firm Foundations of Growth.* Washington, DC: World Bank.

World Bank. 2024b. *World Bank East Asia and the Pacific Economic Update October 2024: Jobs and Technology.* Washington, DC: World Bank.

World Bank. 2024c. *World Development Report 2024: The Middle-Income Trap.* Washington, DC: World Bank.

Measurement of Human Capital, Capital Stocks, and the Productivity Frontier

Introduction

Measurement of productivity is fundamental to the findings within this book. However, measuring productivity is not always straightforward. Productivity (defined as total factor productivity) reflects the part of production that cannot be explained by quantities of labor or of physical or human capital. Therefore, appropriate measurement of productivity also relies on the measurement of physical capital and treatment of labor or human capital. This appendix provides further details on our approach, which leverages recent best practices in the literature and is applied consistently to the various firm-level data sources used in this book (refer to boxes A.1–A.3 for more information).

Box A.1 Challenges in measuring human capital

Although measures of the years of schooling have the advantage of availability across countries—and even availability at the firm level in some East Asia and Pacific (EAP) countries—years of schooling do not fully account for the *quality* of labor input. The latter is influenced not only by the level of education but also by the actual learning and skills acquired as well as workforce health. The quality of formal education and health, and the effects of on-the-job training and learning outside of the education system, are difficult to measure consistently.

(continued)

Box A.1   Challenges in measuring human capital *(Continued)*

In a recent analysis, Angrist et al. (2021) used a globally comparable database of learning outcomes (164 countries from 2000 to 2017) to estimate the role of human capital in explaining income differences across countries, adjusting years of schooling with a direct measure of educational quality. Figure BA.1.1 illustrates the results and highlights the increasingly important role of human capital in driving productivity as countries move up in economic development. This finding underscores the need for EAP countries to ensure foundational skills for current cohorts of students, which will also enable them to acquire more-sophisticated skills relevant to the new services economy.

FIGURE BA.1.1   Contribution of human capital to differences in cross-country labor productivity

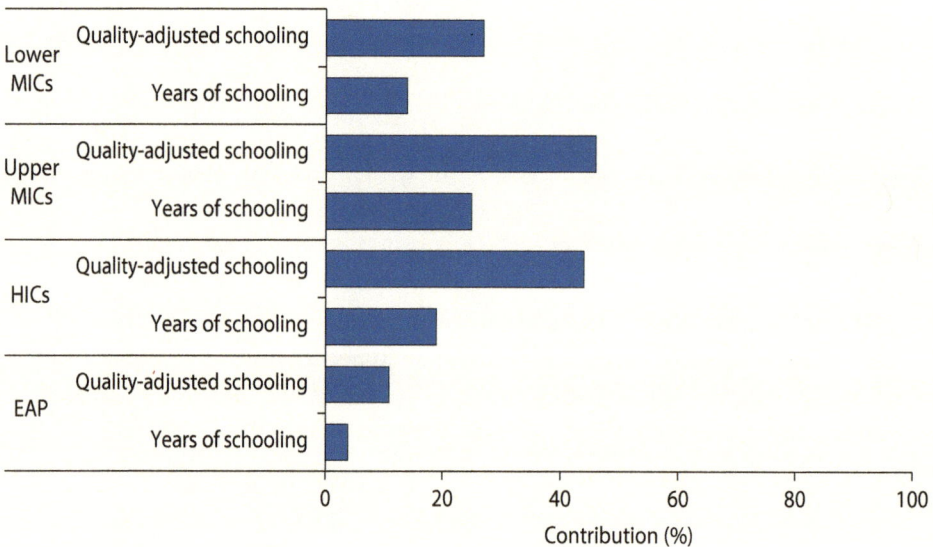

Source: Original figure for this publication using data from Angrist et al. (2021).
Note: "Labor productivity" is defined as real output per worker in US dollars (at 2010 prices) from Penn World Tables v.9.0. The productivity accounting decomposition is based on Var(log[H])/Var(log[Y]), where *H* is one of two measures of human capital from Angrist et al. (2021), and *Y* is labor productivity. Human capital reflects either the average years of schooling in the population ("years of schooling") or a composite measure of the years of schooling and measures of learning outcomes ("quality-adjusted schooling"). The global sample covers 164 countries from 2000 to 2017, including most EAP countries. HICs and MICs also include EAP countries. HICs = high-income countries; MICs = middle-income countries.

Box A.2 Measurement of capital

"Estimating firm productivity," defined as total factor productivity, requires information on net capital stocks and gross capital net of depreciation, which are difficult to measure and are not always widely available.

Capital stocks often are obtained either directly via firm surveys or calculated indirectly using the perpetual inventory method (PIM). PIM is a bottom-up method that uses a time series of the real value of all the asset additions and disposals to calculate the stock of capital. Depreciation is applied to the gross stock of capital, using assumptions on asset lives, to arrive at the net stock of capital. Instead, surveys can ask firms to report the gross and net value of their capital stock directly. Note that capital stocks typically refer to tangible capital such as cars, machines, land, and buildings. Reporting intangible assets, such as software and data or innovative property, is rare.

PIM is the standard approach to measuring capital but requires detailed historic data to be usefully applied. One advantage of PIM is that it allows a transparent calculation, asset class by asset class, which can be important because computers and land have different expected lifespans or different price trends. Unfortunately, PIM requires comprehensive historic data on additions and disposals, and with limited historical data the calculation can be sensitive to the assumed starting capital stock. Direct surveys are much less data-demanding but report accounting values of capital stocks, which can differ from those estimated via PIM. For example, the accounting assumptions for depreciation can be quite different from economically useful asset lives, and price changes are not easily accounted for.

Firm-level information on capital is available unevenly in the East Asia and Pacific region. From our data, we can calculate PIM capital stocks for China and Indonesia and use directly reported capital stocks for Malaysia, the Philippines, and Viet Nam. The Philippines data also report some measures of intangible assets such as software and data. We lack capital data for Mongolia or Thailand and so are limited to measuring firm labor productivity for these countries. For the countries for which we have capital data, information is available for three-quarters or more firms; however, for Viet Nam it is closer to one-third. The imperfect availability of capital motivates our robustness analyses using labor productivity.

Box A.3   Measuring the productivity frontier

"Productivity" refers to total factor productivity (TFP), which is estimated using a value-added production function following the two-step estimator proposed by Wooldridge (2009). The production function is estimated separately for each country and two-digit industry, which allows for differences in production technologies across industries and countries. To allow comparability, all monetary variables are expressed in real 2005 purchasing power parity (PPP) international dollars, using national industry price deflators (rebased to 2005) and the local currency to derive the PPP dollar exchange rate in 2005. The TFP of the global frontier firms has been calculated similarly by the Organisation for Economic Co-operation and Development (OECD) and expressed in PPP dollars (Andrews, Criscuolo, and Gal 2016; Criscuolo 2023).

The national frontier in developing East Asia is defined as the most-productive 10 percent of firms within a given country, two-digit industry and year. The OECD defines global frontier firms as the most-productive 5 percent of firms in each two-digit industry globally. Our comparisons of the national and global frontier are for firms within the same two-digit industry, which abstract from differences across industries (for instance, in their tradability).

The lack of available price data is a common challenge in productivity estimation, so we use monetary values rather than unit quantities in our production function. As a result, we measure revenue-productivity (so-called TFPR), which encompasses both higher-quantity productivity (TFPQ) and higher markups (and so higher prices). Our measure of the frontier reflects both firms with high TFPQ and firms with high markups. High markups may be due to greater market power (for example, of state-owned enterprises) but can also reflect the production of higher-quality varieties or the use of sunk cost technologies—which would be the case if the frontier captures the more-sophisticated firms. However, where price data are available, studies commonly find a strong correlation between TFPR and TFPQ (Eslava et al. 2013; Haltiwanger, Kulick, and Syverson 2018). In addition, firm surveys show that TFPR can be a better measure of firm capabilities than TFPQ (Atkin, Khandelwal, and Osman 2019).

We define the frontier according to the firms' *level* of productivity (in a given country and industry and year) and examine their *changes* in productivity in chapter 3. To do so, we report cross-sections of the productivity distribution, which allows for changes

(continued)

Box A.3   Measuring the productivity frontier *(Continued)*

in the composition of the frontier over time. It is important to contrast this with so-called firm-level convergence regressions. Conventional convergence regressions often show faster within-firm productivity growth for initially less-productive firms, conditional on survival. However, because entering firms can be less productive than incumbents, these conventional convergence regressions may go hand-in-hand with stable productivity distributions over time.

References

Andrews, D., C. Criscuolo, and P. N. Gal. 2016. "The Best versus the Rest: The Global Productivity Slowdown, Divergence across Firms and the Role of Public Policy." OECD Productivity Working Papers No. 5, Organisation for Economic Co-operation and Development, Paris.

Angrist, N., S. Djankov, P. K. Goldberg, and H. A. Patrinos. 2021. "Measuring Human Capital Using Global Learning Data." *Nature* 592: 403–8. https://doi.org/10.1038/s41586 -021-03323-7.

Atkin, D., A. K. Khandelwal, and A. Osman. 2019. "Measuring Productivity: Lessons from Tailored Surveys and Productivity Benchmarking." *AEA Papers and Proceedings* 109: 444–49.

Criscuolo, C. 2023. "Productivity Growth and Structural Change in the Era of Global Shocks." PowerPoint, KDI–Brookings Joint Seminar: Productivity in a Time of Change, April 11. https://www.brookings.edu/wp-content/uploads/2023/04/2.1-KDI-Brookings-Jointt -Seminar-revised-ppt_Chiara-Criscuolo.pdf.

Eslava, M., J. Haltiwanger, A. Kugler, and M. Kugler. 2013. "Trade Reforms and Market Selection: Evidence from Manufacturing Plants in Colombia." *Review of Economic Dynamics* 16 (1): 135–58.

Haltiwanger, J., R. Kulick, and C. Syverson. 2018. *Misallocation Measures: The Distortion That Ate the Residual* (No. 24199). Cambridge, MA: National Bureau of Economic Research.

Wooldridge, J. M. 2009. "On Estimating Firm-Level Production Functions Using Proxy Variables to Control for Unobservables." *Economics Letters* 104 (3): 112–14.

Supplementary Figures

Introduction

This appendix includes figures B.1–B.3 to show the robustness of the results presented in the chapters to alternative specifications.

> **Different decomposition methods show EAP productivity growth has been driven primarily by increases in productivity within firms.**

FIGURE B.1 **Decomposition of aggregate productivity growth, select EAP countries by decomposition method**

Percentage share

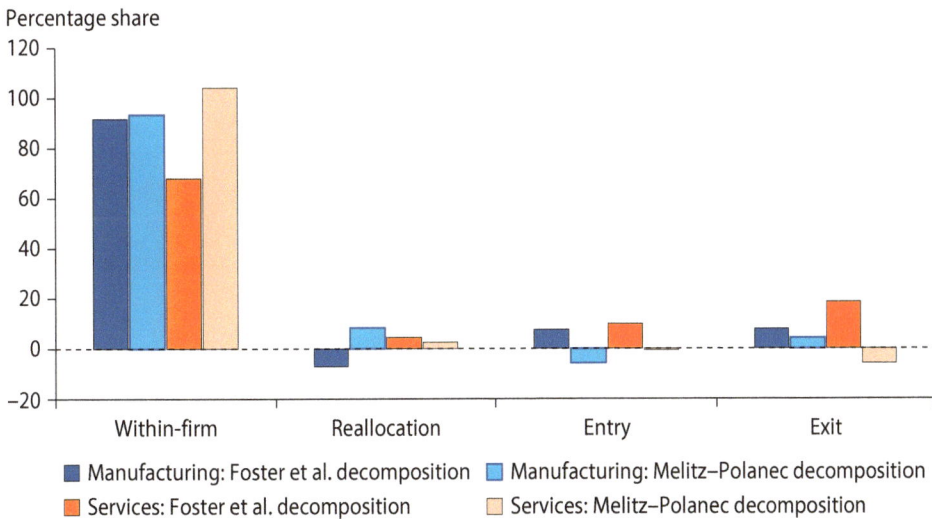

- Manufacturing: Foster et al. decomposition
- Manufacturing: Melitz–Polanec decomposition
- Services: Foster et al. decomposition
- Services: Melitz–Polanec decomposition

(continued)

FIGURE B.1   Decomposition of aggregate productivity growth, select EAP countries by decomposition method *(Continued)*

Source: Original figure for this publication using statistical office microdata for manufacturing firms in China 1998–2007, Indonesia 1996–2015, Malaysia 2000–15, the Philippines 2006–18, and Viet Nam 2001–21, as well as for services firms in the Philippines 2012–18 and Viet Nam 2001–21.
Note: The decompositions are calculated at the two-digit level and aggregated for each country using value-added weights; the figure shows an unweighted average across countries. The decompositions follow Foster, Haltiwanger, and Krizan (2001) and Melitz and Polanec (2015) where specified. The figure reflects the average of 5 or 6 yearly productivity changes (5 or 6 years depending upon country data availability). Entry reflects only entry of young firms (5 years old or less); older firms entering in the microdata due to sampling changes have been excluded. Refer to Figure 1.4 for country-specific results using the Foster et al. (2001) decomposition.

> For Mongolia and Thailand, labor productivity growth of frontier manufacturing and services firms has been slower than that of other firms in the EAP region.

FIGURE B.2   Labor productivity growth along the firm labor productivity distribution in Mongolia and Thailand

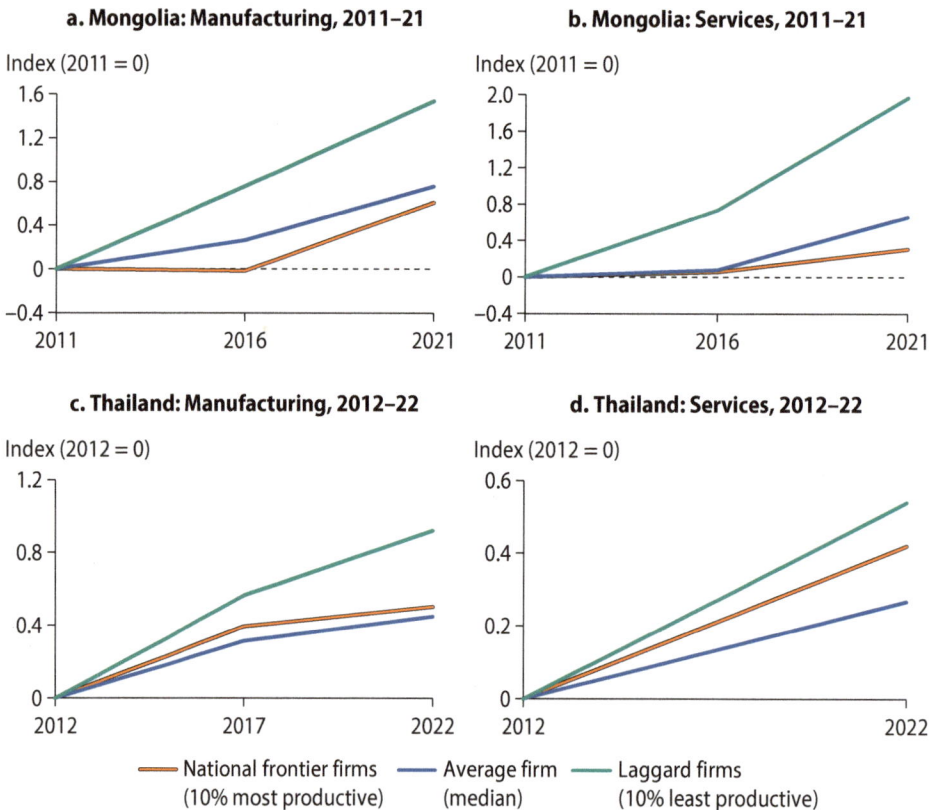

Source: Original figure for this publication using statistical office microdata for Mongolia and Thailand.
Note: "Labor productivity" is defined as real value added per worker in 2005 PPP international dollars. The figure reflects cross-sectional percentiles of the firm labor productivity distribution within countries, by industry, over time. "National frontier firms" refer to the 90th percentile of the firm labor productivity distribution and "laggard firms" to the 10th percentile. The figure reflects an unweighted average across two-digit sectors. Refer to figure 3.6 for labor productivity growth for EAP as a whole. PPP = purchasing power parity.

EAP data investment comprises relatively more database entry and less software development or data analytics than EU countries.

FIGURE B.3   Composition of data investment across EU and EAP countries, 2018

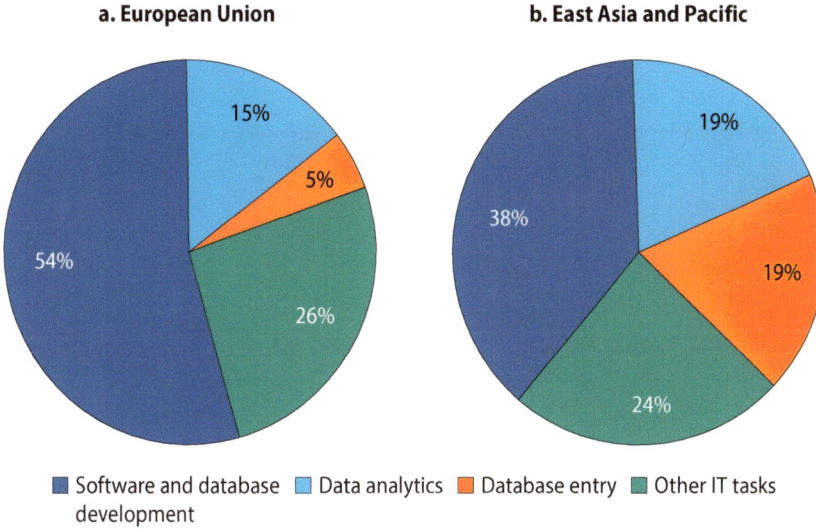

a. European Union

15%
5%
54%
26%

b. East Asia and Pacific

19%
38%
19%
24%

■ Software and database development   ■ Data analytics   ■ Database entry   ■ Other IT tasks

Sources: Original figure for this publication adapted from Goodridge, Haskel, and Edquist (2022) using 2018 data (panel a); calculations from Labor Force Surveys for Indonesia, Malaysia, Thailand, and Viet Nam (using data for 2018 or latest available year), following the methodology of Goodridge et al. (2022) (panel b).
Note: The percentages in the pie charts reflect their share in total data investment. The 4 categories in the pie charts reflect distinct tasks in the formation of data assets, as given by Goodridge et al. (2022). EU = European Union; GDP = gross domestic product; IT = information technology.

References

Foster, L., J. C. Haltiwanger, and C. J. Krizan. 2001. "Aggregate Productivity Growth: Lessons from Microeconomic Evidence." In *New Developments in Productivity Analysis*, edited by C. R. Hulten, E. R. Dean, and M. J. Harper, 303–72. Chicago: University of Chicago Press.

Goodridge, P., J. Haskel, and H. Edquist. 2022. "We See Data Everywhere Except in the Productivity Statistics." *Review of Income and Wealth* 68 (4): 862–94.

Melitz, M. J., and S. Polanec. 2015. "Dynamic Olley-Pakes Productivity Decomposition with Entry and Exit." *RAND Journal of Economics* 46 (2): 362–75.

www.ingramcontent.com/pod-product-compliance
Lightning Source LLC
Chambersburg PA
CBHW050907210326
41597CB00002B/54